ARNIE, SEVE, AND A FLECK OF GOLF HISTORY

ARNIE, SEVE, AND A FLECK OF GOLF HISTORY

Heroes, Underdogs, Courses, and Championships

BILL FIELDS

FOREWORD BY BEN CRENSHAW

University of Nebraska Press • Lincoln & London

Chapters 1–30 originally appeared in *Golf World*, 1994–2011, © Condé Nast.

Acknowledgments for the use of copyrighted material appear on pages 325–27, which constitute an extension of the copyright page.

Library of Congress Cataloging-in-Publication Data

Fields, Bill.
Arnie, Seve, and a fleck of golf history: heroes, underdogs, courses, and championships / Bill Fields; foreword by Ben Crenshaw.
pages   cm
Summary: "Candid profiles and informed observations on golf by one of the sport's best living writers"—Provided by publisher.
ISBN 978-0-8032-4880-9 (paperback: alk. paper)—
ISBN 978-0-8032-5526-5 (pdf)—ISBN 978-0-8032-5527-2 (epub)
ISBN 978-0-8032-5528-9 (mobi) 1. Golf—Anecdotes.
2. Golfers—Anecdotes. I. Title.
GV967.F53 2014
796.352—dc23
2013047891

Set in Scala by Renni Johnson.

For Juanita H. Fields
and
in memory of Gene Fields (1920–1980)

CONTENTS

Foreword by Ben Crenshaw   ix

Introduction   xi

PART 1. TALL SHADOWS: THE GREATS

1. Golf's Gray Ghost   3
2. He Came, He Won, He Died   13
3. The Trials of a Trailblazer   22
4. Man of the Century   33
5. A Place in Time   44
6. King of the Hill   54
7. A Golfer and a Gentleman   66
8. Simply the Best   74
9. Arnie, Now and Then   84
10. Seve: Portrait of an Artist   100

PART 2. INSIDE THE ROPES: COURSES AND COMPETITIONS

11. Changing the Course of History   111
12. The Streak   119
13. He Went Down Swinging   131
14. Homero Blancas's 55   143
15. Lost and Found   151
16. A Champion's Last Hurrah   164

17. Surround Sound   174

18. Devil's Island   184

19. Fortunate Son   191

20. Thoughts from Augusta   198

PART 3. MORE THAN A SCORE: THE CHARACTERS

21. Shades of Greatness   213

22. A Fleck of History   223

23. The Gospel according to Joe Dey   239

24. The Mouth That Roared   250

25. The High Life and Hard Times of John Schlee   256

26. Taking a Stand   267

27. The Detour of a Phenom   275

28. The Journey of Jim Simons   285

29. Still Driven after All These Years   294

30. The Man Who Loved Golf to Death   304

Epilogue: The Tiger Era   315

Acknowledgments   325

It is with pleasure—and it's an honor—to write a few words about Bill Fields and his talented prose. I have always loved golf history, for it is rich with people and places and the famous battlefields where many important events and milestones have occurred.

Bill writes about a wide variety of that history in this collection of some of his best stories. One happens to be about amateur Francis Ouimet's historic victory in the 1913 U.S. Open at The Country Club near Boston against British titans Harry Vardon and Ted Ray. It was The Country Club where I traveled in 1968 to compete in the U.S. Junior Amateur, an experience that heightened my interest in the sport's past.

There is a broad mix of subjects in this anthology. Bill's portraits of Sam Snead, Byron Nelson, and Ben Hogan illuminate America's great triumvirate born a century ago. His profiles of Jimmy Demaret, Billy Joe Patton, and Bert Yancey speak to the rich characters who have inhabited our game. He writes revealingly about the unique putting challenge at Augusta National Golf Club, where generations of champions have tried to solve those baffling greens.

There are very few writers whose words reflect the research and love and sensitivity that Bill's do. They can run the full gamut of heartbreak, pure elation, sadness, and joy, but, in the end, this is the maddening and life-giving game that we all enjoy. Bill's stories have always provided the reader with rich detail, enveloped in a humanizing way that is distinctly his. In sum, to paraphrase the great Bob Jones, who said of golf, "It is the type of game that burns inwardly and sears the soul," so it is with Bill's considerable efforts.

Ben Crenshaw
Austin, Texas
July 15, 2013

When I was fourteen, I met a friendly, fast-talking writer-editor-photographer for *Golf World* magazine named Michael Dann, not long out of the University of Illinois. He was giving free golf lessons for the recreation department at a field not far from my house in Southern Pines, North Carolina, where the magazine was based for many years.

Mike was a good golfer, and, as I would soon find out when we became friends, he had a great job. It seemed even better than being on press row at Atlantic Coast Conference basketball games, which to that juncture had been my career objective if the professional golfer thing didn't pan out.

He traveled the country—even the globe—covering golf tournaments and writing profiles about people in the game. As a teenager, I had no idea if I would ever be able to do something like that when I grew up, but it sure seemed like quite a career.

"The writer on golf is a fortunate being," the *Guardian*'s Pat Ward-Thomas, one of the finest twentieth-century British golf correspondents, said in 1966. I am lucky indeed, having had the opportunity to cover the game for three decades, much of that span for *Golf World*.

Golf provides a deep menu of writing possibilities. Many of its venues are beautiful, its protagonists compelling, its challenges enduring, its competitions riveting, its mysteries fascinating. The late George Plimpton famously said the smaller the ball used in a sport, the better the literature produced about it. A golf ball has a diameter of only 1.68 inches. I'm not going to argue with him.

From Bernard Darwin to Herbert Warren Wind, Peter Dobereiner to Dan Jenkins, Charles Price to Jaime Diaz, Al Barkow to Curt Sampson, golf has been blessed through the years with observers full of skill and perspective regardless of their individual writing styles. The game and those who appreciate it are better off because of their articles and books.

The thirty stories in this volume (a new essay about Tiger Woods serves as the epilogue), published in *Golf World* between 1994 and 2011, are part of my effort to chronicle the game. Although I've spent many coffee-fueled Sunday all-nighters in hotel rooms writing tournament reports on deadline and done scores of 750-word columns for the magazine about issues, competitors, and events, the pieces here are mostly longer profiles and essays about golf people and places, articles a few thousand words in length. Postscripts after each story gave me a chance to update the subject or reflect on the writing process.

There is a bias toward the historical. As William Shakespeare wrote, "What's past is prologue." It is also just plain interesting, or certainly is to me. I am not a golf historian, if such a designation is defined by an advanced degree, but I care a lot about how golf got to where it is today and enjoy studying the personalities who have appeared in and shaped its long arc.

Every great golfer to have graced the game isn't found in these pages—there isn't room, and I haven't written about each one of them—but many are, in stories in which I attempted to probe the best I could about what made them tick. Some of my favorite stories are the ones about people who aren't household names, who didn't win lots of majors, who had troubles, who made a difference behind the scenes, who were exceedingly real. The golf canvas, as I've viewed it, is a human canvas.

Regardless of the subjects' station in the sport, it was a privilege to be able to tell their stories. I hope you enjoy reading about them.

Fairfield, Connecticut
Sept. 1, 2013

ARNIE, SEVE, AND A FLECK OF GOLF HISTORY

1
TALL SHADOWS

The Greats

CHAPTER ONE

Golf's Gray Ghost

Imagine the stories the father could have told the son. There would have been tales of ships, great golf matches, and an America vast and wide, but painful memories too, of the months in a sanitarium when tournament golf seemed as far away as the moon.

They would have laughed about all those silly people in a Boston department store in 1900 who were spellbound as the father hit balls into a net, or the folks in charge at Ganton Golf Club who decided in 1903 to cut the father's weekly pay as club professional from 35 to 25 shillings a week, no matter that he already had won three British Opens and would win a record six. They would have lamented all those strokes frittered away by a frail champion in a Toledo gale over the last few holes of the 1920 U.S. Open, and they might even have cried over a marriage that all the applause in the world could never cheer.

He would have told the boy about home, a small island named Jersey in the English Channel, where he learned to strike lofted shots that floated politely down to earth. He would have tried to explain his father, who could be as chilly as a north wind, and his younger brother, Tom, who showed him the possibility of golf. He would have talked about great rivals J. H. Taylor, James Braid, and Ted Ray, and about a young American named Francis

Ouimet. He would have shown him how to place his hands on a golf club—right pinkie overlapping left index finger—the way he described it in books, the way he demonstrated it to the world.

He would have seen whether the boy had any of the waltz in his golf swing. The son, now seventy-four and good with balls and sticks like his father, can only imagine. Almost seventy years have passed since the friendly gray-haired man with the smile and the presents stopped coming around to see him lest anyone find out the nature of their relationship. He was grown, and his father was dead before he knew, before he finally found out why his Uncle Walter always pointed out so many articles, kept a scrapbook, and was so convinced Harry Vardon was the greatest golfer the world had ever known and so determined that a certain boy in Birmingham, England, know it.

"I was frustrated and I still am," says Vardon's son, Peter Howell. "I thought my mum should have told me while he was still alive, but she couldn't face up to it. In those days, it was hush-hush. I would have liked to have known him."

Even if someone has a love of hickory shafts and shaggy greens, there is a temptation to dismiss the golf played a hundred years ago as an off-key warm-up act for what is now available. It is recognizable, but you need to squint. Everything was so different—the swings, the equipment, the course conditions, the golfers—it's like comparing Kitty Hawk to Chicago O'Hare. The United States Golf Association budgeted just $500 to run the 1900 U.S. Open, which was contested at Chicago Golf Club by sixty players who putted on grass that was as wiry as a stiff hair brush. Then as now, though, there were stars, and nobody was bigger than Harry Vardon.

When he sailed to America in 1900, Vardon became golf's first international star. From the moment he disembarked in New York that January, Vardon attracted attention, first from reporters who amazed him by filling up so many column inches based on his remarks. He came to America to promote Spalding's "Vardon

Flyer" golf ball, but he also pitched muscle balm, golf coats, and health tonics—the first golf pro to endorse products other than equipment.

In Pinehurst, North Carolina, spectators peered intently at the marks his irons made as they brushed the grass after contacting the ball. In New York City the stock exchange closed so brokers could view his exhibition. In Maywood, Illinois, a course laid out two new holes so long—one of 715 yards and another of 962 yards—just so the mighty Vardon, who tapped twenty-five nails into the bottom of each brogan to ensure a solid base for his fluid, upright swing, could not reach the green in the regulation three shots. "His hands, arms, body and legs appear to work as a well-oiled machine," the *American Golfer* said of Vardon's technique, "and there is always present that element denoting complete coordination, ordinarily referred to in golf matters as rhythm."

Vardon set course records from Florida to Maine in 1900, recording drives of up to 275 yards with a one-piece gutta-percha ball that most good golfers were overjoyed to hit 175 yards. Despite the limitations of the ball, Vardon brought the soaring shot to golf, relying more on carry than any player before him. When he got himself in trouble, he usually found a way to get out. At one point in his career, Vardon added a couple of left-handed clubs to his bag to use if the situation demanded it, and as a southpaw he showed little loss of form. Ganton Golf Club, where he was the host pro from 1896 until 1903, had much gorse, and he often practiced a trick shot with a ball sitting atop one of the bushes. Using a niblick he would pop the ball well into the air and watch it land in the same spot.

At 5 feet, 9½ inches tall and 165 pounds, Vardon was cut like an athlete, and his technique oozed effortless power a long time before such a thing was widely seen. Whether off the tee or from trouble, he was in control. "Nothing else but a picture swing," is how the late (Wild) Bill Mehlhorn, who played with Vardon in 1921, summed him up. "He never looked like he rushed it, never looked like he ever hurried it, never looked like he ever tried to hit one hard. He had that one, smooth, slow tempo." Mehlhorn likened Vardon's fluidity to that of Julius Boros later on. In 1900 *Golf* magazine described Vardon's swing this way: "It is wrist power that enables Vardon to lay into the ball at the final moment with such astonishing results; he always gets that indescribable final flick, that whip-like snap, which stands for the difference between good and really first-class driving."

Vardon's velvet power rarely let him down in America. Playing about ninety matches—usually against the better ball of two talented amateurs from the host club—Vardon lost only thirteen times. Only Bernard Nicholls was able to beat Vardon in a singles match.

There was at least one golf course in every state by 1900, but the game was in its American infancy. Golf was still largely a diversion for the wealthy, though Vardon's travels planted the seeds of its subsequent popularity. In Cincinnati golfers caused friction when they took over part of a public park to enjoy the game.

Persimmon was replacing dogwood and beech as the preferred material for wooden clubheads. Gutta-percha balls, which would fade out of golf in just a few years with the advent of the more lively rubber-cored Haskell design, were becoming scarce because the gum from Malaysia was being used for a flurry in the construction of transoceanic cable lines. No doubt the Haskell ball was hotter, but Vardon and some others knew how to launch a guttie. "There were some prodigious shots hit with the guttie," says retired Royal and Ancient Golf Association historian Bobby Burnet. "There was Ted Blackwell, known in the cartoons as 'Smackwell,' who in 1894 drove off the tee at the [par-four] eighteenth hole of the Old Course and put it through the green and up against the clubhouse steps."

But the Old Course also allowed for some run, and the low-ball-hitting Taylor mastered it during the 1900 British Open, beating

Vardon by eight strokes. Taylor followed Vardon back to America soon after, where he would challenge him for the American championship at Chicago. Jessie Vardon, Harry's wife, stayed home.

The Vardons lost a son when he was only six weeks old in 1892, less than a year after the Jersey couple was married. Jessie had a miscarriage in 1896. The sadness over the losses was compounded by Jessie's disinclination to take part in Harry's broadening world. Although Vardon was not an educated man, one who most likely would have spent his life as a gardener if not for golf, his travels schooled him. "When he was playing golf he was mixing with society people," says Audrey Howell, Peter's wife, whose perceptive 1991 biography, *Harry Vardon: The Revealing Story of a Champion Golfer,* describes the gulf that grew between the Vardons. "He came to have a different view of life and he was able to handle it, and I don't think she could. He could handle the different world he found himself in. And she couldn't cope with it and didn't want to."

Back in the United States, the odds were long that anyone other than Vardon or Taylor would win the sixth U.S. Open, but there was no question that the design of Chicago Golf Club favored Vardon over his longtime rival. Many greens were guarded by deep-faced bunkers, nullifying Taylor's bread-and-butter approach, a low shot that skidded quickly to a stop. Though Vardon whiffed a one-foot putt on the thirty-sixth hole of the first day when the stubborn grass stopped his putter head, he led Taylor by one stroke with thirty-six holes to go.

The finale attracted the best of Chicago society, many of the women dressed in fine gowns that were fully detailed next to the description of the play in the *Chicago Tribune.* Vardon, whose caddie was Tom Bendelow, one of America's first course architects, pulled ahead of Taylor by four strokes after the third round. He showed his virtuosity on the seventh hole of the final round. A mammoth drive caught a bunker 270 yards from the tee, designed to catch second shots, but he escaped coolly with a niblick and made a birdie 3. When Vardon completed the final round in 80 for a 313 total, two ahead of Taylor and nine clear of Chicago pro David Bell, a gallery rope was needed to control the crowd.

"His victory was well earned," said Taylor. "He played more consistent golf than I, and deserves his good fortune. He had the advantage of being more familiar with the course than I and had been in this country long enough to become thoroughly acclimated, but that was my misfortune and his good luck."

Vardon pocketed $200 for his victory. American reporters estimated that Spalding had paid him $20,000 for the whole tour, but it is likely that his actual fee was a quarter of that. Vardon, thirty years old when he sailed back home, joined his soccer team in Ganton when he returned, but he was tired. His tour had helped American golf grow up, but it had caused him to grow older. Vardon said that he covered 100,000 miles, which is probably a high estimate, but counting ships, trains, trolleys, cars, and on foot the total was still about 40,000 miles.

"The hard work of the tour took its toll," wrote British golf essayist Bernard Darwin, "and it is doubtful if he was ever so brilliant again." Moreover, upon his return to Britain, Vardon realized more fully that his marriage to Jessie was not going to improve. "Vardon realized that there was nothing he could do or say that would bring them closer together," Audrey Howell wrote, "and his answer was to immerse himself in his golf and his life outside the home."

Vardon's fatigue turned into something worse in 1903. That he was able to win his fourth British Open title that summer remains one of golf's grittiest efforts. Soon to be diagnosed with tuberculosis that would send him to Mundesley Sanitarium on the North Sea, Vardon had lost weight, was weak, and was coughing up blood. He nearly fainted several times in the final round and had to be assisted back to his hotel after the victory presentation.

Taking in the fresh air, resting, and eating well, Vardon got better. As he told his fans in a letter to *Golf Illustrated* in the fall of 1903, "I am staying here for the winter after which they tell

Tall Shadows

me I will be a new man and able to take to the game I love so well." By the following February, Vardon was able to play golf at a course near the sanitarium. In his first round since becoming sick he made a hole-in-one (a feat he used to describe as a "perfect fluke"), the only one he would ever record.

Vardon survived the tuberculosis. He slowed down some but didn't alter his pace too much. "Most of his life had been spent in trains getting to golf courses and then getting on another train," says Burnet. "After the TB, he shouldn't have been dashing around like that, but he did." Vardon believed the disease had drastic effects on his golf. He developed what is probably the worst case of putting yips ever to plague a world-class golfer. Without warning, his right hand would twitch as though it had been given an electrical shock.

"His pathetic inability to bring the clubhead smoothly to the ball on a two-foot putt startled me," said Henry Cotton. "The unbelievable jerking of the clubhead, in an effort to make contact with the ball from two feet or less from the hole, had to be seen to be believed."

But Vardon played on. He began to crouch more and more on the greens, resorting to a putter with only a twelve-inch shaft and hoping "the jumps" would make infrequent visits. He wasn't the dominant golfer that he had been in the late 1890s—when it is believed that he won as many as fourteen tournaments in a row and often routed foes by wide margins—but somehow he continued to win. He claimed his fifth and sixth British Open titles in 1911 and 1914, and, while touring the United States for a second time in 1913, he and Ted Ray were beaten by Ouimet in a playoff at the U.S. Open.

Vardon returned to the United States once more in 1920, and his last American tour, this one at age fifty, included one more appearance in the U.S. Open at the Inverness Club in Toledo, Ohio. Vardon built a four-stroke lead with only seven holes to play, but as suddenly as the strong winds whipped off Lake Erie, he was exposed as an aging champion.

After a bogey on the long twelfth hole, he bungled a two-foot par putt on No. 13. Vardon three-putted the next three holes. He still might have pulled out an unlikely victory, but he found a water hazard on the seventeenth hole and double-bogeyed. His old friend from Jersey, Ted Ray, shot a 75 and finished at 295. Vardon, with a final-nine 42, had a 78 and tied with three others for second place. "I was tired," Vardon said. "My strength left me on the 12th hole."

Inverness was the first U.S. Open for Bobby Jones and Gene Sarazen. The world Vardon orbited for so long soon would be theirs, although he would continue to try to qualify for the British Open until he was in his early sixties. Vardon never took a lesson himself, but when his skills waned he took to teaching. "He bore the deprivation with philosophy and sweet temper," Darwin wrote, "enjoying teaching when he could not play and always anxious to watch the younger players."

In fact Vardon couldn't let go of his place in golf any more than he could leave Jessie. Both of those truths figured when in 1920 Vardon began a relationship with a young dancer named Tilly Howell, who also worked as a hotel housekeeper. Vardon could talk golf to Tilly, and she would listen. The affair was kept under wraps, but it continued despite the tensions of the arrangement. In 1925 Howell became pregnant, and on January 23, 1926, Peter Howell was born when Vardon was fifty-five years old.

Vardon visited his son dozens of times, but when Peter got old enough to ask questions, Tilly asked Vardon to stay away for fear of embarrassment and potential for scandal. As for Vardon, "he hid the truth from Jessie and if she had guessed at events, she decided to remain silent," Audrey Howell wrote. Peter didn't find out the truth until several years after Vardon's death from lung cancer in 1937, when he was sixty-six. The world didn't know until Audrey's book came out.

"My mother spent most of her life trying to keep it quiet because that's what people did in those days," says Peter. "I would like to have thought that I could have talked to him as a young man without letting the cat out of the bag if someone had given me the chance. But it was an awkward situation. My father had a wife, of course, and he loved her as well."

Tilly Howell slipped unnoticed into a back pew at Vardon's funeral, an anonymous mourner in the large crowd of British golf dignitaries who came to honor Vardon. She heard J. H. Taylor, Vardon's toughest rival and old friend, deliver a eulogy. "His style was so apparently simple," Taylor said that day, "that it was apt to mislead. He got his effects with that delightful, effortless ease that was tantalizing."

Peter Howell lived most of his life with more questions than answers until the late 1980s, when he joined his wife while she researched Vardon for her book. On their journey they confirmed Vardon's greatness as a golfer and pinned down many details of his life off the course. His golf, they discovered, may not have been as effortless as it looked.

"It was sort of a personal sadness, really," says Audrey. "He was a man at the top of his profession, yet he had all this heartache in the background. J. H. Taylor had several children, and when [Taylor and Vardon] were playing together and he would have been talking about his family, who knows what Vardon might have been thinking?"

Peter Howell is retired after a lifetime running a frozen foods business. He plays a little golf but spends most of his time playing croquet. He is very good. More important, he knows why.

June 9, 2000

Some years after I wrote this profile, I played in the National Hickory Championship, a tournament in which players use hickory-shafted clubs and replica golf balls from the late nineteenth century. I can only say it was a revelation of how talented Vardon and his contemporaries must have been. I've covered a couple of tournaments at the Inverness Club, and it always causes me to think what it must have been like for the aging Vardon trying to hang on to win the 1920 U.S. Open. Few golfers have truly shaped the sport; Vardon is one of them. Although Tom Watson, with his remarkable run in 2009, came so very close to tying him, Vardon remains the only man to win the British Open six times. This year, 2014, is the centennial of Vardon's sixth triumph, an occasion that no doubt will allow a new generation of fans to find out a bit about this important golf figure.

CHAPTER TWO

He Came, He Won, He Died

He left Scotland in winter and got to America in spring. If Willie Anderson, a budding young man of sixteen, had been looking for a harbinger, there was that, the promise of a fresh season. But as he alighted in New York on March 23, 1896, in what was the snowiest month the city has ever seen, he must have been hoping, more simply, that he hadn't used up all his luck.

The journey was grim, with passengers from first class to steerage perishing during the two-week Atlantic crossing, their deaths reduced to a cold, numbered code on the ship's manifest. Fully twenty-one of the ninety-seven persons aboard the ss *Pomeranian* died en route; at that time, if smallpox didn't kill you, yellow fever or a rusty nail could. So if Anderson arrived in his strange, new land burdened by more than the weight of the three bags in his possession, no one could blame him.

Europeans were pouring into the United States by the tens of thousands that year, men and women sailing with bold dreams for a new world: 68,060 Italians, 45,137 Russians, 39,908 Irish. Of the 3,468 Scots, among the merchants and farmers and bookkeepers was William Law Anderson, "golf club maker," who began his second-class passage in Glasgow. This dark-haired lad, strong as a boxer and quiet as the fog, was on a "protracted sojourn," as the customs form put it, to a place whose people knew less about golf than Anderson did about them.

They would become forever linked, Anderson and America. His new country would become his home, his stage, and, much too soon, his resting place. On the 100th anniversary of the 1905 U.S. Open, Anderson's third consecutive and fourth overall national championship—to go with four Western Opens, then every bit a major—he is as close as golf has to a ghost.

At the cemetery in Philadelphia where he is buried, his illustrated marker is less attraction than directional aid—"Turn left at the golfer"—for people trying to find someone else's grave. Anderson's is a history traced in scant photos, the spidery hand of census records, and brief news accounts. There are 104 enshrinees at the World Golf Hall of Fame in St. Augustine, Florida, not far from where Anderson taught the swells for a half-dozen winters, and officials obtained signatures of 102 of them to reproduce in granite obelisks. Anderson and Young Tom Morris, who died in 1875, had the only signatures that couldn't be located, so their names were inscribed in block letters.

"They don't know me, they don't know me," Anderson said once, in an eerily prescient complaint to a friend.

"I hope you can improve the image of Willie Anderson," Scottish golf historian and collector Archie Baird told me, "but I think you're swimming against the tide."

It turns out, though, that the one detail many people believe they know about Anderson—that a life of heavy drinking essentially caused his death at age thirty-one—might not be so.

Anderson hailed from North Berwick, in East Lothian, Scotland, on the south shore of the Firth of Forth. It was a fishing town that, by the time he was born on October 21, 1879, one of Tom and Jessie Law Anderson's five children, was also popular for golf holidays. The West links, for which Tom Anderson left a job as a train engineer to become greenkeeper in the 1880s, was a short and quirky layout. Its par-three fifteenth hole with a perched green, "Redan," would become one of the world's most emulated designs.

Young Willie seems to have developed his golf talent as if by magic, the way a photographic print assumes a life in the developing tray. Unlike Fred McLeod—three years his junior, whose family lived in the same modest apartment building as the Andersons and who would also immigrate to America and claim the 1908 U.S. Open—Anderson left no golf tracks around North Berwick, where he is presumed to have caddied, or in nearby Gullane, where he apprenticed as a club maker from his early teens.

Exactly what brought Anderson to the United States in the first place also is murky, though the sporting-goods entrepreneur Frank Slazenger, trying to stock America's new avocation with people who knew the game, is believed to have paid for his passage. There was another Scottish golfer on the *Pomeranian*, twenty-three-year-old Thomas Warrender, whose U.S. Open record, unlike Anderson's, was brief and undistinguished: he shot 97-93 in 1896, and his name was never seen again in the Open agate.

Anderson, attached to the Misquamicut Club in Rhode Island, nearly won the 1897 U.S. Open at Chicago Golf Club when he was only seventeen, placing second by one stroke to fast-finishing Joe Lloyd in the thirty-six-hole event. Skillful with every one of the eight clubs he carried, especially a mashie he had doctored with lead solder into something akin to a hybrid club of today, Anderson had a graceful full and flat swing and hit the ball very straight. He was a reserved individual who said little during competition.

But en route to his first U.S. Open title in 1901 at Myopia Hunt Club north of Boston, he erupted in fury when told the pros, whose place on the pecking order wasn't much higher than a servant, were going to have to eat lunch in the kitchen. "Na, na, we're no goin' t' eat in the kitchen!" he said, taking a divot in front of the club. A compromise was reached: the pros dined under a quickly pitched canopy, perhaps golf's first hospitality tent.

Anderson's first national championship was gained with a gutta-percha ball, the next three—at Baltusrol, Glen View Club, and another at Myopia—with a rubber-core model. (He is the only man to win the U.S. Open with both styles.) He is a bit of a gypsy his first few years in the United States, holding club jobs in Westerly, Rhode Island; Springfield, New Jersey; Oconomowoc, Wisconsin; Pittsfield, Massachusetts; and Montclair, New Jersey. At Oconomowoc in 1900, he boarded with a German hotelier and his Austrian wife; at the Country Club of Pittsfield, in 1901, he gave lessons for 75 cents an hour and grudgingly was given the golf ball concession. After a trip to Scotland in the winter of 1903, he settled at Apawamis Club in Rye, New York, for three seasons, then spent another three at Onwentsia Club in Lake Forest, Illinois.

It didn't matter where Anderson was based: in fourteen U.S. Opens he had four wins and seven other top-fives. At the 1902 Western Open, which was as important in golf then as the Masters is now, Anderson shot a record 299 for seventy-two holes. "A splendid exposition of two days' golf," waxed writer Herbert Tweedie, "to be remembered, to be thought of, to be conjured over, and finally to be put on the record shelf."

Golf being a minor sport in those days, Anderson's feats didn't always draw ink. When he won his fourth Open, his local newspaper in Port Chester, New York, adjacent to Rye, didn't even mention his triumph. There were other headlines: "Man, Eating, Finds Pearl; One of the Most Perfect Possible; Will Stand Him in $350." For his fantastic U.S. Open record, Anderson won the grand sum of $1,305 in prize money.

In 1910 Anderson left his winter post in northern Florida and headed to Philadelphia, where he took the pro's position at the Philadelphia Cricket Club, venue for the U.S. Open in June. Philly was consumed with Connie Mack's Athletics baseball team that summer, but those who noticed assumed Anderson's background and local knowledge made him the man to beat. They forgot, perhaps, that he had followed a similar strategy in 1906, but all his familiarity with the Onwentsia Club got him was fifth place, twelve strokes behind Alex Smith in his run at a fourth consecutive victory.

This time Anderson again wasn't on the top of his game, and at the end of seventy-two holes he was five strokes behind Alex Smith, Johnny McDermott, and Macdonald Smith (Alex Smith won the playoff). Willie wasn't even low Anderson. His brother, Tom, nipped him by a shot, and earned $40 for his tie for eighth. "Much to the surprise of the golfing public," reported the *Philadelphia Inquirer*, "Willie Anderson . . . did not even qualify in the money on his own course yesterday. [He] finished at 303, just out of the money, to his great disgust."

There was one victory that week about which Anderson must have been proud. The pros, for the first time at a U.S. Open, were allowed in the clubhouse to eat and change their shoes. But progress in how pros were treated was slow, the dismissive attitudes toward them evident in their meager salaries and the few tournament opportunities. "These were called opens, with a lower-case o," Al Barkow wrote in *Golf's Golden Grind*, "a conceit by which these professional-dominated events were put in the perspective of their time."

At different junctures Anderson designed clubs for Worthington Manufacturing and endorsed the "near indestructible" Champion ball, but unlike British stars such as Willie Park Jr., who got into course architecture after coming to America, he didn't design any courses. Exhibitions were still where Anderson made most of his money. As his thirty-first birthday approached that fall, Anderson traveled to the Pittsburgh area for three thirty-six-hole matches with other leading pros and amateurs. There was a match on October 19, a second on his birthday, October 21, and a third on Sunday, October 23.

Anderson said he was tired, and he had been having bad headaches. He was due to report on November 4 for another season in St. Augustine, but he wasn't going to make it back to the fountain of youth this time. He returned Monday to his home in Philadelphia. By noon the next day, the man who had walked thirty miles while playing 108 holes of golf over five days was gone. The *American Golfer*, taking note of his schedule in his final days, reported that Anderson "may be said to have died in harness."

It was October 25, the same date on which, eighty-nine years later, the life of another multiple U.S. Open champion who could make golf look so easy, Payne Stewart, would end without an autumn.

"Death was caused by a disease of the arteries," the *Philadelphia Evening Bulletin* wrote on its front page on October 26. "Although he had been ill for some time, his illness did not become serious until Sunday." The *Philadelphia Record* reported, "Death was caused by a hardening of the arteries."

For nearly a century it has been written that Anderson died of arteriosclerosis—hardening of the arteries, as it was called then. Even in those perilous times, thirty-one was awfully young to succumb to that affliction. "And so the suspicion exists that it might have been from something less socially acceptable, one theory having been that it was acute alcoholism," golf historian Charles Price wrote in 1980.

Golf professionals of Anderson's era generally were fond of alcohol—famously, Fred Herd had to offer a deposit to assume possession of the 1898 U.S. Open trophy because the USGA worried he might hock it to buy drinks—but the rap against Anderson might have been, at the very least, exaggerated. Indeed most modern descriptions of Anderson's personality (dour) and lifestyle (boozy) seem to emanate solely from one man quoted in one place, a December 1929 profile of him in The *American Golfer*.

"Well, there was this about Willie," said a pro named Tom Mercer, who had been a close friend. "If he didn't like a person, he couldn't pretend that he did. He was not what you would call a glad-hander. Yet he went the route with the rest, and probably his convivial habits had much to do with undermining his health and hastened his end."

There is no way of knowing exactly how much Anderson liked

Tall Shadows

a wee dram or the rot-gut liquor favored then by the servant class, but perhaps he didn't drink himself to death. An obituary in the *Philadelphia Public Ledger* headlined "Golfer Anderson Dead: Phila. Cricket Club Professional Victim of Abscess on Brain" explained, "Although the cause of his death is not certain, it was probably caused by an abscess on the brain, as he had been suffering intensely for the past six weeks with pains in the head."

Could a brain tumor have killed him? More compelling than the *Ledger*'s obit is a salmon-colored, three-by-five-inch "death card" residing in the Philadelphia City Archives. Scores of Andersons passed away in 1910; among the causes of death listed were apoplexy, dementia, gastritis, abdominal hemorrhage, Potts Disease, hardening of the arteries and cirrhosis of the liver. The official cause of death for thirty-one-year-old William L. Anderson wasn't hardening of the arteries, as has long been reported. It was epilepsy.

Pennsylvania had been having a hot spell when Anderson passed, but by the funeral at his home on the morning of October 28, the weather had turned cool and breezy, a good day for golf in the old country. Tom Sr. took care of the arrangements at Ivy Hill Cemetery. He would join his son there three years later, at age fifty-nine, after thirteen years as pro at Montclair Golf Club in New Jersey, followed in 1915 by Tom Jr., who was killed in a car accident when he was twenty-nine. Tom Jr. wasn't nearly the golfer Willie was, but he made up for that with a sartorial splendor of such magnitude that at the 1912 U.S. Open, Walter Hagen was so taken with Anderson's flair he spruced up his own attire.

The Anderson men were buried next to each other, Willie on one side and the Toms—junior on top—on the other. Between them is a substantial monument for Willie erected by the Eastern Professional Golfers Association that carries a likeness of a golfer in his follow-through. He is wearing a golf coat, something Anderson, whose distinguishing fashion was a cap pulled low to hide his large ears, rarely did on the course.

Willie was said to have been married and the father of a little girl. They aren't named in the news accounts or in the death notices, where it was customary for immediate survivors—such as "beloved wife of John" or "devoted husband of Jane"—to be mentioned. Could they have been estranged, or was it merely Scottish reticence? Why didn't Mrs. Anderson end up next to her husband at Ivy Hill? In the 1911 Philadelphia directory, there are a dozen or so "widows of Wm Anderson." Was she Anna or Bessie, Rebecca or Harriett? Or one of the five Marys?

By 1940, when the PGA Hall of Fame was formed, it couldn't locate any survivors and gave his plaque to the Onwentsia Club, whose grillroom also is the home of a wonderful photo, circa 1909, of Anderson with six members having drinks at a patio table. When Anderson was inducted in 1975 into the World Golf Hall of Fame, then located in Pinehurst, North Carolina, Gene Sarazen, a former Apawamis caddie, accepted for him. That was the last time most anyone thought anything of Anderson until 1990, when Curtis Strange made an unsuccessful bid to equal Anderson's U.S. Open trifecta.

"He undoubtedly never thought golf would ever come to this," said Strange at the time, "but I think he is kind of looking down from wherever he is and really enjoying all this."

Of the four-time U.S. Open champions (Anderson, Bobby Jones, Ben Hogan, Jack Nicklaus), the Scot, because of the antiquity of his time, a disregard for the quality of his competition, and disgust with his off-course behavior, is a poor cousin. Even in his hometown. "He's completely forgotten," says Douglas Seaton, a fifty-seven-year-old North Berwick resident and part-time historian. "The generation before me completely shunned him. Anybody born in the 1920s or '30s was not interested in him because of the drink, which is a damn shame because everybody of that period—the caddies, the pros—was drinking. They were never far away from drink. But there's not even a plaque on the wall, not a thing on the wall."

Tall Shadows

A month after Anderson's death, *the Rye Chronicle* reported on plans for a fundraiser for Anderson's wife, a Rye native who met her husband while he was the pro there. The program was going to feature "a series of moving pictures of the late Mr. Anderson in competitive action. The pictures have been shown in the west, and are expected to create the same wealth of interest here as there."

If only the benefit for the Widow Anderson could have shown a scene from California 1899. Touring with 1895 U.S. Open champion Horace Rawlins, playing the kind of exhibitions he would be engaged in at death's door a decade later, Anderson kept beating Rawlins, but the older man still believed he had more game. Rawlins's self-confidence persisted, as *Golf Illustrated* reported, until the day when a stranger with a pocket full of walking-around money set a golf ball atop a beer bottle on a hotel lawn and offered Anderson $50 if he "could knock the ball off without a foozle."

Anderson would make his reputation by playing better than anyone when everything was on the line, so this bet was like panning in a stream rich with gold. "The trick was something Anderson had never tried before," the magazine wrote. "Taking a full swing, Anderson, on each trial, would send the ball flying from the bottle top for fully 200 yards. Not once did he touch the bottle."

June 10, 2005

Discovering through my research what happened to Willie Anderson in his last days, and debunking the popular notion that he might have drunk himself to death, was very satisfying because many myths get transported through the years, in golf and other sports. The fact that two champions, Anderson and Payne Stewart, each died tragically young on the same date, October 25, is beyond eerie. Through the 2013 season, no one has been more successful in the U.S. Open than the championship's first four-time winner—and only Bobby Jones, Ben Hogan, and Jack Nicklaus have as many titles.

CHAPTER THREE

The Trials of a Trailblazer

For a few weeks in the summer of 1925, in several tournaments around his native Philadelphia, an old name resurfaced in the golf scores. He was only thirty-three, but more than a decade had passed since he had left the sport. Not many people remembered what he had achieved, and fewer still knew what had become of him. Yet from out of somewhere, pulling up the caboose end of fields that he once would have ruled—the Philadelphia Open, Shawnee Open, Pennsylvania Open—there he was.

He had been the best golfer in the United States—eager to practice hard and even more keen to beat you—who fought for the honor of American golf as if he were trying to conquer Bunker Hill instead of a few bunkers. He was a magician with the mashie. Jack Burke Sr. told columnist Red Smith a story about the man's legendary accuracy with his irons, how he could hit a few dozen balls and gather them simply by folding up the newspaper he had used as a target.

"Which newspaper?" Smith wondered.

"Oh, any tabloid would do," Burke said.

Now his behavior, not his shotmaking, was out of the ordinary. He was sullen one minute, laughing oddly the next. He was yesterday's news, a listing in tiny type.

Until John J. McDermott, a tough and talented man from working-class Philly, came along, the U.S. Open was ruled by the British as though it was some distant colony. Immigrant or visiting golfers from Great Britain claimed the first sixteen U.S. Opens, but McDermott changed America's luck. After losing a playoff in 1910 when he was only eighteen, McDermott, at nineteen years and ten months, won the 1911 U.S. Open at Chicago Golf Club. He successfully defended his title in 1912 at the Country Club of Buffalo, becoming the first golfer to finish the championship under par.

Golf was just being unwrapped in America, and McDermott held the ribbon in his hands. He was winning $1,000 challenge matches when a house in his neighborhood rented for $20 a month. Companies paid him to endorse their products, a first for an American-born golfer. Resort guests ponied up $100 for the privilege of playing with him. At a time when most American clubs still preferred that Brits hold forth, McDermott had a coveted job at Atlantic City Country Club.

Then, a little more than two years after McDermott won his second consecutive U.S. Open on December 5, 1914, there was news from the Jersey shore: "McDermott retires from seashore job. Noted golfer leaves Atlantic City Country Club—sticks are sent home. Friends say McDermott will quit the game for a while."

McDermott was born on August 12, 1891, the son of a mailman who settled his young family in West Philadelphia, a streetcar suburb so packed with Irish immigrants—the population more than doubled from 1900 to 1920—your neighbors could hear you dream. Amid the bustle, McDermott discovered golf at the old Aronimink Golf Club, then located near his grandfather's farm not too far from where McDermott lived with his father, John Sr.; mother, Margaret; and sisters, Alice and Gertrude, at the orderly address of 1234 South 50th Street. A caddie by age nine, he was befriended by Aronimink pro Walter Reynolds, but McDermott loved the loneliness of golf.

"There was an apple orchard along the seventh fairway," remembered Morrie Talman, a fellow caddie and one of McDermott's few friends, "and Jack had laid out a practice area with three or four tin cans for cups. All our free time, we were there. But if any other caddie came in the orchard, Jack would just walk away."

McDermott dropped out of high school after his sophomore year to pursue golf against the wishes of his father, who wanted him to study a trade. With Reynolds's help he learned how to make clubs and give lessons, but he was drawn to playing the game and absorbed in its challenges. "Golf was McDermott's life," James Finegan writes in *A Centennial Tribute to Golf in Philadelphia*. "He rarely drank, and though an excellent 'buck and wing' dancer, he seldom dated. There is sketchy evidence that he was once engaged to a girl in Boston, but nothing came of it and he never married."

After a short stay at Merion, McDermott held jobs at Camden County Country Club and Merchantville Country Club in New Jersey. He later applied for the pro's position at Philadelphia Cricket Club, site of the 1910 U.S. Open, but the job went to Scot Willie Anderson, the four-time U.S. Open champion who wanted the position so he could learn the course. (The tactic didn't work; Anderson finished eleventh and soon was dead at age thirty-one.) In 1909, when he was just seventeen, McDermott finished fourth in the Philadelphia Open and the next year beat Anderson by one stroke to win the title.

McDermott stood five-foot-eight and weighed 130 pounds, but he had the hands—broad, with long, strong fingers—of a larger man. His clubs had oversized handles, and he utilized an unusual grip in which the pinkie and ring fingers of his right hand overlapped his left so that only eight fingers touched the club. He played the ball back of center, cocked his wrists early, and used his big muscles more than the Brits. His face contorted at impact, his mouth agape, as if trying to marshal energy into the hit. "Every

Tall Shadows

time he made a full swing at the ball, he would give a little 'Ah-eeh,'" says Jerry Pisano, a Pennsylvania pro who played regularly with McDermott many years later. "I never forgot that. Almost like one of those karate-chop things."

McDermott's right side chased down the line after impact in a move that was ahead of its time, a tendency that may have contributed to his pinpoint control. "I have never seen a man who, when called upon to hit a ball a given number of yards, could do so with such damned irritating consistency," said Ted Ray, the 1912 British Open champion who witnessed the full fury of McDermott's skill when he and fellow Englishman Harry Vardon were routed by the young American at the Shawnee Open in the summer of 1913. Still, like all golfers of the day, McDermott was a handsy player. "Like a man flicking a fly from a horse's back," A. W. Tillinghast wrote in 1911. "McDermott used his wrists. He is the best exponent of the value of the wrist in America today, and this, coupled with his supreme confidence, is the secret of his astonishing play."

Just how brash was McDermott? After losing the 1910 U.S. Open playoff by four strokes to Alex Smith, according to John Kiernan of the *New York Times*, McDermott wasn't in the mood to be consoled.

"Hard luck, kid," Smith told the young challenger.

"I'll get you next year, you big tramp," McDermott responded.

McDermott kept his promise, although he put himself in a hole with a first-round 81 the following June. He rallied quickly with a 72 in the afternoon. The final thirty-six holes the next day were contested in a driving rain. At the end of seventy-two holes, McDermott was tied with George Simpson and another home-bred hopeful, Mike Brady, at 307. McDermott's quest for a quick buck (a $300 bonus offered by the maker of the Colonel ball brand) nearly was disastrous. He switched from his usual Rawlings Black Circle model on the first hole of the playoff and immediately hit two shots out of bounds. But he recovered to shoot 80, beating Brady by two shots and Simpson by five.

In the *Philadelphia Inquirer*, McDermott's historic victory—"This is the first time a native-born golfer has won the honor"—shared space with longer stories about Connie Mack's Athletics baseball team and Charles Durburrow's eight-mile swim "from Million Dollar Pier to Ocean City in rough sea." McDermott's age was incorrectly reported as twenty-one.

The following year, still not yet twenty-one, McDermott repeated his success by beating 128 golfers in Buffalo—the first time the Open field topped one hundred—with a 294 total, two better than Tom McNamara. The key blow was a five-iron on the 155-yard sixteenth hole to ten feet, which allowed him to play the final two holes with a two-shot cushion.

McDermott's U.S. Open defense made up for a dreadful attempt in the 1912 British Open. Able to travel across the Atlantic thanks to donations from an admiring public, McDermott crowed that he was going to make history abroad as well. Exhibitions got him acclimated to links golf, and he felt comfortable enough to play, as he did at home, without a jacket, but you couldn't have guessed it from his qualifying round at Muirfield. His reliable draw turned into an uncontrollable hook in the heavy wind. He didn't break 90 and failed to make the field.

McDermott returned to the British Open and finished fifth in 1913, then the best showing by an American. A couple of months later, Vardon and Ray were on McDermott's home turf for a series of exhibitions. Because they were getting $150 a man per exhibition, some Americans thought they were being "held up" by the famous Brits, but they customarily received $500 each on their native soil. At the Shawnee Open in Shawnee-on-Delaware, Pennsylvania, a tune-up for the U.S. Open that September, the duo might have wished they were home: McDermott beat Alex Smith by eight strokes, Vardon by thirteen, Ray by fourteen.

But it was the aftermath that made real news as the papers reported the words of an arrogant winner. "We hope our foreign visitors had a good time," McDermott said, "but we don't think they did, and we are sure they won't win the National Open." Some accounts were more incendiary: "The Open champion, with a sneering twirl of his mouth, jumped on a chair and said the visiting English golfers may as well go back home, as their quest of the American championship honors will get them nowhere in particular." McDermott, whom the *New York Times* noted was "worried greatly over the affair and has almost broken down under the strain," claimed he was misquoted, his words taken out of a joking context.

United States Golf Association officials, miffed by McDermott's arrogance, threatened to reject his U.S. Open entry but relented. McDermott placed eighth at The Country Club, as Massachusetts amateur Francis Ouimet defeated Vardon and Ray in an epic underdog achievement that quickly displaced McDermott's Open history to a distant shelf in the eyes of many—even though McDermott had offered encouragement to the twenty-year-old caddie. "Just play your own game," the one American told the other. "Pay no attention to Vardon and Ray."

McDermott had worries other than his place on golf's throne. Stock investments had gone badly, erasing the financial gains that accompanied his national titles. In 1914 he sailed to Britain for another shot at the British but missed a ferry and a train that would have gotten him to Prestwick in time for qualifying. Officials offered to bend the rules for him, but he declined, saying it would be unfair to the other competitors.

Then, just as his return voyage back to America on the swift *Kaiser Wilhelm II* was beginning, the ship was struck by a grain carrier in the foggy English Channel. Although the ship suffered a large gash, it made it safely back to England. Some passengers, including McDermott, who was in the ship's barber shop when the collision occurred, were put in lifeboats. Physically McDermott was okay, but his mind was fragile. "Everything had hit within a year," his sister Gertrude explained. "First the stock failure, then the awful results of the Shawnee tournament, then the Open and finally that wreck."

"Johnny entered the 1914 U.S. Open," Finegan writes, "but the indomitable—some would say abrasive—self-confidence that had always marked his demeanor was nowhere in evidence." McDermott finished in a desultory tie for ninth at Midlothian Country Club near Chicago. In mid-October, his mind cracking, he collapsed at the pro shop in Atlantic City. On Halloween his parents came to bring him home, but soon he was taken to two mental hospitals in Massachusetts and another one in Philadelphia. On June 23, 1916, less than two months from his twenty-fifth birthday, McDermott's mother committed him to the State Hospital for the Insane in Norristown, Pennsylvania. She was ordered to pay $1.75 a week "for support of said lunatic in said Hospital, until further notice."

The Norristown hospital opened in 1880, with a series of buildings, some ivy-covered, connected by ground-level tunnels spread over a thousand acres. "Norristown was considered a good state hospital and compared to other state hospitals had a fairly good reputation, but they were all grossly overcrowded at the time," says Dr. E. Fuller Torrey, a research psychiatrist who has authored twenty books on mental illness. "It would generally be pretty chaotic." By the end of McDermott's first year at Norristown, there were nearly three thousand patients in the wards.

"There were some states, Georgia and others, where he would have been worse off," says medical historian Gerald Grob, author of *Mental Illness and American Society: 1875–1940*. "The Pennsylvania hospitals were by no means snakepits." There were diversions. Patients got to play baseball on Wednesdays, and Vitagraph movies were shown weekly. Ice cream was served every two weeks in the summer, and Easter eggs were given on Easter. The Red Cross provided Christmas packages for "soldier patients," and cigars were available thanks to a donation of ten thousand annually by a Philly businessman.

McDermott, according to Finegan, was one of the calmer patients: "[He] was labeled in the hospital reports variously as paranoid, delusional, catatonic, hallucinatory, incoherent, apa-

Tall Shadows

thetic, silent, retarded, passive, preoccupied, seclusive. He made no contact with staff or patients. Indeed he rarely spoke. He spent endless hours scribbling unintelligibly in notebooks, claiming he was writing his mother's and father's names."

Mental institutions, when McDermott was stricken and for decades thereafter, were basically holding cells. Restraints and sedatives were used to subdue the aggressive and violent, and some patients were wrapped tightly in a sheet, which was then drenched with water so that it would shrink and bind the person even tighter. "They thought water calmed people down," Torrey explains, but it is hard to fathom why McDermott received hydrotherapy after his trauma in the shipwreck.

The Norristown facility housed people from all walks of life, including actors, brass founders, dyers, hucksters, nuns, soldiers, and watchmen. In 1922 its professional golfer got a makeshift, six-hole course measuring 1,232 yards. Following a fundraising exhibition for McDermott in Philadelphia, Walter Hagen came to the hospital and played golf with him. McDermott told Hagen, "I don't think I ever saw a more beautiful view than from here. Tell the boys I'm getting along just fine."

In 1925 McDermott emerged to play his final competitive rounds. He broke 80 one round in the Philadelphia Open but finished last. At Shawnee he shot 342 for seventy-two holes, next to last and fifty-nine strokes behind winner Willie Macfarlane, the reigning U.S. Open champ. Bud Lewis, a longtime Philadelphia area club pro who was fifteen at the time, was in attendance at Merion in late July when McDermott shot 329 and beat six players. "Holed one putt on the twelfth green, about thirty feet," recalls Lewis, "and he just laughed all the way to the next tee."

Although his final-round 87 was his last competitive score, McDermott continued to play. Lewis became a playing partner in the late 1930s. "I'd pick him up at Norristown," Lewis says. "He'd have his golf shoes on. He'd come down ready-made, wearing a suit and tie. We'd play, then I'd take him back. He would shoot in the 80s. He had big grips, still the biggest I've ever seen." Lewis's conversations with McDermott were short and sometimes frustrating. "If you talked about anything serious, his eyes would water up. He kind of stuttered. He knew what was going on, but he couldn't say it. He couldn't really talk." But when Lewis brought up the U.S. Open victories, he thought it registered with the champ. "When you mentioned it, he'd give you the smile and the laugh."

On late Sunday afternoons that were fit for golf in the summers of 1956 and '57, Jerry Pisano, then a young assistant pro at Overbrook Golf Club in Philadelphia, would wait for Gertrude and Alice to drop off their brother at the club. It was part of Pisano's job to play nine holes with McDermott, who would arrive in shirt and tie, his sleeves rolled up not quite to the elbows.

"He was an old man, kind of scrawny looking," Pisano says. "But he stayed right up with me, give or take a club. He could drive the ball 225 yards. No matter how goofy he looked or how goofy he sounded, he played golf. He would go around in 39, 40, 41. And Overbrook was a tough track. He just did it out of instinct." Pisano, eager to glean some wisdom from such a trailblazer, tried to ask McDermott golf questions—but with little success. "I'd start conversations with him," he says, "and he'd carry conversations with me but abruptly fade out."

Whether it was the effect of medications or the fact that about half of schizophrenics improve as they age, McDermott spent more time out of the hospital the last fifteen years of his life. But his mind was still limited. "He didn't know what year it was," says Pete Trenham, the longtime pro at St. Davids Golf Club who has written a history of the Philadelphia PGA section. "I was talking to him one time, and he said, 'I saw [Bobby] Jones at Merion the other day. I think he's going to be pretty good.'"

In June 1971, sixty years after his breakthrough victory, McDermott went to Merion and watched Lee Trevino beat Jack Nicklaus in the U.S. Open. He was a forgotten relic in outdated clothing, shooed out of the pro shop one day because he didn't look as though he belonged. Less than two months later, on August 1, eleven days short of his eightieth birthday and a day after he played nine holes at Valley Forge Golf Club, McDermott's heart gave out. His passing received three paragraphs in the following day's *Philadelphia Inquirer*. Seats weren't hard to find at his funeral.

After McDermott's death, his devoted sisters gave his 1911 U.S. Open winner's medal to Leo Fraser, patriarch at Atlantic City Country Club. A couple of times a year in the 1950s and 1960s, McDermott visited his old club, and Fraser would come see him in Pennsylvania. When Fraser died in 1986, his family found the medal in his desk. They displayed it for years—once getting a $50,000 offer from a collector—before donating it in 1997 to the United States Golf Association.

McDermott was buried in the vast Holy Cross Cemetery in Yeadon, Pennsylvania, one of scores of men with the same name laid to rest there. The John McDermott who is still the youngest man to win the U.S. Open is in the golf-appropriate section 18. On a recent spring day following a lot of rain, bright green grass the height of U.S. Open rough lapped at the base of the monument, making it hard to see the inscription on one side.

First American Born
Golf Champion
1911–1912

Alice, who died in 1973, and Gertrude, who passed away in 1979, are buried next to their brother, but when Gertrude died there was no one left to make sure her name got on the stone. If you don't ask, you don't know she is there.

June 11, 2004

In 2011, on the centennial of Johnny McDermott's first national championship victory and forty years after his death, I remembered the troubled star again during the U.S. Open at Congressional Country Club. I discovered a 1916 reflection about McDermott from famed sportswriter Grantland Rice. "There isn't any question," Rice wrote, "but that McDermott would have been to American golf what [Harry] Vardon is to British play if John J. had not been forced out through fate just at the moment when he was coming upon the uplands of his career." Rory McIlroy, twenty-two, scored a runaway victory at Congressional. It was a phenomenal achievement, but a century later McDermott, who won his two titles before turning twenty-one, remains the youngest U.S. Open champion.

CHAPTER FOUR

Man of the Century

Golf's oldest legend lives quietly in Marco Island, Florida, in a comfortable fourth-floor apartment flush on the Gulf of Mexico, with a view almost as expansive as the life he has led. He was born before the airplane, raised before radio, a star decades before television. He drops more names by accident than most people do with a full sweat. Harry Vardon? Played with him. Bernard Darwin and Grantland Rice? Interviewed by them. Ed Sullivan? Caddied with him. Howard Hughes? Taught to fly by him. The sand wedge? Invented it. And for modern-day gladiators who gauge success by White House visitations: Warren Harding asked Gene Sarazen to stop by in 1922. "I'm the oldest living *everything*," Sarazen says.

Sarazen is ninety-three, and if the weather is too hot or too cool or, as on this October day, too damp, he has to take the view from inside. His mind is still sharp, and he doesn't even wear glasses. His face, despite all those decades in the sun, is remarkably unlined. He still has a car and occasionally drives. But when recalling the past these days, he edits his stories for brevity, to save his strength as much as anything. Sarazen has lost some twenty pounds in recent years—he had to have his trademark knickers taken in two inches in the waist—and he is concerned about his ebbing appetite. "I don't eat much," he says, "but I like this new spaghetti, this angel hair."

He is also bothered by arthritis, particularly in his shoulders, an affliction that limited his golf to two swings during 1995—sendoff shots to start the Masters in April and the Sarazen World Open a couple of weeks ago. "It's so painful that I don't like to do it," he says. "I don't know how I managed to get that ball off the first tee at Augusta."

The week prior to the Sarazen, Donald Panoz, who began the event in 1994 to honor the old pro, was concerned that Sarazen might forgo his duties as honorary starter. "But I was talking with him and asked how many people would be traveling up on the plane with him," Panoz says. "And he said, 'I'm traveling light. It's just going to be me, my grandson, and my driver.'" For the record, Sarazen ended the season as he began it, with a drive down the middle of the fairway, never mind the cortisone shots he had to take just to be able to take his cuts.

Sarazen has lived so long that his annual appearance at the Masters—he became an honorary starter in the early 1980s, at first playing a full nine holes, and more recently merely striking one tee shot in the presence of those whippersnappers Byron Nelson and Sam Snead—is Sarazen's calling card to a generation of fans. There he is, getting Snead to tee up his ball. There he is, bunting one down the sprinkler line one more time, with just enough hand action left to illustrate why Harry Vardon—yes, *the* Harry Vardon—once said of him, "His swing is perfect, and he has that clasp-knife sort of snap in hitting iron shots that distinguishes the very great golfer from the merely good."

"I feel like an exhibit in a museum," Sarazen observed at Augusta a few years ago. That was about the same time he told Hord Hardin, then chairman of the Masters, that he was getting too old to hit a shot. "Gene," Hardin told him, "they don't want to see you play; they just want to see if you're still alive."

There wasn't a Masters when Gene Sarazen was born, the

youngest of two children of Federico and Adela Saraceni on February 27, 1902, in Harrison, New York. Golf was about as new to the United States as the Saracenis were. Gene's birth name was Eugenio Saraceni, which he would change when he was sixteen and starting his unlikely way in golf. "I made a hole-in-one, and the newspaper had a headline with Eugenio Saraceni," Sarazen recalls, pronouncing the name with a proper Italian accent, "and I thought that sounded like a violin player. So I changed it. G-e-n-e S-a-r-a-z-e-n. That wasn't in any phone book. I liked the way it sounded, and I liked the way it looked. It sounded like a golfer."

Sarazen became a golfer against all odds, not the least of which was Federico's opposition to the sport. Federico Saraceni had studied in Rome to become a priest but had to change his plans when both his parents died in the same year. In America he earned a living as a carpenter by day, then retired to his basement each night to read the Italian classics. He believed that his son's station in life would also be as a tradesman. "He wanted me to be a good carpenter," Gene says. "He wasn't for the country club crowd. I don't think he ever was in a clubhouse."

Sarazen's father saw his son play one stroke in his entire career. It was at the 1923 PGA Championship at Pelham Country Club outside New York City, a tournament Sarazen won. Federico stood on a road adjacent to the tenth hole and peered through a fence. "He was looking over from a highway," Sarazen says, "and I had about a forty-foot putt which I missed. When I got home that night, he said, 'To think you get paid for what you're doing. You missed that putt.' I told him I was lucky to get down in two shots in that position, but he didn't know. He took a swipe at a ball once and he fell down. He almost broke his leg."

Despite the discouragement from his father, Sarazen loved golf almost from the time he was eight and caddieing for the first time at Larchmont (New York) Country Club. Because of better opportunities at nearby Apawamis Club, Sarazen moved there, where one of his fellow caddies was Ed Sullivan. One day, Sarazen and Sullivan got called down for the next twosome, and Sullivan jumped at the bigger and flashier of the two bags. But by the end of the day, sportswriter Grantland Rice had given Sarazen $3—three times what Sullivan got—and begun a lifelong friendship with him.

Sarazen's caddieing money went toward the Saracenis' bills. His heart, however, got deeper into the game, inspired by Francis Ouimet's stunning victory in the 1913 U.S. Open and stoked by matches on a makeshift neighborhood course with tin-can cups and schoolyard games so persistent that his teachers would set fire to the kids' wooden-shafted clubs. Whereupon Sarazen, who used the interlocking grip favored by Ouimet, and his friends would retrieve the clubheads, scour up some replacement shafts, and have golf again.

Sarazen wasn't in school very long, forced to drop out in the sixth grade to earn more money for the Saraceni household. In 1917, when he was fifteen, the family moved thirty-five miles to Bridgeport, Connecticut, home of bustling wartime manufacturing. Gene caught on at Remington Arms, drilling holes in wooden crates in which shells were sent to Europe. In January 1918, he caught a cold, which became pneumonia and later developed into pleural empyema. Sarazen was so sick he received the last rites. He stabilized, but to drain the fluid from his chest and to prevent the onset of tuberculosis, he underwent an operation in which two holes were drilled through his back between the ribs. When he was finally discharged from the hospital in May, his doctor, John Shea, told Sarazen to get an outdoor job. To Sarazen, that meant golf, but the game, despite Ouimet's triumph, was still tough for homebreds to enter. The Scottish and English immigrant pros ran the roost. But Sarazen persisted, honing his game at a nine-hole public course in Bridgeport called Beardsley Park. Before long, thanks to the help of its pro, Al Ciuci, Sarazen was able to get a job as a shop boy at Brooklawn Country Club.

Two of Brooklawn's most prominent members, Archie and Willie Wheeler, convinced their pro, George Sparling, that Sarazen was something special, and he was on his way to a life as a competitive golfer, with one more detour. In the winter of 1919, Sarazen returned to Bridgeport Hospital during the middle of an influenza epidemic. He had the grim task of delivering the dead to the morgue. "The patients that were going to die during the night, the doctor would put a red light over their bed," Sarazen remembers. "And when they were gone I would take them down. I would take shots of whiskey so I wouldn't catch the flu. There was nothing else you could do. There was no vaccine, no pill to take."

Sarazen's game advanced quickly. By 1922, when he was just twenty, he had tasted victory and life on what passed as the professional circuit. Working as the pro in Titusville, Pennsylvania, he caught the eye of Emil Loeffler, the greenkeeper, and William Fownes, the founder of Oakmont Country Club in Pittsburgh. Fownes bankrolled a trip for Sarazen to play Skokie Country Club in Chicago, in advance of the 1922 U.S. Open there.

"I got back to Pittsburgh," Sarazen says, "and I told Mr. Fownes that the course was built around my game. I was fortunate. But in order to win those things, you've got to be fortunate." When Sarazen won the 1922 U.S. Open, he also started what would be a lifetime of good relations with the press. He was a good quote when quotes weren't the lifeblood of newspaper stories. "All men are created equal," Sarazen said after winning the Open in 1922. "I'm just one stroke better than the rest." When Sarazen was in his prime, favorable attention affected the endorsements and exhibitions that a golfer might get to supplement his paltry purse winnings—to this day, Sarazen speaks fondly of his 1930 Agua Caliente Open triumph in Mexico that paid him an unheard-of $10,000—and he knew how to play the game.

When Sarazen insured his hands for $150,000 or suggested that the hole be eight inches in diameter instead of 4¼ inches, it brought him headlines. His peers were jealous and at times suspicious of Sarazen. His publicity seeking coexisted with a pep-pery on-course demeanor obscured at times by a Cheshire-cat grin. "That grin of his," wrote legendary British golf writer Ber-nard Darwin, "is the mark of a sunny and delightful nature, but not of an altogether placid one." If Hagen was the showman and Jones the gentleman, Sarazen rounded out American golf's troika of the 1920s as a competitor who gave no quarter.

Sarazen was in fact as solid as the calves that supported his five feet, five inches, a man who always took care of his body. He strengthened his golf muscles by swinging a weighted practice club—an idea he got from a chat with Ty Cobb. But Sarazen's real heavy lifting was simply in blazing a trail as an Italian Ameri-can during a time when not everyone liked pasta. And if he had changed his name for reasons other than not to sound like a vio-linist, no one could have blamed him. But Sarazen was forever giving people a reason to pay attention. When he traveled the world during the 1930s, taking golf to South America and Asia, Sarazen was not only making money but, as Donald Panoz points out, "being a globetrotter before globe-trotting was cool." It was risky business and meant flying in dicey planes, driving on dan-gerous roads, and hitching a ride on the occasional freighter. He made friends easily in the foreign lands, and the Japanese (per-haps, Sarazen reasons, because he was more or less their size) took a special liking to him. He can remember playing in Japan in the late 1930s, several years after he invented the sand wedge. Sarazen would play a bunker shot, and when he walked out of the trap, the Japanese would filter into the sand and take their place in the stance he had carved.

Every golfer who blasts out of a bunker and saves par ought to thank Sarazen for creating, in 1931 and 1932, the first modern sand wedge. His inspiration: the way the tail of the plane was adjusted upon take-off one day when he was learning to fly with Howard Hughes in Florida. Sarazen also credited watching ducks land on a pond, skimming the surface with rounded bellies.

Tall Shadows

A model with a concave face, eventually ruled illegal by the United States Golf Association, existed earlier, but Sarazen soldered a thick base, or flange, onto a niblick, creating a clubhead that would bounce rather than stick in the sand. The new design revolutionized the way pros viewed sand bunkers; now they weren't a crapshoot. Although the advent of steel shafts coincided with Sarazen's invention and has to be taken into account, the average winning score in the ten U.S. Opens from 1932 through 1941 was 6.6 strokes lower than the winning average in the U.S. Opens played from 1922 through 1931. For Sarazen, the only drawback was that he never made a dime off his invention. Since he was under contract to Wilson Sporting Goods—he was signed in 1923 and remains under contract to this day—the company reaped the benefits. The same thing happened when Sarazen popularized the use of "reminder" grips.

Sarazen once said that inventing the sand wedge was his biggest contribution to golf. It was a singular achievement, ranking right up there with a stroke he played during the final round of the 1935 Masters—at the time a fledgling little invitational tournament whose only real attribute was that golf's recently retired hero, Bobby Jones, had begun it.

Augusta National Golf Club's par-five fifteenth hole was then 485 yards, and as Sarazen reached his second shot, he knew he needed to birdie three of his final four holes in order to tie leader Craig Wood. Today golfers routinely reach the green with a middle iron for their second shots, but Sarazen had about 235 yards to the hole, over the small pond that fronts the green. The distance called for his three-wood, but the snug lie demanded a four-wood, a club not yet as popular with golfers as the longer two-wood, or brassie, but one that Sarazen had embraced for some time.

Although only twenty-three people were standing by the green— Sarazen's count, including Jones and Walter Hagen—Sarazen's stroke was one of the first "shots heard round the world." The double eagle got Sarazen into a playoff with Wood, which he won the following day for his last major title. His Masters triumph, combined with his earlier victories in the U.S. and British Opens and PGA Championship, also gave Sarazen the distinction of being the first golfer to win all four modern "Grand Slam" events. Ben Hogan, Jack Nicklaus, and Gary Player are still the only others to have done so. [Tiger Woods made it a fivesome in 2000.]

At the time, Sarazen was hoping for a plaque to mark the spot from which he struck his historic blow, but the divot was merely filled in with grass seed. But twenty years later, in 1955, the small bridge on which golfers cross the pond on the left side was named in his honor. By then Sarazen was fifty-three, long removed as a regular player on tour and fifteen years from his last serious run at a major, the 1940 U.S. Open, when Lawson Little beat him in a playoff. Sarazen was still fit and would have made a killing if there had been a senior tour. He was doing occasional television commentary for NBC—Sarazen prematurely congratulated Hogan for winning the 1955 U.S. Open with the eventual winner, Jack Fleck, still on the course—but mostly spent his time on his farm in upstate New York.

Sarazen had lived with his wife, Mary, and their children, Gene Jr. and Mary Ann, on a farm since 1933—first in Brookfield, Connecticut, and later in upstate New York. He got his nickname, "The Squire," in the process. He always liked the moniker, and the irony that it stuck on someone who grew up a poor city boy was never lost on him.

He was all but out of public view by 1961, when Shell Oil decided that a golf travelogue show would be good for business. *Shell's Wonderful World of Golf*, which ran on NBC-TV from 1962 through 1970, featured pros playing matches in exotic locales. It brought host Sarazen into the dens and grillrooms of a new generation of fans. It was a lot like his worldly travels decades earlier, only this time the ride was smoother and the seats in first-class.

"The show really gave him a new lease on life," says Fred Raphael, producer-director of the Shell series who later started the Legends of Golf, the precursor to the senior tour, in 1978. "He didn't just

Tall Shadows

represent Shell; he represented golf. Because he had already been around the world, it was like that show was created for him."

Sarazen also had a hand in the formation of the Legends tournament. He and Raphael were dining after the second round of the 1963 Masters when Sarazen left the table to call for his starting time. "He came back," Raphael remembers, "and said, 'Tomorrow the old legend, Gene Sarazen, will be paired with the future legend, Arnold Palmer.' The word 'legend' got me thinking."

Raphael has many memories of the Shell days, none more vivid than one particular trip to Rome. Sarazen's father, by then in his nineties, had returned to Italy many years before, disenchanted with American politics. He received a regular check from Gene, but the father and son who never got along hadn't seen each other in a long time. So Gene Sarazen went to have dinner with Federico Saraceni. Sarazen gave his father a television set. It was the last time he ever saw him. "That was a great moment for him," Raphael says. "He was as happy that night as I ever saw him."

Sarazen is now about the age that his father was then. But other than the bittersweet reality of outliving most of his friends, he has few regrets. "I wouldn't wish to start over again for anything," he says. "I won the four majors and I'm satisfied." Not factoring in the aging process, Sarazen's life hasn't been the same since 1986, when Mary, whom he married in 1924, died shortly after suffering a heart attack. She had the formal education he never received and a love and trust in him that wouldn't quit. "Here I was, the Open champion, and I only had a sixth-grade education," Sarazen says. "Then I met this girl, and she was so well-educated. I married her quick. I was very fortunate. But the last eight years have been lonely."

A housekeeper shares Sarazen's apartment. His daughter, Mary Ann Ilnicki, and her son, Gene Martin, live on Marco Island and see him often. Sarazen's grandson is particularly close to him, an aide-de-camp really, who travels with him on his infrequent out-of-town trips. Sarazen is looking forward to the reopening this year of The Island Club, at which he maintained an office he visited daily to handle correspondence and eat lunch until a fire destroyed it almost two years ago. He lost some memorabilia in the fire, as he had in 1976 during a blaze at home in New Hampshire, where he summered. And if not for the quick thinking of some golf-savvy firemen, who covered some important articles with a tarp, the loss would have been greater.

Sarazen tends to his various charitable concerns—primarily a scholarship program at Siena College and the Urgent Care Center on Marco Island—and watches plenty of news and golf on television. He kept up with the O. J. Simpson trial and judiciously says, "When people ask me what I thought of the verdict, I say I believe in the American system. I don't want to take sides." He handles letters and autograph requests, the latter increasing after The Squire has made a television appearance because, he admits, it is evidence that he is still alive: "They say, 'I thought that guy was dead.'"

Of the current crop of golfers, Sarazen enjoys watching Greg Norman the most. He also admires Corey Pavin, whose stature is similar to Sarazen's and who proved this year in the U.S. Open that he also knows what to do with a four-wood. But Sarazen most enjoys watching televised senior golf. He is a little bit more familiar with that cast of characters, and they seem to play faster. Sarazen always champed at the bit when he played, and he believes everyone else should too. He is uncertain whether he will attend the Masters next spring, when he will be ninety-four. "That's a long ways off," he says.

Sarazen's life has been so long and so rich, it longs for something to tie it together. That would be the Marco Island phone book. Gene Sarazen is listed, the only Sarazen in its pages, just as he had diagrammed those many years ago when he picked a name that sounded like a golfer. Even a double eagle disappears into the dark, but how wondrous the ride.

November 24, 1995

Gene Sarazen died May 13, 1999, at age ninety-seven from complications of pneumonia, having lived a life only the biggest of dreamers could have imagined. "It felt like meeting history," LPGA legend Nancy Lopez said of Sarazen when he passed away. Indeed it was, and I'm so glad I also had the opportunity. If you have a chance, search the Internet and try to find the footage of Sarazen, then seventy-one, making a hole-in-one during the 1973 British Open on the "Postage Stamp" par-three eighth hole at Royal Troon. It remains one of golf's magical moments, a shot struck by one of the game's most enduring personalities.

CHAPTER FIVE

A Place in Time

Glenna Collett Vare was different. It wasn't just the pearls she wore when she played, the balletic action of her left foot as she swung, or the magical ability she had for finding a four-leaf clover. "She had a way of just scanning the rough and going, 'There you go,'" says her son, Ned. Or even the way she helped people begin to understand—at a time when most had little inclination to do so—that an attractive woman wasn't less so with some sweat on her brow and a three-wood clutched assuredly in her hands.

There was something else. As the years turn into decades and they gray way beyond their achievements, many champions crave to be reminded of their glory the way a baby needs milk. How do we know Vare was not that way? In front of a multishelf trophy case in a house where she once lived hung a beige curtain. With a pull of a string, the preeminent American woman golfer of the 1920s and early 1930s could shutter her past and sit down to savor a drink or a novel or a game of bridge, free from the silvery glints that recalled her phenomenal golf accomplishments.

"Golf, when she wasn't playing or getting ready to play—it was over," Ned Vare said in a recent interview. "When a round was over, it was over. She didn't want to talk about her shots or hear about yours. My father and I would talk endlessly at dinner about how we played, and she would be bored sick. For Mom, it was enough to do it."

Vare, who died in 1989, chiseled her performances in an era when women's golf was more sorority than vast corporate tool, yet they are no less arresting: the record six U.S. Women's Amateur championships she won between 1922 and 1935; the stunning 1924 season in which she won fifty-nine of sixty matches, the only loss occurring on the nineteenth hole of her U.S. Amateur semifinal against Mary K. Browne, when Browne's ball caromed off Vare's and into the cup; and her pitched battles abroad with legendary British star Joyce Wethered. Combined with her graciousness and spirit, Vare's success elevated her into the stratosphere of the golden age of sports. She was "the female Bobby Jones," a woman who penned two books, wrote articles for *Vanity Fair*, and posed, as an "empress of the links," for photographer Edward Steichen.

She won her first five national championships as a single woman, Glenna Collett, personifying the ideal, as Herbert Warren Wind wrote, "of the American girl." She won her last in 1935 as Mrs. Edwin H. Vare Jr., a thirty-two-year-old mother of two who, in the final, conquered seventeen-year-old newcomer Patty Berg, who would become the pepper-pot star of a new generation, one to which golf would be more than the avocation it was for Vare.

"Much as I love golf," Vare wrote in her 1928 book, *Ladies in the Rough*, "I consider it merely a pastime. . . . If you have common sense and the ability to compromise, you can be a model husband or wife, and admirable parent, and a stunning golf-player all at the same time. Just because I am interested in golf, there is no reason for me to limit my association and activities to the fairways."

Born in New Haven, Connecticut, and reared in Providence, Rhode Island, Vare was the daughter of a former national bicycling champion, George Collett. After forgoing the chance to open Providence's first Ford auto dealership, he had gotten into insurance and had the resources to join the Metacomet Club, where the athletically minded Glenna was first exposed to the sport she would soon dominate.

As a young girl, she would scavenge for old golf balls, bringing them home and washing them with a lye solution, then painting them to an "angelic whiteness" before setting them on her mother's cake rack to dry. By fourteen she had put away her baseball glove, which she'd worn with aplomb, and started taking golf lessons from Metacomet's pros, Alex Smith and John Anderson, whose instruction included a ditty sung to the tune of "Yankee Doodle Dandy": "Mind your music and your step, And with your clubs be handy." She also learned how to hit the hell out of the ball.

As Vare explained in *Golf for Young Players*, "There is something quite natural about a youngster taking to this game, for there is a big stick with which to make a lusty hit, there is a quiet, demure and rather harmless-looking ball to whack, and there is a wide expanse over which to roam."

Maturing quickly after shooting 132 in her first important championship, Vare developed an eye-catching swing—one not given its due in the instructional photos taken during her prime. It was brisk and powerful, with a full backswing marked by a distinctive up-and-down twirl of her left foot and an impact position at which she was up on both toes throwing all of her 125 pounds into the hit. Once, with an assist from the wind and packed turf, she hit a drive measured at 307 yards.

"She was beautiful," says ninety-five-year-old Gene Sarazen, recalling his introduction to Collett at a Rhode Island pro-am in 1919. As a player or a person, I asked Sarazen. "Both," he said, the intervening years clouding his memory not a bit.

"She was a good, long driver," recalls ninety-year-old Maureen Orcutt, one of Vare's amateur rivals. "But her spoon [three-wood] was her best shot. She could do about anything with it. She was wonderful with that club." Like Jones, Vare had to tame a youthful temper. She endured some lapses against opponents she was supposed to beat easily, but she kept improving. "No one pays much

Tall Shadows

attention to the fact that she always keeps her *mind* on the ball," The *American Golfer* reported. "She just goes after it with a grim determination and wallops it hard, and if she gets into a bad place, why she wastes no time worrying or thinking of consequences, but just keeps her mind on the ball, goes after it and wallops it hard again."

To be a champion, Vare believed, a person needed "a love of combat, serenity of mind and a spirit of fearlessness." She could win going away, as she did over Virginia Van Wie, 13 and 12, in the scheduled thirty-six-hole final of the 1928 U.S. Women's Amateur, displaying "a brand of golf that would have put Bobby Jones to work," Grantland Rice observed. And she could win from behind, as she proved by rallying from four down with four holes to go in defeating Dorothy Higbie in the 1929 U.S. Women's Amateur quarterfinals. The only thing Vare wasn't able to do was beat Wethered.

Wethered was Vare's opposite across the Atlantic, another strong and stylish golfer who hit the ball off her toes and had "the best swing I've ever seen," according to Jones. While Wethered, four-time British Ladies champion, never ventured to America to meet the challenge of Vare in her home country, Vare resolutely sailed to the United Kingdom to try to unseat Wethered. Wethered beat Vare, 4 and 3, in the third round at Troon in 1925, even though the American was only one over par for fifteen holes. Four years later, at St. Andrews, Wethered came out of retirement to meet Vare's challenge. The two stars ultimately met in the thirty-six-hole final, a match many believe was the best ever played in women's golf.

Battling not only Wethered but a boisterously partisan gallery and an Old Course stretched to 6,600 yards, Vare was under par in surging to a five-up lead after eleven holes. But the American lost an opportunity to expand her lead when she missed a short putt on the twelfth, and Wethered fought back to only two down at lunch. By the turn of the afternoon round, Wethered had built a four-up lead. Things looked bleak for Vare, but she quickly won two holes. On the fifteenth hole, Wethered holed an eighteen-foot par putt to keep her lead, and she eventually closed out the match on the seventeenth, the Road Hole, 3 and 1.

Three years later the two foes met for the last time, in the singles of the first Curtis Cup match. Wethered won easily, 6 and 4. "[Glenna] never could find a way of beating Joyce," says Orcutt, "but I always wondered why Joyce didn't come over here and play in our Amateur. I think Glenna was tops. I don't know how she would have done against Babe Zaharias or some of the girls now, but I wish we could find out."

Well after she stopped breaking records, Vare continued to play avidly, mixing rounds with her other sporting interests, trap and skeet shooting, and accompanying her husband on field trials. One day in 1954 Ned Vare played in a group ahead of his parents at Point Judith Country Club in Narragansett, Rhode Island, near the family's summer home. He walked off the eighteenth green having shot 69—and feeling rightly proud.

"I told my father," remembers Ned Vare. "He said, 'Match cards with your Mom,' who was then about fifty years old. She beat me, 2 and 1, and I think she might have had a 68, which was the course record. From the men's tees, which she always played."

By then golf was mostly a conduit for her friendships. During the Point Judith Invitational, a tournament she played in for more than sixty years, Vare hosted a lobster dinner for perhaps twenty people. After the main course was served, the very proper women from the right zip codes in Philadelphia and Long Island would sidearm the shells into a bowl in the center of the large table. "Golf was a vehicle for maintaining and enjoying her friends," says her son. "And what better way was there than by playing golf and then having a meal?"

But the legendary golfer didn't necessarily attract new friends with ease. As she grew older and more set in her ways, new acquaintances could have a hard time getting to know her. "I always found her a little bit hard to talk to," says 1973 U.S. Women's Amateur winner Carol Semple Thompson, one of the last of the lifelong amateurs. "She was older, sort of gruff and sure of herself. She was wonderful, but she would have scared me to death if I had to play against her."

Vare downplayed her competitiveness, but there was no doubt that she possessed the mind as well as the body necessary for athletic success. Prior to her arrival on the scene, most women golfers, bridled up in tight corsets and by even more restrictive attitudes—the Nineteenth Amendment was passed just two years before Vare's first national title—were content with a conservative strategy. "She taught us a new game," observed the British champion Dorothy Hurd Campbell. "Before Glenna, we ladies used to aim just for the green. Glenna showed us that ladies can play for the flag."

And though she was a graceful winner and a dignified loser, there was no doubt that Vare wanted to win—and knew *how*. She captained the 1950 U.S. Curtis Cup team, which included a young and timid Peggy Kirk, now Peggy Kirk Bell, the renowned teaching pro in North Carolina. Kirk didn't want to be picked to play a singles match, but she pleaded her case without success.

"I call the shots," Vare told her. "I'm the captain. You're playing." On the sixteenth hole of her match with Jeanne Bisgood, Kirk informed Vare that she was one down. Vare left but returned presently with a four-leaf clover and said simply to her young charge, "Go get her." Kirk won the match, one up.

Even in more informal settings, Vare's drive and spirit could surface. Ned Vare recalls partnering his mother in a mixed-foursomes match sometime in the early 1950s and losing track of the score. "I made the mistake of asking her how we stood in the match," he recalls. "Mom looked at me very crossly and said, 'What do you mean, how do we stand? Why am I playing with you? This is why we're here, to beat these people. We're three up and we're going to get to four up.'"

In the 1960s Vare was a regular in the U.S. Senior Women's Amateur, beginning with her runner-up finish to Orcutt in the inaugural championship in 1962. Vare continued to better her age well into her eighties. Her distance disappeared, but her full turn never did, and she still danced on her left foot. "Bobby Jones had wild feet like that too," Ned Vare says. "That was the style. She did it all her life, never changed. And nobody was going to tell her, 'Glenna, I think you'd be better off if you keep your feet flat.' She would have melted them with that stare she could have."

Vare stuck with traditional clubs but had a revelation once when someone noticed the slick, leather grips on her old clubs and replaced them with a set of tacky, composition style. "She said, 'God, it's a whole new game,'" says her son. "She had such an easier time holding the club. She hadn't realized that putting new grips on would make the game that much easier."

The girl who learned to drive a car at ten was a woman who still loved to drive at eighty. She favored a Cadillac and often shared the front seat with her terrier, Jimmy, one in a long series of pet dogs, riding shotgun. But it was his master who had some bark behind the wheel. "Glenna was one of the fastest drivers I ever had the bad experience to ride with," recalls the longtime amateur and golf-course designer Alice Dye. "She passed between a car and a mailbox more often than anybody I've known. She was a speedster. She loved anybody who played golf—as long as they played quickly."

Around her winter club, Gulf Stream Country Club, the dawdling drew her wrath. "Glenna used to barrel through every group on the course," says Thompson. "She'd stand in the fairways tapping her toes waiting for people to move aside so she could go through." Even as she grew older, Vare liked to spend her hare-footed rounds in the company of better golfers, which led to a long friendship and regular games with Judy Callaghan, a 1973 Rhode Island state champ and a fellow Point Judith member.

Though Vare was seventy-four when Callaghan first played with her in 1978, vestiges of the old champion would occasionally pop through: an iron would be struck as crisply as a winter wind; a putt would be willed into the hole; or the octogenarian would straddle an out-of-bounds fence to play a recovery shot. "She had that old-fashioned swing and hit *down* on the ball," Callaghan says. Mostly, however, Callaghan had to imagine what the young Glenna had been like as a golfer.

"I would try to pump her for information once in a while, but she didn't like questions about herself," Callaghan says. "But one day I was sitting in the cart with her and the dog, and I asked her, 'Ever had a hole-in-one?' 'Of course,' she said. Then there was a pause. 'Six of them.' There was another pause. 'And they were all in tournaments.'"

Vare picked up the requisite honors for being the pioneer that she was: the Bob Jones Award for sportsmanship from the United States Golf Association in 1965 and induction into the World Golf Hall of Fame in 1975. Interviews had worried her in her youth, despite what could be fawning coverage. ("Most women who spend a lot of time playing in tournaments get a kind of baked look," the *New Yorker* wrote in 1927. "Well, Glenna Collett isn't like that. She is a very nice-looking girl. There is nothing about her that reminds you she is a golf champion except her hands, with their short, strong fingers and the little pack of muscle on the outside curve of her palm.") Later in life, she dreaded public speaking.

"She was shy," says her daughter, Glennie Kalen, "but if she got to know you she was as open as all get-out." When Jack Nicklaus's Memorial Tournament honored her in 1982, she spent a dozen anxious months fretting about her two-minute speech. "She was vastly pleased that they chose to honor her, but she worried about that speech," Kalen says. "I have a lovely picture of her and Mr. Nicklaus just after it, and I can still see the nerves in her smile."

Vare resisted most attempts by others to coax recollections, but she allowed that her epic match with Wethered in 1929 had been her favorite, even though she had lost. "The match was so exciting," she recalled in 1975. "There were so many Scots watching the match and in those days the crowds followed the matches very, very closely. I was lucky to have a few friends, strong ones, who linked arms to keep the gallery from getting to me. Even still, I was very lucky to ever see a shot land. When I was winning, the silence was deafening. When she started to win, there was a noise like I had never heard."

In the mid-1980s writer James Dodson began an annual pilgrimage to Vare's summer home, hoping to be granted a round of golf with her, but she would have no part of it. Instead Vare asked Dodson about his life or enlisted his help in chopping carrots or served him a bowl of her homemade tomato soup. To see Glenna the golfer, Dodson had to sneak glimpses by peeking over a hedge.

"She was the most forthright woman I've ever met," Dodson says. "She'd talk about players she had played against, but not herself. She felt like she had outlived her time. There hadn't been many stories done on her in her later years. I think she felt golf had forgotten her."

Vare was eighty-five when she died of lymphoma on February 2, 1989. Her daughter received about two hundred letters from people around the world who had been touched by her mother, not so much for what she had done as for who she had been, someone with a sense of humor who did great things and was able to seal them up with a smile. For casual sports fans, Vare's death brought merely a mild tilt of the head that greets the passing of someone who so outlived her headlines.

By the time she passed away, it was getting easier for boys and girls to get into golf, even if they weren't born on the right block, but tougher and tougher to find any clover on a golf course. The Vare Trophy, for the LPGA player with the lowest scoring average, was being given each year on a dais crammed with other awards named for watches, sports drinks, and hotels.

"There are a lot of golfers coming up now who don't even know who Glenna was, and that's sad," says Jody Anschutz, an LPGA player who competed in the 1984 Curtis Cup at Muirfield, Scotland. "I know some gals on our tour who don't even know who [LPGA Hall of Famer] Mickey Wright is. Those women back then kept the fire burning."

Almost eighty-one at the time, Vare attended the 1984 Curtis Cup and played in an informal match pitting former players and current officials of the two sides. Having prepared for the occasion with extra walks and more golf than usual, Vare won her match, then spectated with an old rival from that inaugural 1932 Curtis Cup, Molly Gourlay. "Every time there was anything happening," Vare recalled in *The Illustrated History of Women's Golf,* "they'd pull out two chairs for Molly and me and there we'd sit, these two old dames, to be pointed out to everybody."

By then Vare had returned the important cups to the USGA and taken many of her other trophies—the ones she chose to hide behind that curtain—and had them melted down. The glory, compartmentalized now the way Vare always liked it to be, was reduced into a handsome, quite substantial silver tray. It listed the places where she had reigned in the spring of her four-leaf life and that of women's golf, spots like Pinehurst and Palm Beach and Shennecossett and White Sulphur Springs, during that time when women were just beginning to flex their golf muscles, no one better than she.

November 28, 1997

I didn't know that much about Glenna Collett Vare before I began researching this article, one of the most enjoyable I have ever worked on. She was a true trailblazer who, by her talent and her verve, convinced other women that there was nothing wrong with being a tough competitor on the golf course, that playing with gusto was a good thing. Vare noted that it was natural for youngsters to be attracted to golf, but she would probably be amazed at how well young women have performed in recent years, golfers such as Lexi Thompson and Lydia Ko, who haven't been intimidated competing against players twice, or three times, as old as they are. I hope every woman golfer in this century finds out a bit about Vare, a person to whom they owe a debt for helping the women's game evolve the way it has.

CHAPTER SIX

King of the Hill

Sam Snead's swing used to resemble a Faulkner sentence. It was long, laced with the perfect pause, and blessed with a powerful ending. Now that he is eighty-four years old, it is only slightly less so. He is driving off a tee beside me, on a piece of Florida land that was a swamp way back when, and he still purrs.

That will be Sam Snead's legacy, more than his glorious swing, the scads of tournaments he won, his Appalachian roots, or the funny way he putted. Like no one else, Sam Snead lasted.

"He has muscular rhythm, a flow of movement—all those things the advertising copy writers attribute to an automobile engine." Snead's swing has wrinkled a little since that description of him in 1950, and his eyes fail him so much that he needs help locating the flagsticks, but his action is still very smooth. And on this warm November day, he is plenty capable of opening my wallet. Snead doesn't need my twenty bucks for affirmation of what he used to be, and what he remains, but he will get them. As he has said about so many other matches, it will be "like pickin' corn."

The swing he styled. The bets he collected. The straw hat that covers the bald head. The eighty-two official tournaments and scores of others he won. The U.S. Open he didn't. The country roots from which he sprang. The world that golf let him see. The long, winding road that took him out of the Virginia mountains, an athletic boy in a pasture swinging sticks whittled into golf clubs, and took him on a magical trip to being rich and famous, is filled with this and that.

"They called me the God of Golf in Japan," Snead says. And while his Japanese hosts sat on pillows, the God of Golf got a chair.

So many memories. They flow like water over a fall, interrupted only occasionally by the rocky edge of age. Snead might forget someone's name, but in the same hour he will remember, with startling recall, details that boggle the listener: how a St. Louis taxi driver nearly got him disqualified; how they stuck needles around the hole in Peru so the Americans' putts would not drop; how he used four caddies in the course of winning the 1946 British Open; how an ostrich followed the play once in Argentina; how his mother, Laura, who was forty-seven when Sam was born, could heave a 192-pound barrel of flour into a wagon.

In conversation with Snead, he often returns to the early days in Virginia, just outside Hot Springs, where he was born and raised and still lives, on a 250-acre farm now, in a house on top of a hill like the Stetson Straw sits on his head, as if that is where it was always meant to be. Snead returns to his mother, to trapping a Noah's Ark of animals when he was a child, and to his oldest brother, Homer, gone now, who was as good with circuits and wires as Sam was with clubs and balls.

"Homer had more talent than all of us put together," Snead says. "You could dump a truckload of radio and television parts out and he could build you either one. He wired almost all the houses around us, put Delcos in, stuff like that. But he wanted me to go collect his money. And all most of those people had were a few sheep and a couple of cows. Before my mother died, she told me I would have to look after Homer, even though he was older. She said, 'He don't have the do.'" Sam, the youngest Snead, always had the do.

"I came and saw Mom after I got on tour in '37," Snead says, "and I asked her if she thought I ever would amount to anything.

She said, 'Yes, you never were still. You were always building something, doing something.'"

Snead is still building, still doing. Affiliated once again with the Greenbrier in White Sulphur Springs, West Virginia, he carries the title of golf professional emeritus at the resort he represented for almost forty years during his heyday. His current job description includes clinics and autograph sessions. "Yeah, it's been fun, but they ran my ass off for three years," Snead says. "I was going to Japan, Chicago, Palm Beach. I was bushed. But they really didn't put it on me this year. It's been a whole lot better."

Nearly every day Snead makes the forty-minute trip from his home to the Greenbrier. Robert Harris, the director of golf, has a stack of pictures, programs, and golf flags for him to sign. Over at The Sam Snead Collection in the hotel, Snead-logoed clothing and autographed memorabilia sell well. A fan can pick up a Snead-model straw hat for $35 or a reprint of Snead's first book, originally published and sold for $1 in 1938, for $29, or $54 if it's signed by Slammin' Sam. Snead likes the receipts, but the autograph craze bewilders him.

"I'll go in the store to sign," he says, "and they'll do $5,000 worth of business in an hour and a half. People have gone completely nuts over this autograph stuff. I don't get it." He allows that he has collected three signatures in his long life: one from a Hollywood star whose name he can't recall, which he got the first time he visited the Brown Derby, and ones from Presidents Eisenhower and Nixon.

Meister, Snead's thirteen-year-old golden retriever who has been a constant companion for a decade, doesn't give autographs. But the eighty-pound pet enjoys the life of a celebrity, accompanying his master nearly everywhere he goes, living, as Snead says, "the best life of any big dog ever." Meister rides shotgun in the golf cart each time Snead plays, and he looks on intently every time Snead hits a shot. Twice a day Snead hides an anti-inflammatory pill in a piece of bologna and gives it to Meister for his arthritis. "Damn,

I'll miss him when he's gone," Snead says. "If he lives one more year, he'll be lucky. I don't know if I'll want to get another dog."

Snead will always be a product of the old school and the Old South. He's still keen on telling an R-rated joke or story when the mood strikes him; his fellow Masters winner Gene Sarazen says he heads for the other side of the room at the annual champions dinner in order to stay out of storytelling range. But Snead's affection for his pet is among other evidence that the years have mellowed the old pro.

"I have the only house I know of," Snead says, "that I can sit on the toilet and see a turkey in the back yard."

Until a couple of years ago, Snead would have taken out a gun. His eye was sharp. Years after playing golf with Richard Nixon, Snead ran into him. The shot the former president recalled was the rock Snead threw to pick off a snake. Now he leaves the hunting to others and picks up a powerful pair of binoculars that rests on a table in his living room, with one of the best views around. Snead was quite a hunter. His basement is a testament to his earlier kills—a stuffed Kodiak bear, elephant tusks, and a zebra-skin rug decorate one big room—but he has changed his thinking.

"I like looking at things so well," Snead says. "I just didn't want to kill anything anymore. I don't even want to kill a snake now. I shot an elephant. And lions. But Jesus Christ, there aren't many left now. Why do I need to kill anything? People are the cruelest thing that walks this earth. You just look at what they do to each other, to animals. Animals don't do that—animals kill to survive."

Snead, who grew up trapping all manner of small game in the woods not far from where he is sitting now to put meat on his family's table and to sell the hides, is still fascinated by wildlife. A few days earlier, not far from Snead's home, a motorist struck a black bear and walked up to the animal to check its condition. Injured but alive, the bear mauled the man, causing serious injuries. "What was that person thinking?" Snead asks. "That bear tore him to pieces. That man's got to know better than that."

But most people do not have the feel for the natural world that Snead does. Playing in Florida once, he spotted a small wildcat and captured it with his hands. Not long ago he took pride in befriending a bass in one of his farm ponds. Two friends were visiting, skeptical of his pet bass. Snead took them to the pond. "I knelt down," Snead says, "and the bass came up and took my finger. I started rubbing his belly. I picked him right out of the water. Fish never moved a muscle. I put him back in the water, and he wanted to go again. I don't know why, but he liked to get out of the water."

There is much of the surprising and the improbable sprinkled throughout Snead's life. He never did bury his money in tomato cans, one of the many stories his old manager, Fred Corcoran, propagated to sell the image of his homespun client, who was never quite as countrified as people were led to believe. But it is true that he has a vault in his house, one with eight-inch steel walls, suitable, perhaps, for a small bank. "When [Dan] Quayle came to play golf with me up here," Snead says, "his people asked me if they could put him in there in case something happened." Quayle didn't have to hide out, but there is an autographed copy of his book, *Standing Firm*, on Snead's coffee table.

Not far from the vault are shelves of jigsaw puzzles, hundreds of them. They are a clue to Snead's younger son, Terry, forty-four, who is learning-disabled as a result of a fever that struck him when he was two and a half. Snead, his late wife, Audrey, and their other son, Jack, now fifty-two, who lives in a house down the hill from his father and oversees Sam Snead Enterprises, were in Florida when Terry became ill and nearly died.

"The doctor down there said he'd never seen a child that sick live," Snead says, regretful that his son didn't have more extensive care after his illness. "Two or three doctors looked at him, and they said if Terry had one-on-one [teaching] from the start, he would have been able to go to school. He's smart—you'd be surprised what he comes up with. But you turn around and ask him his name, and he'll say he doesn't know. He puts those jigsaw puzzles together. I tell you, he's fantastic the way he can do that."

I asked Snead if Terry knew what his father used to do for a living. "Oh yeah. He'd say, 'Daddy plays golf.'"

Snead can't explain exactly how he came to possess such a talent for golf. He always liked sports and excelled at them; he set some track records at his high school that still stand. Many of his relatives were big and strong for their day, and one uncle is said to have grown to 7½ feet and 350 pounds. Snead himself is 5 feet, 10½ inches, but he might have been taller if not for two misaligned vertebrae in his lower back. His arms, requiring thirty-five-inch sleeves, are those of a taller man, and while they have prompted some ribbing—once on *Shell's Wonderful World of Golf*, Jimmy Demaret said, "If he had a little more hair, he'd be hanging in a tree"—the length of Snead's arms may have given him a fundamental and aesthetic advantage.

He figures that some of his athletic grace was helped by his love of music. When he was a kid, he paid 25 cents every time he could and eventually owned a $50 Gibson banjo (a rare instrument that is said to be worth $64,000 today). Later on he learned to play the trumpet, often jamming with the jazz band in the Old White Tavern at the Greenbrier. Snead also was a product of the cadence of his land, of stories told slowly and porch swings moving gently.

The package made Snead a mesmerizing man with a golf club in his hands. One can argue the relative effectiveness of Snead versus contemporaries Byron Nelson and Ben Hogan, both of whom were born in 1912, like Snead, but Nelson had that distinctive dip and Hogan a brisk, city-sidewalk tempo. Snead was easiest on the eyes. Something few knew, though, was that Snead was missing a beat on the inside.

"I've had a heart skip since I can remember," Snead says. "My heart'll go pluck, pluck, pluck-uk. Pluck, pluck, pluck, pluck-uk. Then it might go, pluck, pluck-uk, pluck. I just hope it keeps on plucking. My doctor told me I had two heart attacks years ago and I didn't know anything about it. Thank god I didn't get the big one."

In golf, of course, that has always been the second part of the sentence when Snead's career is concerned. Unlike Nelson and Hogan, Snead could never win the U.S. Open. Second four times, he found all kinds of ways to lose, and it usually had something to do with putting. Snead grew up a wrist putter, developed the yips by the time he was thirty-five, and was always on the defensive on quick U.S. Open greens.

"I more or less believed in predestination," Snead says. "What's going to be is going to be. If I had let every one of those losses rake me like they have other people, I wouldn't have won anything. I said, 'It's my turn or it's not my turn.'"

In every other way, "his turn" was arguably better than anyone else's. Consider that in 1974, the year he turned sixty-two, Snead finished third in the PGA Championship and threatened to win a couple of regular events. Five years later, at Quad Cities, he became the first player to break his age in a tour event. He was sixty-seven.

"I was in the Waldorf-Astoria in New York one time," Snead had told me, "and a guy is running down the hall yelling, 'Mr. Hogan, Mr. Hogan. Can I have your autograph?' I told him I wasn't Mr. Hogan. He said, 'Well, you're somebody.' And I said, 'You'd better believe it.'"

Snead is on the practice range at the Meadowood Golf and Tennis Club in Fort Pierce, Florida. It is where he and Meister spend the winter. He always loved Virginia—never wanted to leave home for good—but he always liked to warm his bones come cold weather. As I walk toward Snead, who is striking irons, with Meister in the golf cart near him, I am struck by just how much he still looks like a pro, like the God of Golf.

He is wearing gray golf slacks, a light-colored striped shirt, white shoes, and the ever-present Stetson, size 7½. I can sense his timing from thirty paces. I am already fretting: Should I ask for any strokes or not? He is, after all, old enough to be my grandfather.

But he also shot a 59 two weeks before I was born in 1959, a 60 when he was seventy-one, and a 66 earlier this year. Playing him even is a decision born of pride, not common sense.

Though he stayed near the top of the sport longer than anyone else, tournament golf is a memory for Snead. This day, twenty-six clubs rattle around in his familiar Wilson staff bag, and we're rolling the ball in the fairway. I help him with hole locations, though once he has an idea what he is aiming for, he is seldom off line by much. He thinks the stroke-and-distance penalty for hitting a shot out-of-bounds is too severe, but when I sail a tee shot sixty yards right of the white stakes on the fourth hole, it is clear we're playing by the current rule. "Shoot again," Snead says quickly.

Snead is having, for him, a lousy front nine. After a beautiful forty-yard bunker shot on the first hole, he misses the five-foot par putt. At the sixth, which plays 177 yards from the blue markers, he hits a wood into a front bunker and makes a bogey to go one down. Before driving at the eighth, he bounces the ball he had been playing, along with a fresh one, on the cement cart path. He changes balls and pulls even with a bogey after I thrash out of a palmetto thicket and make a 6. "This is some golf," he mutters, heading off the green. "This is the worst I've ever played. You gave that one to me."

One reason Snead doesn't hit the ball very far is a dislocated left shoulder suffered in his tragic car wreck driving to Augusta, Georgia, for the 1992 Masters, in which he ran a stop sign and collided with another car, the driver of which was paralyzed from the neck down. Snead was advised not to have surgery on his injury, and it has resulted in a loss of strength in his left arm. "My left feels like a rope," he says, dangling the arm at his side. "I used to do everything in golf with my left arm. Everything."

Just a few minutes later, though, it's apparent that my opponent is still Sam Snead, a legend who hasn't forgotten how to play, or how to win—bum arm or not. With his ball in the fringe of the ninth green, fifty feet away and faced with a downhill then uphill slope to the hole, Snead walks off the eight-iron chip from both sides and gets down into a semi-squat to check the slope one more time. The shot, hit with nearly perfect pace and line, finishes a foot away. Snead has his par and has put the pressure on me.

"You're hitting those shots out of memory, aren't you?" I say, aware now of just how poor his vision is. "Yeah, memory," Snead says. "And feel."

My ball is on the same line as his, ten feet closer. I feel nervous for the first time all day, and my putt dies four feet short of the hole. He toys with the idea, for a millisecond, of giving me the putt.

"That's not quite in the leather."

"That's not inside Rocky Thompson's driver," I say, alluding to his club with a fifty-two-inch shaft. Snead laughs, then watches as I push my par putt, losing the hole and the front nine.

Snead enjoys a Bacardi and Coke as we take a leisurely fifteen-minute break in the clubhouse grillroom, then fills a twenty-ounce Styrofoam cup with water for Meister. As we talk about everything from course design (Snead is amazed at how many balls "choppers" lose on some of the new modern courses) to golf tees (he says they yield a surprisingly high profit for the club pro), I remember something he had said earlier: "I don't know why, but I always seemed to play the back nine better, even if it was harder. When I shot the 59, I had 31-28."

I don't know if it's the rum, the fact that his muscles fully loosened in the 85-degree heat, his life-long propensity for a better second nine, or my four-putt on the thirteenth that spurs Snead on, but he starts playing more like his old self. I build an advantage but lose it quickly. Although he had taken his time earlier in the match, his attention seems keener on the back. His tee shots, with an oversize metal driver, fly higher, and he gets perhaps 225 yards on his most solid strikes. No doubt he could add some distance by using a solid ball with a hard cover, but he sticks with a wound model because he likes the way it feels on short shots.

He also putts better on the incoming holes. Putting sidesaddle—the method he has used for nearly thirty years, after the United

States Golf Association banned the croquet style he found for rescue from "the twitches"—he starts to hit most putts with authority, particularly an eight-footer for par to halve the fourteenth and set up the whipping he is about to give. Snead adds three more pars, then tacks on a birdie on the eighteenth after an exquisite six-iron from 145 yards covers a flag he could hardly see and finishes three feet from the hole.

Despite the uplifting finish, every round Snead plays offers him more evidence of his deteriorating vision. Retina problems first blurred the vision in his right eye thirteen years ago, and the left, he says, is worsening as well. "Next year I don't think I'll be playing golf," he says, "unless they come up with some glasses I can see with. Never had any that suited me. But if they just give me something and it'll help, I'll use it." Snead grows serious, his face lengthening when talking about his eyes. "If I get to where I can't see nothing, I fear that more than dying."

Even playing partially blind, it had been an off day for Snead—but his 81 won both nines and took me, 2 and 1, for the 18. After adding up my 86, I deliver a $20 bill to Snead, and he settles down with a whiskey sour in the bar.

"Good swing, you've got a good swing," he told me. "But you're hyper, quick, very tense. The hardest thing to do is relax, but that's what you have to do."

Soon Snead clasps my right forearm with both hands. "That's as hard as I grip the club," he says, exerting what to me is a surprising force. If he were holding a bird, the analogy he's used for years to articulate grip pressure, I imagine at the very least a cardinal that has spent plenty of time at a full feeder. The next instant, he really clamps down. "You don't want to hold it like this." Then he strokes my arms. "You don't want steel," he says. "You want 'em to be soft, real loose."

Going on, Snead describes his philosophy on full shots. He was one of the longest hitters of his day, but he didn't do it with brute force. "Trying to hit the ball as hard as you can is bullshit," he says. "I played at 85 percent, and if I played a par five, I could get another fifteen or twenty yards. I believe I could take John Daly, if he'd listen, and have him winning. Hey, this go-for-everything attitude is bull. If chances are you make a double bogey or a bogey, you play safe. You watch Greg Norman—when he tries to hit a drive really hard, nine out of ten times he moves his body ahead and the ball goes to the right. Golf is rhythm and timing."

Snead can't fathom the wave of new golf instructors, many of whom never enjoyed competitive success and, he believes, often make the game more complicated than it needs to be. In a sense, he is the tournament player's version of Harvey Penick. "I've had success telling people just to swing the club up and pull it down," Snead says. "I think I know every aspect of the game, but I'm not going to change a guy just for the sake of change. You keep it simple. If you're a bad putter, you putt until you think you're a good putter. Putting is number one, driving is number two, and being a good wedge player is number three. If you've got a good wedge, you're bodacious."

On television, Snead's nephew, J. C. Snead, is playing in the Senior Tour Championship. Lately, J.C., who used to learn from his uncle, has been visiting other teachers. "He's driving the ball beautifully," Sam says, "but he's helpless on his short irons. I tried to talk to him, but he doesn't want to listen to me. I told him he can't buy a damn swing."

Snead is incredulous at the news that Norman has begun taking lessons from David Leadbetter. "What's he ever won?" Snead asks. "He'll have Norman so screwed up. Norman's crazier than hell. There's nothing wrong with his swing."

The irony: photographs of Snead are tacked up where lessons are given around this land still, decades after his prime. A couple of years ago, during a presentation at a golf instruction conference, Mac O'Grady pointed out all the possible flights and directions of a golf shot. Many golfers had mastered some of them, O'Grady said, but only Snead could hit them all.

Early in the week of the Memorial Tournament this year, Tom Watson was at the Greenbrier doing a corporate outing. As he used to do when he was a young buck on tour and Snead, in his sixties, still came out to test himself against a new generation of golfers, Watson took the time to watch Snead hit some balls. Six days later, Watson won his first PGA Tour event in eight and a half years.

The day after I played with Snead, I stopped by a practice range on the way to the airport. I hit some good shots and some bad ones. I tried to keep his words in my head and his movements in my eyes, and every so often I paused to try to feel the grip of Sam Snead's hands on my arm. Not too firm and not too loose. Just right.

November 29, 1996

Sam Snead was four days shy of his ninetieth birthday when he died on May 23, 2002. In his obituary for *Golf World*, I wrote that his game had been "as well-preserved as a smoked Virginia ham." So it had been, languid and lasting, one of golf's magnificent sights produced by one of its unique giants. Snead's old friend Bill Campbell, the great West Virginia lifelong amateur, eulogized Snead beautifully: "Sam was a physical phenomenon with boundless energy and stamina. He had the eye of an eagle, the grace of a leopard, and the strength and heart of a lion." As the 2013 season concluded, Snead, at fifty-two years, ten months, and eight days when he won his eighth Greater Greensboro Open in 1965, was still the oldest winner of a PGA Tour event.

CHAPTER SEVEN

A Golfer and a Gentleman

The mastery exhibited by many sports legends is often coated with a considerable layer of mystery, but that was not the case with Byron Nelson. His golf swing was likened to an efficient machine; his playing record, compressed by choice into a truncated prime, shone like a neon sign decades after he produced it; his character, according to those who knew him well, was more unswerving than any of the sure and solid shots he ever struck.

Although Nelson won more silver trophies than all but a handful of golfers, many of them in his fantastic 1945 season—when he claimed eleven consecutive tournaments among eighteen victories—he was most proud of a long life lived by the Golden Rule. "If whenever people mention great players, they think of Nelson, too, that would be nice," he said. "But I prefer being remembered as a nice man with a lot of integrity, as somebody people could love and trust, as being friendly and a good Christian man."

Nelson, ninety-four, died of natural causes on September 26 at his Fairway Ranch in Roanoke, Texas, slightly more than sixty years after moving there following the most concentrated period of dominance the game has known. In three seasons—1944, 1945, and 1946—Nelson won thirty-four of the seventy-five tournaments he entered, was runner-up sixteen times, and only once finished out of the top ten. Ruling the tour in 1945, Nelson had a stroke average of 68.34 (a mark that stood until Tiger Woods broke it in 2000) and a final-round average of 67.45.

Among Nelson's 52 PGA Tour victories—which place him sixth on the all-time list behind Sam Snead (82), Tiger Woods (79, through the 2013 season), Jack Nicklaus (73), Ben Hogan (64), and Arnold Palmer (62)—were five major championships: 1937 and 1942 Masters; 1939 U.S. Open; and 1940 and 1945 PGA Championships. He was "in the money," the equivalent of making a cut in the modern game, 113 straight times, a record that stood until Woods bettered it.

"He was a legend who transcended generations and was loved and respected by everyone who knew him," said PGA Tour commissioner Tim Finchem. "His legacy spans across his historic performances, the gentle and dignified way he carried himself and his tremendous contributions to golf and society."

Nelson carved his place in golf history with an individualistic swing against fellow icons Snead and Hogan, with whom he shared a birth year (1912) in an era when the purses were small, course conditions ragged, and travel hard. The circuit visited cities such as Corpus Christi, Durham, Tacoma, and Gulfport, and the pros usually got from one place to the next by car. It was a far cry from the life led by current pros who came to play in the Byron Nelson Championship, for which Nelson had been the host and soul since 1968.

In *Golf's Golden Grind*, Nelson described the travel: "We would drive Sunday night, Monday, and Tuesday sometimes. Once you got to the tournament it took two days before you got rid of the shakes in your hands and the golf clubs quit feeling like the steering wheel. It's a wonder anybody could putt at all."

But in some ways the journeys between tournaments weren't as arduous as Nelson's path to adulthood. Born February 4, 1912, on his family's 160-acre cotton farm in Long Branch, outside Waxahachie, Texas, John Byron Nelson Jr. was momentarily given up for dead during a difficult delivery. Before he was a teenager, Nelson had survived a bite from a rabid dog and typhoid fever (the latter making him sterile, which, he said, is why he and his first wife of fifty years, Louise, didn't have children).

Golf became part of Nelson's life after his family moved from the country to nearby Fort Worth when he was ten. At age twelve, Nelson became a caddie at Glen Garden Country Club, where one of his fellow loopers was Ben Hogan. When Nelson was fifteen, he beat Hogan by one stroke in the final match of the caddie championship.

Nelson might not have pursued a golf career at all, but having quit school in the tenth grade he lost his job as a railroad file clerk when he was seventeen. By late 1932 he had earned his first check as a pro, $75 for a third-place finish in a tournament in Texarkana. The next couple of years were lean, but Nelson was in the process of developing the swing that would take him to the game's pinnacle.

Golf had been the province of players relying on active hands and wrists and perfect timing to control hickory-shafted clubs. With the advent of steel shafts, Nelson sought to turn a complex equation into simpler math by using his lower body to drive the clubhead squarely through impact—along the target line for several inches before and after impact. Nelson fought sieges of shanking initially until he learned to curb the movement of his head with that of his legs and hips through the ball; even after he perfected his action, he would occasionally hit a lateral.

By then, though, his technique was producing the most accurate shotmaking the game has seen. Instructor Harvey Penick wrote that Nelson's dollar-bill divots, rectangularly precise and paper-thin, were like few he had ever observed. Nelson's shots drifted little right or left, and his judgment of distances was as adroit as anyone's. Playing in the second Masters, in 1935, Nelson watched from the adjacent seventeenth fairway as Gene Sarazen holed a four-wood shot for his famous double-eagle 2. Two years later, when Nelson closed with a final-nine 32 to overtake Ralph

Guldahl and win his first green jacket, he started hitting plenty of great ones himself.

His accuracy became the stuff of lore. Nelson recounted to Dave Anderson the time in the late 1930s when he was pro at Ridgewood Country Club in New Jersey and the caddies challenged him to hit a shot off a slate patio at a flagpole a hundred yards away. Nelson chose a three-iron and hit the pole on his second try. During the 1939 U.S. Open at Philadelphia Country Club, which he won in a playoff, Nelson hit the flagstick six times with six different clubs.

The legend of the British icon Harry Vardon was that he played two seasons without missing a fairway and often hit shots into divots he had made previously. Nelson, who learned how to grip a club properly when he was a kid by studying a book on Vardon's technique, once duplicated the star when he toured a course for the second time in a day. "I'll be darned," Nelson said, "I've landed in my own divot. I've equaled Vardon at long last."

Nelson's precision—True Temper, and later the United States Golf Association, would simulate his swing in the mechanical "Iron Byron" testing device—coexisted with a predilection for a nervous stomach that was heightened on key tournament days. Prior to the 1942 Masters playoff with Hogan, Nelson threw up during the night. "There were easier people to have a playoff against than Ben Hogan, you know," Nelson recalled years later to *Sports Illustrated*.

The straight hitter's competitive desire was sometimes hidden. "Even though folks couldn't always see it," he told the *New York Times*, "I had a very big desire to achieve. I got pretty steamed up inside." Once, at a 1936 tournament in the Pacific Northwest, Nelson was so ticked off after missing short birdie putts on the first six holes that he hurled his putter and it got stuck in an evergreen tree.

At his best, though, he kept the frustrations to a minimum. Ruled 4-F and ineligible to serve in the military during World War II because his blood took an unusually long time to clot, Nelson crisscrossed the United States doing Red Cross and USO exhibitions (110 in all) and dominated the play that went on while some of his peers, notably Lloyd Mangrum, Hogan, and Snead, were serving in one capacity or another.

"They try to put an asterisk by his record," eighty-two-time LPGA winner Mickey Wright once observed, "but just look at some old film of the conditions of the golf courses back then. And look at the scores he shot."

Snead played in six of Nelson's eleven straight victories and nine of his overall titles and won six times himself in 1945; Hogan, who won five times, competed in five of the events Nelson won. Citing the greater depth of fields in more recent years and the relative peace he had—compared to modern media demands—as his streak grew, Nelson was modest about his stunning season. "Put today's players against me in 1945," he told *Golf Digest* in 1996, "and I would have won more than six. I think I would have won nine tournaments."

The eighteen that he claimed in large measure paid for his dream ranch. Louise, skeptical of Byron's ranching skills and wary of losing any of their investments, told him he would have to pay cash for a ranch if he wanted one. His dream spread cost $87 an acre for 630 acres. He paid $55,000 and said goodbye to full-time tour life after the 1946 season, when he was only thirty-four. Proceeds from his 1946 instruction book, *Winning Golf*, helped stock the ranch with cattle.

Nelson claimed he had just had enough of the travel and achieved most of his goals. In 1952, six years after his retirement, he acknowledged that the grind of competition had taken a toll. "The body takes a severe beating, but it is the wear and tear on the nerves which gets you," he said. "Day after day, hole after hole, with no let up in the pressure. It got me. That's why I quit while I have my health."

Although he played only a couple of events a year into the mid-1950s, Nelson kept his game sharp and perpetuated his reputation as a gentleman golfer. One of his protégés, Ken Venturi, recalled that when Nelson visited a course to play an exhibition, he always asked who held the course record. If it was the home pro, Nelson would never break it.

"For many, Byron will be remembered for his incredible record as a professional golfer, including winning eleven tournaments in a row," said Tom Watson, who became a pupil of Nelson's in the mid-1970s, shortly before he became the best player in the game. "But he will be most remembered for the genuineness and gentleness he brought to all those around him."

After Nelson joined ABC Television's broadcast team in 1963, Roone Arledge urged him to modify his Texas twang, but Nelson kept talking like he always had. His voice carried like one of his long irons; Donna Caponi backed off a crucial five-footer on the seventy-second hole of the 1969 U.S. Women's Open after she heard Nelson say which way the putt was breaking. (She made the putt and won the tournament.) Plexiglas was installed to dampen Nelson's calls soon thereafter.

Nelson had his name attached to the PGA Tour event in the Dallas area since 1968, but he was much more than a figurehead. Staying active and on hand even into his final year, when he required portable oxygen and had difficulty walking, his recall of events sixty years ago was extraordinarily sharp, his interest in the current scene keen. "I got my last call from him only about two months ago," said Loren Roberts. "It was after I won the Senior British Open." Roberts, who won Nelson's tournament in 1999, was one of scores of players to receive handwritten notes from Nelson through the years, thoughtful expressions of congratulations or encouragement.

Tiger Woods, who was a teenager when he met Nelson, got his first of about fifty notes from him after winning the 1994 U.S. Amateur. "He wrote a nice letter," Woods recalled. "I was just shocked. Here is a legend of the game writing to some little amateur a handwritten letter, which I . . . never, ever forgot."

But it was the face-to-face contact that today's generation treasured even more, whether it was a handshake by the eighteenth green or getting met by Nelson at the Dallas–Fort Worth airport, as Retief Goosen was in 2005. "He was so kind-hearted, so kind and so soft and so genuine," Woods said. "He always looked at you and talked to you with extreme interest, and you don't find that with everybody you meet. He just had a softness about him that was very unique."

The captain of the 1965 U.S. Ryder Cup team, Nelson made wooden keepsakes with a psalm on them for members of this year's American team. According to family friend Jon Bradley, Nelson had fourteen clocks at various stages of completion in his woodworking shop on the day his second wife, Peggy, whom he married in 1986, a year after Louise's death, found him passed away on their back porch. Asked by the *Fort Worth Star-Telegram* this year how he had stayed so active into his nineties, Nelson said, "I never drank, never smoked, never chased women. And I've never had a sitting-down job in my life. . . . I weigh 181 now, and I weighed 179 when I left the tour when I was 34. My life, for 94, is still very, very full. And I love it."

Nelson's philanthropic efforts—his namesake tournament has raised $94 million for the Salesmanship Club's efforts for troubled youth—were recognized the day after his death, when the U.S. Senate approved a bill to grant him posthumously the Congressional Gold Medal, Congress's highest civilian award. He was one of the original thirteen inductees into the World Golf Hall of Fame in 1974. Also that year he won the United States Golf Association's Bob Jones Award for sportsmanship and the William D. Richardson Award from the Golf Writers Association of America for his outstanding contributions to golf.

More than 2,200 people attended Nelson's funeral on September 29 at Richland Hills Church of Christ, which was both a tribute to a humble man and the end of an era. The fiftieth anniversary of his 1945 success had put Nelson back in the reflected glory of his accomplishments and afforded newer generations the chance to appreciate him anew. "I don't have many worries," he told *Golf World* in 1995, "but the biggest is that I'll wake up like Rip Van Winkle and find out this has been one long dream. Or that I'll forget every wonderful thing that ever happened to me."

He needn't have worried. Nelson lived it all: superb golf and solid citizenship, a streak that was only beginning with eleven tournaments in a row.

November 13, 2006

It is hard to imagine any golfer living a better, more meaningful life than Byron Nelson, a genuine American hero. I spoke to Nelson for the last time by phone from his ranch early in 2005, on the sixtieth anniversary of his phenomenal season. "I never wanted to let anybody down," he told me, "because I haven't been let down." Nelson, to be sure, kept his end of the bargain. To shake one of his powerful hands was to touch a man with much inner strength.

CHAPTER EIGHT

Simply the Best

Mickey Wright, who turned sixty-five last Valentine's Day, doesn't get around as much as some her age. She's not big on crowds. She's not keen on dining out. And she hasn't been in an airplane since 1978. Lenny Wirtz, who ran the LPGA that Wright dominated in the 1960s, remembers a helicopter ride from Biloxi, Mississippi, to New Orleans for a television interview, and Wright's knuckles weren't white, they were translucent.

In Wright's heyday, everyone drove. The long trips from one tournament to the next weren't fun—she'd have to putt at a water glass on the motel-room carpet from the time Walter Cronkite came on until he said good-night just to get the road shimmy out of her stroke—but these were her hands on the steering wheel and her eyes on the road.

Wright always appreciated the unpredictable bounces and other vagaries golf offers, the way the challenges change like the weather—or how they used to, anyway, before designer grasses and smart mowers. "You never see a bad lie now," she says, "and when one of these guys hits it in a divot, you'd think the gods had thrown down lightning. It just breaks me up." Yes, Wright could deal with a bad break, but she also liked to be in control.

When Wright was over a shot, it was a dictatorship. Her opponents remember: equal parts satin and steel, that's what her golf swing was, as pretty as it was powerful. They remember the sound of club meeting ball, loud and crisp, like it was amplified. They remember the flight of her shots, high and soaring, so different from every other woman. When someone told Wright she hit it like a man, she smiled.

To this day the golfers who played against Wright—the golfers who tried to beat her—haven't forgotten what it looked like. "She could play shots other women could not play," says Hall of Famer Betsy Rawls. "Her swing had speed, and she could hit the ball at exactly the right moment. There was not wasted motion."

This was a year for remembering. The LPGA celebrated its fiftieth anniversary, honored its founders, explained how it got from then to now. More than once in 2000, old pros gathered, told a few lies, had some laughs, imagined what it would be like to win a check with so many zeroes. Wright took everything in from a distance, from her comfortable but modest home on a golf course in Port St. Lucie, Florida, where a day might include hitting golf balls, gardening, checking the stock market, playing penny poker, and wondering how some of her friends spend so much time online.

"I don't want to sit at a screen for four or five hours," Wright says. "I have a computer, but I have no interest in going online. I have friends who get in these chat rooms and get so wrapped up in it. I don't like what I see in them when they do it. That's not for me."

Wright likes to look people in the eye when she talks to them. She punctuates her sentences with a little twinkle or slight grin. Unless, that is, the other party is a reporter, which is seldom, and in that case, the conversation is on the telephone. She was not tempted in the least to join the LPGA festivities. "Not a bit," Wright says. "It's wonderful and nice, but it's hype, and I'm just not into that. But it is absolutely incorrect to think that I am a recluse. The people who know me know that's incorrect. I don't hide out, put on sunglasses, and pull a cap down when I go out or anything like that. I just like life simple."

Her peers hoped Wright would go with them down Memory Lane to discuss the eighty-two victories, which include thirteen major championships. She always got along with the women she played with. Although they were sometimes demoralized by what they were up against, her opponents knew Wright as humble in victory and gracious in defeat, despite a lack of practice at the latter. "We had a great feeling for her and what she was able to accomplish," says Marilynn Smith, one of the LPGA's founders. "She wasn't ever arrogant. We would have loved to have had her around this year, talking about old times."

But Wright doesn't want to get anywhere near a dais or a microphone. "I never heard Mickey give anything but outstanding speeches," says Rawls, "but she works herself to death to do it. She's not going to put herself through that anymore. She doesn't want to be applauded. She doesn't need that."

Wright gave enough talks to the Rotarians and the Civitans, checked her swing in enough cheap mirrors, holed enough putts that meant something to win another tournament before getting in the car to go someplace else to try to do it again—sometimes for ten to fifteen weeks in a row.

"The four consecutive tournaments I won twice were done four weeks in a row," she says. "It wasn't win one, take a week off to rest, come back and win another one." Wright averaged ten victories a year from 1960 through 1964, "the best run anyone has ever had," says Tom Watson. Wright's expectations were high, but those of others were out in space. "When other people have unrealistic expectations," Wright says, "you tend to transfer them to yourself. Anybody who tries to live their life with unrealistic expectations is asking for trouble."

In 1963, the year that Wright turned twenty-eight, she won thirteen tournaments. The roster of wins reads like an atlas of the United States: Sea Island, St. Petersburg, Muskogee, Waterloo. But the gorgeously efficient swing and the cocoon of concentration Wright put herself into during play masked the churning inside. She developed an ulcer, but the symptom was easier to treat than the cause. "If I didn't play well one week, I didn't think less of myself," says Rawls, "but unfortunately for Mickey, she did. Her self-worth was pretty much tied in with winning golf tournaments. She was never a contented person when she was on the tour."

Carol Mann, who was a rookie in 1961, spent some of the long trips from one event to the next in a car with Wright, one cigarette after another, windows down, belongings rustling in the backseat. There was always a dictionary handy. Wright would ask Mann to choose a word and read aloud its meaning. Then Wright would use it in a sentence. "I recall her insecurity with her golf game," Mann says, "and there was a sense of quest, a pursuit of mastery, in her whole being, not just her golf. It created an unsettledness about her."

Once Mann and Wright pulled in for a night's rest in Fort Worth after a long day on the road. "We stopped at a hotel and she said to me, 'Do you want to play cards?' I said, 'Oh, I don't care.' She threw something against the wall and yelled at me, 'You have to care. You must care.'"

It would have been easier for Wright if she had cared less—about her appearance or her swing plane, the sponsors or the reporters. "She would have been quite happy to play at dawn in front of nobody and shoot a score," says Kathy Whitworth. That was impossible, of course.

Women's professional golf wasn't a hot ticket. Wirtz, who was the LPGA tournament director, its de facto commissioner, from 1961 to 1969, had to scrounge for events. When a sponsor ponied up, it expected Wright, the main draw, to be there. She usually was: for three years beginning in 1962, she played thirty-three, thirty, and twenty-seven events.

Along the way she agreed to Wirtz's idea to restructure tournament purses so that the winner would receive 15 percent of the pie instead of 20 percent, all so the end of the field would at least win gas money to get to the next tournament. Wright often went fishing with Wirtz to get away from everything. But the giggles would fade as she left the lake, replaced by a dread. The burdens, like the fish they caught, went right back to where they had been.

"It was a lot of pressure to be in contention week after week for five or six years," she says. "I guess they call it burnout now, but it wore me out. Unless you're a golfer, you can't understand the tension and pressure of tournament play. And it was the expectations. It was always, 'What's wrong with your game?' 'Are you coming apart?' Second or third isn't bad, but it feels bad when you've won forty-four tournaments in four years."

Although Wright would be plagued by wrist and foot problems that also influenced her decision to scale back her competitive schedule, an occurrence in Albuquerque in August 1964 had a lot to do with triggering her retreat. In the first round of the $10,000 Swing Parade tournament, a television cameraman hounded Wright throughout the day. Several times he asked her to pause while he readied his camera, and at others he lay on the edge of the green just opposite the hole while she putted. Exasperated and playing poorly through the distractions and already edgy because she was trying to quit smoking, Wright lost it at the sixteenth hole, backhanding her way to a six-putt. She shot an 86. But she showed up the next day, paid the $200 fine levied by Wirtz, and completed the tournament, all the while realizing she had to get away soon.

"I had completely lost control of myself," Wright told *Sports Illustrated* the following year, "and I figured it might happen again. Everything I had built up over the years, all my care about my public image, would be out the window. This finally made me decide to quit the tour."

The quest had begun in San Diego, where Wright was the only child of a well-known attorney named Arthur Wright. Her father, a lover of sports and cards and life, was fifty-two when she was born. Her parents divorced when she was three, but a galvanizing force soon came into her life. "I wanted to be the best woman golfer in the world," she says, "and that was from age ten on."

Early on, her game was shaped largely by men, with refinements suggested by women once she joined the tour in 1955. She grew up with smooth-swinging Gene Littler, six years her senior. Starting when she was fourteen, Wright took lessons from Harry Pressler, who was based 120 miles away in San Gabriel. Each week Wright would be driven to San Gabriel for a Saturday morning lesson. The sessions lasted thirty-five minutes, and Wright hit no more than thirty-five balls. Pressler preached good footwork and a square clubface, and Wright, who would grow to be five-feet-nine with long arms, had the gift of athletic grace.

"I grew up with Sam Snead, Jackie Burke, and Mike Souchak and, of course, Gene [Littler]," Wright says. "They were aesthetic. I grew up liking pretty, I think. And I guess I still do. There are not so many golf swings out there now that I think are so great. But I think an efficient swing produces clubhead speed. Clubhead speed is the answer to it."

Burke, who watched Wright hit some balls when she was a teenager, encouraged her to hit the ball as high as she possibly could. As Rhonda Glenn, who wrote definitively about Wright in *The Illustrated History of Women's Golf*, described, Wright then grooved her high-carrying shots by clearing a tall tree in practice. Later on, Chicago instructor Stan Kertes and Earl Stewart from Dallas helped Wright. Her swing not only approached the ideal that she sought, it came to define it.

Ben Hogan called it the best swing he ever saw—man or woman. Others raved about it as well because of its mix of strength and flow, a blend that allowed Wright to strike wonderful long-iron shots.

"It was just so gracefully athletic," says Mann, who became a well-known instructor after she quit the tour. "Where the club was coming from, how fast it was going, and the unloading right at the moment of impact was extraordinary. She was a swinger, but she had one of the volatile impacts. It was almost like a whole new category."

Fascinated by learning the full swing, Wright for years neglected her putting. "If she had been an exceptional putter," says Littler, "she would have won every week." As did Hogan, Wright had some contempt for golfers who scrambled their way to success. "She didn't respect the short game at all when she came on tour," says Rawls, who helped Wright come to think otherwise. "[Ultimately] she realized that was a sure way to fail, that it took as much talent to hit good putts as good drives."

Wright improved her putting—becoming, like Jack Nicklaus, one of the best at making putts when they had to be made—but she remained enthralled at striking the long, high shots that were her trademark. She watches a lot of televised golf these days and doesn't always like what she sees in the current generation of women pros, some of them with golf bags bulging with five or more fairway woods.

"I don't think there are too many of the ladies who hit it like a man now," Wright says. "You don't see the driving of the legs, the use of the lower body. So much looks like it's just arms back and through. A good golf swing can take a two-iron and hit it high, carry it over traps, and make it land softly on the green. A good swing can do that."

The clinical precision melded with a keen mind to form a golfer who didn't overextend her career because, fellow competitors say, she couldn't have tolerated being less than what she once was. "She absolutely couldn't cope with playing average," says Hall of Famer Judy Rankin. "Mickey can't be described as a grinder. When Mickey was having a bad day—and they weren't that often—it was hard for her to grind it out."

Rawls is more blunt. "I would have hated to be around her on a downward slide," she says. "It wouldn't have been pretty."

Wright played her last full season of golf, twenty-one events, in 1969. For the next decade, after moving to Florida with her best friend and housemate, Peggy Wilson, she played a smattering of tournaments each year. Her eighty-second and final victory came in the 1973 Colgate Dinah Shore Winner's Circle. Whitworth, who eventually would surpass Wright with eighty-eight career wins, made a point of congratulating her that Sunday night. Whitworth, happy to see her friend and rival back, believed Wright would play a fuller schedule. "But she didn't," Whitworth says. "I was so broken-hearted." Today Whitworth is among a few peers who stay in touch with Wright on the phone.

Wearing tennis shoes because of her painful feet, Wright lost a playoff to Nancy Lopez at the 1979 Coca-Cola Classic. She made her final appearance in an LPGA event in 1980, finishing thirty-third in the Whirlpool Championship. When Wright started, tournaments carried the names of the cities, but when she finished they were named for dishwashers. "When to quit is a personal thing, but I hate to see people hang on too long," she says. "I don't like to see great ones hang on and have me feel sorry for them."

She wouldn't have had to do much this anniversary year. Walk into a room. Hit a couple of five-irons. If the motion didn't match the memory, it wouldn't have mattered, right? "If you put it on display," Wright says, "it better be good. No matter how realistic you have to be about your game, if you've ever played golf well, you don't want to put something less than that on display."

The fact is, Wright worked herself ragged getting ready before playing in the Sprint Senior Challenge each spring for three straight years beginning in 1993. She had not competed since playing with Whitworth in the 1983 Legends of Golf, but she showed up still hitting the ball high and hard, her swing producing plenty of shots that were, as the Canadian shotmaking savant Moe Norman likes to say of his own, "pure as the driven snow."

In each of the three Sprint appearances, a flock of current LPGA players absorbed every swing of Wright's that they could. She used her 1962 Wilson Staff irons, the grooves worn to a visible bull's-eye from so many shots hit right on the button. Wright had the same putter she won every one of her titles with, a putter she got in 1956. After the 1995 event, she drove off in her Cadillac knowing she would never compete again. "I figured [age] sixty was a good time to stop."

Wright has not played even a casual round of golf since. "Earl Stewart told me a long time ago to practice on your own time, not to take it to the course and learn there," she says. "If I went out and played once a week, there is no way I could play well. And that's just untenable to me."

Golf, like the past, is still with her. Almost every morning as the sun is just beginning its climb she hits balls off an artificial turf mat on her back patio toward a nearby hole of the Club Med Sandpiper Sinners course. "If I hit a hundred balls full-tilt I can't hit 'em the next day," she says. "I have to take a day off. When you're sixty-five, things hurt more, even if you don't want to think they do."

But Wright doesn't miss too many days. "Wedges, seven-irons, five-irons. It depends on which way my mat is headed. I have to hit the ball out over traps and these high trees. If they don't cut the rough I can't hit five-irons because I can't find the balls."

Although Wright has not played a round of golf since her Sprint appearance in 1995, she doesn't rule it out. "I've got friends from Indiana who come down every winter," she says. "If they need someone to fill out a foursome and they asked me, I'd probably go play with 'em."

If Wright does play, few will know. Her reluctance to share herself with the public in retirement is very similar to two of the three great women golfers who preceded her. Babe Zaharias was a showman, her life cut short by cancer. But Glenna Collett Vare and Joyce Wethered lived quietly after their playing days. Vare curtained off her trophies and later melted down most of them. When Wethered died, some of her neighbors knew her only for a wonderful garden, unaware of her golf heroics.

"I really don't want my privacy invaded," Wright says, explaining her preference to be left alone. "Rhonda Glenn spent three days with me doing her book. I spilled my guts. There is just not much more to say. My life now is not that exciting or interesting. The interesting part was in the 1960s."

Cordially but firmly, Wright soon brings a thirty-five-minute interview to a close. "I think we've done all the conversing we need to do," she says. "I'm really worn out with it. I think I've given you about all I can give you."

That's all she ever did. All the efficient effort came at a price. That's why she's tired, and that's why she's happy.

November 24, 2000

I continued to periodically talk on the phone and correspond with Mickey Wright following the interview for this story in 2000, and she has never been anything but courteous and insightful. That I have been unable to coax her into letting me visit her in Florida remains a professional disappointment. But a bigger regret is not having seen her play during that sublime reign from 1960 through 1964. Some years back, *Golf World* asked a group of legendary golfers to note their "five favorite swings." One of Wright's was the free-swinging and powerful Argentine, Angel Cabrera, well before he won the 2007 U.S. Open at Oakmont Country Club. Yes, she knows her golf. In 2011 Wright donated more than two hundred artifacts from her fabulous career to the United States Golf Association. The Mickey Wright Room at the USGA museum in Far Hills, New Jersey, opened the following May. True to her private nature, she did not attend the opening reception. The room, however, is a fine testament to her greatness.

CHAPTER NINE

Arnie, Now and Then

Golf was ready for Arnold Palmer in 1958, and he was ready for
it. Like the larger world, which got fast food and faster travel in
the 1950s, the pro game was in transition. A generation of players
who had carried it since before the start of World War II, including titans such as Ben Hogan and Sam Snead, were getting older.
Other golfers were trying to nudge their way toward center stage,
but most of them were businesslike performers in a business that
didn't pay very well.

"The best I ever finished on the money list was fourth in 1956
when I won a little less than $25,000," says eighty-five-year-old
Fred Hawkins. "We were all just trying to scratch out a living;
we all could have made more money doing something else. The
purses weren't worth anything, and they only paid about twenty
places. Many weeks I made more gambling in the practice rounds
than I did in the tournament. We all had to be kind of crazy to
play, but we all loved the game."

By and large, though, Hawkins and his peers kept their feelings close to their cardigans. "Most of the good players back then
were more stoic," says Don January, who joined the tour in 1956.
"They tried to hide their emotions. Arnold threw his out there for
everybody to see. He'd hitch up his pants with his elbows. He'd

hit and have that finish with everything twirling, and his nose would be snorting like a bull in heat."

Palmer's gusto was combined with a simple grace that connected him with fans eager to latch onto a hero—it was the social equivalent of his golf mantra to hit the ball hard, find it, and hit it again. "He likes people and conveyed that to them, and they naturally liked him," says longtime friend Dow Finsterwald. "It's easy to like somebody when they like you. It was just his way, his natural way. What you saw was what you got, and it was pretty damn good."

Had the substance of Palmer's game not matched his appealing style, he would have remained a curiosity instead of becoming a champion. "Hard as nails," January says of Palmer's competitive grit. "He was always a player with a great set of nerves. He'd get in that funny, knock-kneed stance putting on a green that was half grass and half dirt and run a thirty-footer six feet by and just climb on the other side and pour it back in there. Boy, that takes some talent."

Finsterwald has known Palmer, and about his talent, since 1948, when his college team went to North Carolina and had a match against Palmer's Wake Forest team. "He shot 29 the first nine against me," Finsterwald says. "Yeah, I knew early on. Others on tour had their reservations, a wait-and-see attitude. The old guard was still around. They said, 'Let's see.' And they saw."

After winning the U.S. Amateur in 1954, Palmer joined the tour the following year. He won the Canadian Open in 1955, followed by six victories during the next two seasons—including titles such as Insurance City, Azalea, and Rubber City that sound quaint in today's corporation-heavy culture.

But the tournament with the simplest name of all, the Masters, had Palmer's keen attention. He tied for tenth place in his initial visit, was twenty-first in 1956, and tied for seventh in 1957. Augusta National enthralled him from the first time he saw it. "Everything was just nice," he says. "I had heard so many things about Cliff Roberts and how tough he was. The way the course was manicured, the setting overall. I played all winter in some pretty rough conditions and spent the whole time looking forward to getting to Augusta. Everything about Augusta turned me on."

"I'm not much for spending a lot of time in the office," Palmer says, pausing between wedge shots about 3 p.m. on a recent Wednesday at the Bay Hill practice range, the Orlando club he bought in 1976. "It makes me stiff and sore and usually irritable. Eleven o'clock is checkout time."

"That's nice work if you can get it," someone says.

"Hey, I've been working seventy-eight years to get it," Palmer says. "I figure I ought to be able to check out at eleven."

Palmer is a little grouchy at having stayed in his small upstairs office in the Bay Hill clubhouse longer than is his custom. Just before leaving for the day, a man had come in and offered to donate $5,000 a hole to one of the hospitals Palmer is involved with if Palmer would play nine with him. "Usually my price is a little higher than that," Palmer says, admitting that such off-the-street propositions happen more frequently than you might think. "But that's a pretty good offer, isn't it? We usually don't turn those babies down."

Palmer is hitting balls from a small roped-off area on the extreme right end of the tee. His cart contains two Callaway staff bags loaded with dozens of clubs. He also has brought from the workshop at his nearby home another set of x-20 Tour irons, which he has just wrapped with leather grips. Before each shot with one of the new irons, he sprays the grip with a can of multipurpose adhesive.

Nobody's hands have ever looked more at home on the handle of a golf club than Palmer's meaty, oversize mitts that got golf-strong through thousands of boyhood swings at Latrobe (Pennsylvania) Country Club. "They're the hands of a blacksmith or a timber cutter," his father, Deacon, observed in 1960. "You can only get hands like that by swinging an ax or a golf club."

"Hell, if he wanted to bend a shaft, he didn't need a vise," Finsterwald says.

Early in his career Palmer adjusted his left-hand grip on the club to a slightly weaker position on the advice of Lew and Herman Worsham. He also took care that his tempo didn't get too quick, maintaining the swing and attitude that his father forged. "My father was my sport psychologist," Palmer says. "The one thing he said to me when I left to go play the tour was, 'You go out there and listen to those guys, and you can still drive that tractor back here when you're finished.' That was what he said, and he meant it. 'Stick with what you had and work with it.'"

On this cloudy, muggy afternoon Palmer is still working at it, but the labor doesn't generate the results it used to. "Not enough clubhead speed," he says after a not-so-crisp eight-iron. "I started noticing it big-time when I was seventy, and when I turned seventy-five, [the problem] really started showing up. It's so difficult to concentrate now. I used to be able to just stand here and lock on and not have a problem. Now, that concentration is difficult."

Palmer had an 81 the previous day in "The Shootout," the daily game for Bay Hill regulars in which foursomes and fivesomes square off. "I think recently he has been playing the yellow markers, which is a concession I didn't think I'd ever see," says Finsterwald, "but hey, he's facing up to it."

Says Jay Haas, who teamed with Palmer in February's Wendy's Champions Skins Game, "He's still Arnold, he just doesn't want to accept that he's not thirty-eight years old. He's seventy-eight. He just does not want to accept that. As far as loving the game and the competition, I would be hard-pressed to say who was more in love with the game than Arnold or Gary Player. Arnold has played as much golf in his lifetime as anybody in the history of the world. If everybody had that kind of passion, there wouldn't be any tee times left."

Once Palmer loosens up, more of his shots have zip. There is not much of his backswing left, but into his follow-through he

is as familiarly unique as ever. He seems insulted when someone observes that a nice-looking three-hybrid has gone 165 to
170 yards. "I hope it's farther than that," he says. "I would like to
think it's about 190."

A few shots later, a club employee straightening up the range
approaches. "It's still a pleasure to watch you hit, Mr. Palmer,"
he says.

The fact is, it still can be a pleasure for the man swinging
the club. "Oh yeah, I still enjoy a good shot," Palmer says, "even
though it's not anywhere near what it used to be. You can always
tell when it's a good shot. If it weren't for that, I wouldn't be here
hitting balls. You can feel it. It may not go as far, but when you
hit it like that, you know."

Early in the 1958 season, Palmer loitered near the top of the leader
board several times, finishing second in Tijuana, seventh in Pan-
ama, second in Baton Rouge, and third in New Orleans. In late
March, Palmer broke through at St. Petersburg, closing with a 65
to edge Hawkins and Finsterwald by a stroke. The week before the
Masters, at the Azalea Open Invitational in Wilmington, North
Carolina, he completed seventy-two holes tied with Howie Johnson.
"I wanted to have a sudden-death playoff," Palmer says, recalling
his eagerness to make the drive south to Augusta, "but nobody
was listening."

On a Cape Fear Country Club course in spotty early-spring
condition, particularly the bumpy greens, neither golfer played
well in the playoff. "Palmer was good to me today," Johnson said
after winning with a 77 to Palmer's 78. "When you beat a guy like
Palmer with a 77, you've got to have some luck."

Palmer's frustrating day included calling a penalty stroke on
himself on the fourteenth green when his ball moved. "I put [the
loss] out of my mind," says Palmer. "That wasn't something that
bothered me, because I was anxious to get to Augusta, and it was
cold—damn, it was cold at Wilmington."

Tall Shadows

As Palmer remembered it in his 1999 memoir *A Golfer's Life*, Finsterwald already had set up a practice-round game against Hogan and Jackie Burke Jr. by the time Palmer got to Georgia late Monday night. Finsterwald played well and the younger duo took $70 from the Texans, but after the match, in the locker room, Hogan wondered aloud—loud enough for Palmer to hear—how Palmer even got in the Masters.

"I was a little disappointed Hogan talked that way," says Palmer, who was never close to Hogan and was irritated Hogan wouldn't call him by his first name. "He said, 'How the hell did Palmer get in the Masters?' That was tough, sort of a blow to my ego. Up until then, even though Hogan and I weren't buddy-buddy, we were not enemies either. You can guess for yourself how that motivated me."

Finsterwald wasn't within earshot when Hogan took his verbal jab at Palmer. "I can't believe [Ben] was serious," Finsterwald says. "I'm inclined to think Hogan was pulling his chain. Maybe the way Arnold played that particular day raised some questions, but Hogan couldn't seriously wonder. Arnold wasn't at his best that Tuesday, but things sure got better."

Even before Hogan poked him, Palmer was fueled by other critiques of his game. "I was determined to play good at Augusta because I knew my game was pretty good and people were talking that I didn't have the game that was required to win there," Palmer says. "I hit the ball low with everything—with the driver, with the irons. It was a foregone conclusion that anybody who did that could not win the Masters. That was probably a bigger factor in my desire to win than even what Hogan said."

What Palmer didn't have in trajectory he made up for with power. "Anyone who had some length off the tee had an advantage at Augusta," says Doug Ford, whose more conservative style had earned him a green jacket in 1957. "For Palmer—and it was the same for Jack Nicklaus—par was 68."

Practice-round form didn't always mean much at Augusta during that period. "For the practice rounds they'd leave the greens a little longer," Hawkins says. "We would all basically shoot under par in practice. The night before the tournament, they'd lower the mowers and triple-cut the greens. Next day, you'd think you were in a different world. That's the way they wanted it."

As Palmer was about to hole a short putt to close out his victory at St. Petersburg in 1958, the silence was broken by the loud cry of a baby. "I mean scream," he said later. "I thought to myself, 'I bet that's Peggy.'"

In fact it was his two-year-old daughter, Peggy, who already was starting to show she was as strong-willed as her famous father. "He never agreed on anything with me," she says, "and I never agreed with him."

As the tides smooth stones, years can smooth relationships. On a sun-splashed afternoon at Bay Hill fifty years later, Peg Palmer Wears is in her dad's gallery again. Palmer stopped competing in his PGA Tour event four years ago, but he is in the Arnold Palmer Invitational pro-am in a pairing with former Pennsylvania governor and homeland security chief Tom Ridge and two other amateurs, Cabot Williams and Craig Smith. Wears's daughter, Anna, eleven, and son, Will, thirteen, who call their grandfather "Bumpy," are with her. "At seventy-eight, it's thrilling to see him out here," Peg says. "This is as good as it gets. It's all good."

Growing up as one of Arnold and Winnie Palmer's two daughters—Peg's sister, Amy, is two years younger—was a complicated existence. Their father relished the activity and attention that came with his sports-hero status; their mother coveted privacy and a normal routine that money couldn't buy. The intersection of fame and family, of contrasting priorities, was not always smooth.

"I felt bad for my mother but always understood [him]," Peg says. "It made total sense to me that he didn't want to be sitting around Thanksgiving dinner hearing about everybody's backaches. He always wanted to be doing something. The guilt involved in being a family man, and balancing your life—yeah, that's all true,

Tall Shadows

but you have to want to do it. If you don't want to do it, it just isn't that meaningful. He didn't want to be there; he wanted to be out on the golf course, and we were welcome anytime. It was hard for my mother, but there was a thrilling side that she loved in spite of her issues. Everything's a trade-off."

Although from the tips, the pro tees that Palmer used to command, Bay Hill is way too much golf course for him—a driver followed by a three-wood at the 441-yard first hole left him fifty yards short of the green—the couple of hundred loyalists in tow applaud his good shots and ignore the bad ones. "I like to walk along and hear what people are saying about him," says Peg. "It used to not always be fun. We used to be in a crowd six or eight deep and there would be two guys behind us willing him to miss a putt because they were just crossing over to catch Nicklaus. It's really hard to hear people talk mean about your dad."

There are no harsh comments this afternoon, just the occasional observation that Palmer, who exuded youth for so long, looks his age. Abandoning style for function, he covers his head with a floppy hat. He bends over slowly when teeing up a ball or picking it out of the cup. He requires hearing aids in both ears, and even with them misses snatches of conversations and asks people to repeat themselves.

"Have *you* had a hard time aging?" Peg responds when asked how her father is handling it. "I've had a hard time aging. I think he's had a real hard time aging. It's a bummer. When you've made culture happen, it's really hard when you can't do it as well anymore. But he does still have a good time, and he just wants to be out here and wants people to care about him. It's a beautiful thing, and they still do care, which is an even more beautiful thing. It never ends that he's thrilled by it."

On the back nine, Palmer—who spoke vigorously against the use of carts on the senior tour—gratefully catches a ride between holes. After No. 15, Amy, who manages Bay Hill with her husband, Roy Saunders, joins her sister in the gallery after hosting a lunch for PGA Tour wives. Palmer tells his daughters, "I think I can make it the last three holes—I'm not sure."

In 1997, the week before Tiger Woods won his first Masters, Palmer, Woods, and Palmer's longtime agent, International Management Group vice chairman Alastair Johnston, were playing a round at Bay Hill. The past and future lords of the game had a $100 bet over these same three holes. "Arnold lost 16, then won 17," Johnston remembers. "And on 18 Arnold was determined to be farther off the tee and hit the s— out of a drive. Arnold took a three-wood out for his second at the eighteenth. He had no chance of putting a three-wood on that green and keeping it there, but he was determined to go for the green. Tiger was sitting in the cart with me and said, 'Look at the old man grind.'"

More than a decade later, from the Tiger tees, the green is within reach in regulation only in Palmer's memory. Still, the last drive of the day is the one you remember tomorrow. He cracks a tee shot, high and solid, his best of the round. At his other home, Latrobe Country Club, with any luck, this one would have carried the creek that crosses the fairway on No. 12. When he was in his late sixties, Palmer vowed to quit the game once he couldn't fly that stream.

"It's about 240, depending on which side you go on," he says. "Last summer, I hit it over the creek once or twice and that made [my year]. If I don't hit it over some time during the year, I will quit."

Once the 1958 Masters began, there was no evidence Palmer had a hangover from his defeat in Wilmington or the dig from Hogan. While Ken Venturi, the hottest player on tour, with three victories when he arrived in Augusta, led after a first-round 68 and a thirty-six-hole score of 140, Palmer was firmly in contention with a 70-73 start. By shooting a third-round 68, Palmer took a share of the lead with Sam Snead.

In a room on the fifth floor of the Paley Center for Media in New York City, a ninety-minute CBS broadcast that originally aired

Tall Shadows

on Sunday, April 6, 1958, to a world of Zeniths and rabbit ears plays on a video monitor. Unlike then, when it would have been science-fiction fantasy, you can pause the show, rewind it, fast-forward through some of the tediously awkward moments—the confusion of accounting for how golfers stood by noting their total strokes rather than relation to par, for instance—that were part of early sports telecasts.

Jim McKay, the TV host, looks ridiculously young. The "analyst," 1948 Masters winner Claude Harmon, wears his champion's green jacket—even when doing live commercials for American Express outside the clubhouse. "You sign here when you buy them and here when you spend them," he says during a pitch with Peter Thomson for the company's travelers checks. Describing the golf without a script, Harmon has a relaxed, straightforward delivery but still has some game of his own too. "I guess the portly veteran can still make one every once in a while," Harmon says after McKay compliments him on his ninth-place finish earlier that afternoon.

As Palmer and Venturi played the eighteenth hole, Harmon was as candid with his assessment as a current-day Johnny Miller. "In the head-to-head battle it was Arnold Palmer who whipped Mr. Venturi into the ground," Harmon said. "They were going at it hammer and tong. . . . It seemed that the eagle Arnold Palmer made at the thirteenth hole was just too much for [Venturi]."

Bobby Jones would call Palmer's 230-yard fairway-wood shot at No. 13 the best he had witnessed since Gene Sarazen's double eagle on No. 15 in 1935. Writer Herbert Warren Wind later described the shot this way: "He met the ball squarely, and it rose in a low parabola. There was some draw on the shot, and it curved from right to left as it crossed the creek and landed comfortably on the green."

Television viewers—CBS had cameras only from the fifteenth green forward—didn't get to see Palmer hit that three-wood to No. 13 or sink his pivotal eighteen-footer, jump into the air, and raise his arms as if he had scored a touchdown. They didn't get to see the tangled situation at the par-three twelfth, when Palmer, leading Venturi by one stroke, hit a six-iron over the green, where it plugged in soft turf.

Palmer asked official Arthur Lacey for relief from the embedded lie, citing wet-weather rules that were in effect for the tournament. Lacey denied Palmer a free drop, telling him to play the ball from the depression. Palmer disagreed with Lacey's call. He chopped his way to a 5 from the original lie, then took relief and made a 3 with his second ball.

At first a double bogey was posted for Palmer on the leader boards, dramatically changing the complexion of the tournament. Not until 15, when Palmer met with tournament committee members, was the situation resolved in Palmer's favor and he was given a 3 on No. 12. Other players and fans were confused.

Venturi played his way out of the picture by three-putting the fourteenth, fifteenth, and sixteenth holes. Palmer looked solid as he played the eighteenth with the lead, but his approach with a short iron was long and right. The ball bounced through the gallery and finished on the rear of the green sixty feet from the hole, a position from which Harmon said it "will be nearly impossible to get down in two from there. I would say Arnold Palmer has his work cut out for him."

Palmer hit a poor putt that was off-line from the start, leaving himself a seven-footer for par. "That putt is going to break at least two or three inches to the left," Harmon predicted. It did, and Palmer's par effort didn't come close to dropping. By making a bogey, he gave hope to Ford and Hawkins, playing together about forty-five minutes behind.

Ford, who putted with a pop stroke, as did most of the pros of the day, including Palmer, endured his own problems on the greens down the stretch. He three-putted the thirteenth for par after hitting a better wood to the green than Palmer, then missed a three-foot birdie on No. 17. Still, Ford and Hawkins came to the eighteenth within a stroke of Palmer. They circled their birdie attempts like hungry lions but missed, Hawkins from sixteen feet, Ford from slightly closer.

If Venturi was angry about what had transpired at the twelfth hole, he masked it completely after Palmer tapped in for bogey on 18. Venturi shook Palmer's hand and kept holding it as they walked several steps. When the handshake was over, Venturi put his right arm on Palmer's shoulder as they continued off the green. "I knew Palmer was entitled to lift his ball," Venturi told reporters that afternoon.

Yet over the years, the memory of the situation lingered within Venturi like a bad case of indigestion. In his 2004 memoir, *Getting Up and Down: My 60 Years in Golf,* he noted that, while Palmer was entitled to relief, he violated the rules by not declaring he was going to play a second ball before he hit the first one. Venturi wrote, "I firmly believe that he did wrong, and he knows that I know he did wrong."

Palmer has maintained he declared his intentions in advance as required. Even if he had not, Rule 11-5, as written at the time, stated that if a competitor failed to announce his intentions, the second-ball score would count. "Guys told me I should protest," Ford says, "but how do you protest something like that? It was water under the bridge for me. I got second money, and I was a 'cash and carry' kind of player then. All I wanted was the cash— you can have the trophies. I see Fred four or five times a year, and we never talk about it."

At twenty-eight, Palmer was the youngest winner of the Masters since Byron Nelson in 1937. "He's a very young boy and very deserving of being a Masters champion and wearing one of the green coats," Harmon said in his closing remarks on the broadcast. "I think he will go on to great heights."

With $42,608 Palmer topped the 1958 money list. In that November's *Golf Digest,* in an article for which he was paid $55, he told the magazine's readers how to putt.

Bay Hill is Palmer's kind of place. No guard gate, no hats in the clubhouse, and a jumbo chili dog for four bucks at the halfway house. When he is in Florida part of the year, Palmer lives in a townhouse, comfortable but not grand. More tour pros lived at Bay Hill years ago, before they started moving away to bigger houses in gated communities. The clubhouse dining-room menu reflects Palmer's meat-and-potato tastes. The "Palmer Salad" is a wedge of iceberg lettuce and bleu cheese dressing, the type of starter someone who could afford a steak liked to order in 1958.

Deacon Palmer, who loved to escape the Pennsylvania winters that he endured for a lifetime, died at Bay Hill in 1976 of a heart attack at age seventy-one after a full day of golf. On a morning of questions at his office there, some about golf, some about life, Deacon's son is asked if he considers his own mortality.

"Why don't you tell him 'Hell, no,' to that?" his business associate and friend Jim Hinckley interjects from an adjacent room.

But Palmer does not demur. "I certainly think about it, because I talk to Jim," Palmer says, "but I don't dwell on it. I just want to go like my father did. Quick."

Palmer's life, which used to keep the schedule of a traveling circus, is not conducted at the pace it once was but is still full. A man who helps keep it that way is Johnston, who has managed Palmer's business affairs since 1976. "I often tell Arnold my grandfather retired at eighty-five, and somebody gave him a television set as a going-away present," says Johnston. "He then spent the next year of his life watching television and died. That was because essentially he always had been an active guy.

"I'm the guy who takes the heat about ensuring Arnold remains active," Johnston continues, "because from a business standpoint, he's got to do some appearances to keep the business element going. And also from the standpoint of keeping his mind aware of what's going on. At the end of the day, it's somewhat pioneering to represent a professional athlete who is closing in on eighty years old and still perceived to be, and would like to be, active in his profession.

He's challenged, of course, at the best of times because his hearing isn't particularly good. That's become increasingly frustrating."

Palmer is still involved in his golf-course design business and has endorsement deals with Callaway Golf, Administaff, Rolex, and Wyndham Hotels. "Oh, yeah, and Ketel One," says Johnston, with a grin, of the premium vodka. "But that's a very natural connection."

According to the 2007 Golf Digest 50, a ranking of the top money-makers in the sport, Palmer was No. 5 with an annual income of $29,550,000. In Japan trendy young women wear designer clothing licensed to carry Palmer's name, a name of status. "If you go to downtown Tokyo," says Johnston, "there are sixteen Arnold Palmer stores, all of which target fifteen- to twenty-eight-year-old women. I go and meet the designers. They've got purple hair and nose rings. He told me a couple of years ago that he hadn't been to Japan with me in a while and asked if I wanted him to come. I said, 'I don't think so.' I think Arnold appreciates that the royalties are very healthy."

Spend even just a little time around Palmer, whose yellow Labrador, Mulligan, is frequently at his feet, and it is clear he likes company. "I don't think he gets lonely," Johnston says. "He uses crowds, uses visitors—they are absolutely still a source of energy for him. Kit [Palmer's second wife] is a great companion. He's surrounded by a lot of people on his staff. I don't think Arnold really enjoys his own company. He's never really enjoyed being on his own, and he makes sure he never is."

That is not universally true, however. Three years after his fiftieth and final competitive appearance at Augusta, Palmer kicked off the 2007 tournament as honorary starter. There has been talk that Jack Nicklaus should join him in the role, in a reprisal of the way Byron Nelson, Gene Sarazen, and Sam Snead started off the event together for years. Asked if he thinks that would be a good idea, Palmer says, "No, I think one starter is enough. When Jack's ready, I'll step aside."

A question to Palmer: "If there was a ten-foot putt that had to be made, would you rather putt it, have Jack Nicklaus putt it, or have Tiger Woods putt it?"

The answer comes quickly, and with a smile. "Any one of the three," Palmer says. "Tiger is one of the best putters I've ever seen, and so is Jack. And I could hold my own."

Woods passed Palmer on the PGA Tour career victory list a few weeks ago and would surpass Palmer's four Masters titles with a triumph at Augusta next week. Woods's rousing, last-hole win at Palmer's tournament last month recalled Palmer at his dramatic best.

"I think he would see a lot of himself in Tiger," says Johnston, "but I also think Tiger has things Arnold never had and Arnold knows that. Tiger has had the ability to focus and really remove himself from distractions that Arnold couldn't. Arnold enjoyed being Arnold Palmer, and back then there was not as much money, not as much spotlight, not as much pressure as Tiger has."

Out on the Bay Hill range, Palmer has worked his way through his bag to the driver, always the best club in his bag. "If I could have hit the irons equal to the driver," he says a bit wistfully, looking down range, "I would have won a lot more than I did."

Hinckley has pulled up in a cart to watch Palmer hit a few drivers. One of them is particularly pure, flying farther and higher than the rest.

"Are you going to write it up that he was just pounding it down the fairway?" Hinckley asks.

Actually, yes, for a seventy-eight-year-old man, he was pounding it. In fact, in the summer, at the course where he learned to play on a certain hole with a creek, like a certain strong-armed, narrow-hipped young golfer fifty years ago, it would have potential.

April 4, 2008

I saw Arnold Palmer hit a golf ball for the first time when I was a boy in the early 1970s, at the short-lived U.S. Professional Match Play Championship at the Country Club of North Carolina. Palmer was in his forties at that time, his swing still full of fury, his charisma vast, his grip on the golf club perfect. Some thirty-five years later, when I spent time with Palmer in Orlando while working on this story, only the swing had changed. Palmer, Jack Nicklaus, and Gary Player are together on the first tee at Augusta National now, each hitting a ceremonial tee shot to get the Masters started.

CHAPTER TEN

Seve: Portrait of an Artist

Severiano (Seve) Ballesteros played the sport with a tenacious flair, pugilistic in its intent and painterly in its method. For both spectators cheering him and competitors trying to beat him, the Spaniard made an indelible impression. His confidence—"I knew I was the best," he admitted—rubbed off on a continent, while his virtuosity mesmerized the world. "Seve plays shots," American Ben Crenshaw once said, "I don't even see in my dreams."

The talent both to improvise recovery shots and scramble like no one else around the greens, combined with what British golf writer Peter Dobereiner termed a "fanatical ambition" to succeed, took Ballesteros to golf's summit. He won five major championships (the 1979, 1984, and 1988 British Opens along with the 1980 and 1983 Masters) and captured a record fifty tournaments on the European Tour and nine titles on the PGA Tour (his five majors count on both tours). Inducted into the World Golf Hall of Fame in 1999, the first golfer from Spain to be so honored, Ballesteros was at his best in the Ryder Cup. Europe's inspirational leader, he compiled a 20-12-5 record in eight appearances as a player and captained his side to victory in 1997.

Ballesteros lost a two-and-a-half-year battle with brain cancer on May 7, passing away at age fifty-four in his hometown of

Pedrena on the northern coast of Spain one day after his family issued a statement saying his condition had drastically deteriorated. "We heard at the Masters Champions dinner that it was not good," Fuzzy Zoeller said, "that it was only a matter of time before we got word."

The Spanish legend, who retired in 2007 after years of struggling to rediscover the greatness that had left him prematurely, collapsed in the Madrid airport on October 5, 2008. Diagnosed with a malignant tumor above his right temple, Ballesteros underwent four surgeries that attempted to remove as much of the growth as possible and reduce the swelling around his brain. After spending more than two months in the hospital, he had chemotherapy and radiation, but the treatments ultimately could not thwart the disease.

"We can only imagine how difficult this battle has been for him and his family the last few years," said Jack Nicklaus, "but I know Seve faced it with the same grit, fight and spirit he approached his golf career."

Ballesteros lost much of the vision in his left eye and suffered some paralysis on his left side. He spent most of his time at home, where he played a little recreational golf, but was unable to travel to the British Open last summer for a much anticipated return to St. Andrews. It was at the Home of Golf in 1984 when a seventy-second-hole birdie led to victory over Tom Watson and a celebration that became one of golf's most iconic scenes as the British gallery erupted for a golfer it loved as if he were a countryman. Ballesteros's jaunty fist pump when the winning putt crept into the hole became his corporate symbol, and he liked the pose so much he later had it tattooed on his left forearm.

"For golf, he was the greatest show on earth," said contemporary Nick Faldo, a six-time major winner. "I was a fan and so fortunate I had a front-row seat."

That joyous moment in St. Andrews was the zenith of Ballesteros's career, one at times roiled by turmoil that contrasted the instinctive grace with which he played and the joie de vivre spectators sensed and were drawn to in good times.

On and off the course, Ballesteros wasn't always sweetness and light. At different junctures he warred with the European Tour over appearance fees and the PGA Tour about how many tournaments he had to play. While he could be generous to other pros, he gave no quarter in the heat of battle, particularly in the Ryder Cup.

"Some pros are harder to play with than others, and the worst was Seve Ballesteros," two-time U.S. Open champion Curtis Strange told *Golf Digest* in 2006. "His gamesmanship was irritating, and he never let up. He'd do outrageous, childish things, like coughing as you got set to swing, and if you objected, he'd act wounded and escalate the situation. . . . There was only one Seve, and a little of him went a long way. But I'll tell you this, he could back it up."

Robert Green, who tracked Ballesteros's career for a quarter-century, described his multifaceted personality in a 2006 biography, *Seve: Golf's Flawed Genius*. "He is a complex character— charming and manipulative, gregarious and withdrawn, open and suspicious, generous and mean—depending on how the mood takes him," Green wrote.

Given Ballesteros's unlikely rise from humble means in a sleepy Spanish fishing village (majors would be the "big fish" to Seve) to become one of the most famous sportsmen in the world, it is not surprising that his journey included some dark corners.

It was in Pedrena equipped with only one club, a wooden-shafted three-iron, but boundless imagination where Ballesteros began to forge the game that would make him a star. The youngest of four brothers, forced to leave school when he was twelve following an altercation with a teacher, according to Green, he accelerated his golf education. Ballesteros caddied by day at Royal Pedrena Golf Club and practiced when he could sneak on the course, sometimes in the wee hours.

Ballesteros had a right arm a tad longer than his left, a physique that made it seem as if he was born to hold a golf club. His ingenuity came from the countless hours spent hitting shots with his one club out of various types of lies, often on the sandy beach not far from his house. Turning professional shortly before his seventeenth birthday, he hadn't played at all on the amateur circuit, his competition limited to the caddie championship at Royal Pedrena.

It didn't take long for Ballesteros to win as a pro, taking the 1974 Spanish Under-25s Championship at seventeen even though he had reinjured his back—first hurt in a boxing accident three years earlier—with incessant practice in damp, cool weather. Ballesteros successfully defended his title in 1975. In 1976 he became more widely known with his second-place finish to Johnny Miller in the British Open at Royal Birkdale, where the Spaniard played a deft and daring chip between two bunkers on the final hole. It was a shot many players might have tried in a practice round, but few would have attempted with so much riding on the seventy-second hole.

The stroke presaged what was to come: bold, inventive shots that would distinguish Ballesteros from his peers. "He goes after a golf course like a lion at a zebra," the Los Angeles Times's Jim Murray wrote of Ballesteros. "He doesn't reason with it; he tries to throw it out of a window or hold its head under water 'til it stops wriggling."

In a few weeks Ballesteros won for the first time on the European Tour, at the Dutch Open. Later in 1976, he closed with a back-nine 31 to overtake Arnold Palmer and win the Trophée Lancôme. While continuing to excel in Europe, Ballesteros ventured to the United States for the 1977 Masters. He returned to America in the spring of 1978, shooting a final-round 66 to win the Greater Greensboro Open and become the youngest winner on the PGA Tour since Raymond Floyd in 1963. The next week, at Augusta National, Ballesteros impressed Tom Weiskopf in the first round. "He's so long and so smooth and so effortless, he's unbelievable," Weiskopf said. Nicklaus played with Seve in the second round, noting that Ballesteros, who would finish tied for eighteenth, often outdrove him by twenty-five to thirty yards.

Attacking courses with the charismatic aggression Palmer had brought to the PGA Tour a quarter-century earlier, Ballesteros had a magnetic expressiveness. "You knew you were in the presence of something special," said CBS announcer and former European Tour player David Feherty. "There was sort of a feline grace to everything he did, kind of an animal-like quality. You felt like he could change the weather with his mood. He would be thunderous one minute, his face would be purple. When he smiled, the world lit up. He came in, a caddie who came from nothing, and just transformed European golf, dragging it into the modern era the same way that Arnold did in America."

Ballesteros's major breakthrough came in the 1979 British Open at Royal Lytham and St. Annes. Dueling Hale Irwin in the final round, Ballesteros sprayed his tee shots all over the place. One of his errant drives, at the par-four sixteenth hole, flew far right of the fairway and ended up among cars in a parking lot that had been added to accommodate the final-day crowds. Frank Hannigan, former executive director of the United States Golf Association, said he was once told by Keith Mackenzie, former secretary of the Royal and Ancient, that the R&A had intended to mark the car park as out-of-bounds that day but did not do so. The area was through the green, Ballesteros got free relief from the automobiles, and hit a routine short iron onto the putting surface and rolled in the birdie putt en route to victory, the first in the Open by a continental European since Frenchman Arnaud Massy in 1907.

"I watched the guy hit three fairways all day and win the British Open," Irwin said after Ballesteros's death. "It wasn't because he was lucky—it was because he created some shots that were unbelievable."

Phil Mickelson was a boy watching the Masters on television when he became enthralled with Ballesteros. "Watching him stroll up 18, giving it the fist pump, and chipping in on the last hole, I remember saying to my mom, 'I want to win the Masters,'" Mickelson said. "'I want to do that like Seve did it. I want to be like that.'"

Although Mickelson would produce his own portfolio of great escapes and short-game magic once he joined the tour, Ballesteros was the original get-out-of-jail artist of modern golf. "Even when I was in trouble, I could always see more shots than anyone else," he told *Golf Digest* in 2000. "When you are in trouble, it is not only about ability or aggressiveness. It is more than that. You have to see a certain shot. Some people don't have that."

Crenshaw is still awed by a one-armed, backhanded shot from next to a tree Ballesteros pulled off against him in the 1981 World Match Play final at Wentworth. "Everyone thought he was going to chip out about ten yards," Crenshaw remembered. "Then he took a full swing, hooking it 150 yards up the fairway. I'd never seen anything like it."

For Feherty, his Seve highlight reel is topped by a greenside bunker shot Ballesteros executed at Royal Birkdale. With his ball thirty feet from a tight pin, Ballesteros aimed 45 degrees right of the target line, as if playing a bank shot in pool. He hit a hard, low-liner into the revetted bunker face, and the ball bounced up and to the left, clearing the bunker, landing gently on the green, and rolling next to the hole. "I remember standing there going, 'Who the bleeping hell thinks of that?'" Feherty said.

Irwin once watched Ballesteros hit a hard-to-fathom bunker shot from a buried lie with spin. "I asked him how he did it and he wouldn't tell me," Irwin said. "I understood. That was part of the mystique and part of the fence between the American players and Seve." Denis Watson approached Ballesteros one time, telling him he had gotten a bunker lesson from Tom Kite, a golfer also known for his fine wedge play. "'What do you think?'" Watson asked Seve, demonstrating the technique Kite had taught him. "He said, 'I'm Seve. I am the best. Let me show you.' He tossed one into a deep bunker and hit it about two inches from the hole."

Ballesteros's miracle-working from trouble was for years an adjunct to his solid long game. He was never Hogan-like in his precision, but Seve wouldn't have compiled the record he did without being a solid ball-striker. His competitive decline—he won his last major, the 1988 British Open, on the strength of a sterling final-round 65 when he was thirty-one, and recorded his last regular win at thirty-eight—quickened because he began to hit the ball all over the place all the time.

Always the most natural of swingers, Ballesteros attempted swing changes with numerous instructors—from David Leadbetter to Mac O'Grady to Butch Harmon. He insisted he would have been able to successfully evolve his swing if not for his bad back. "The back was the only reason my game and my golf swing would deteriorate progressively," Ballesteros insisted to *Golf Digest*'s Jaime Diaz last year. "The only reason. To change the swing is not that hard if you have talent, but you have to be very good physically. I wasn't. I couldn't do it."

Harmon spent two weeks with Ballesteros in 1995. "I thought he had gotten too robotic in his swing from his work with some other guys, and I was trying to get him back to natural-feeling shots," said Harmon, who positioned himself about fifteen yards in front of his pupil and called out shots—low hooks, high fades—for him to hit. "[He hit] every one perfect. He was just seeing the shot and doing it. But I walked away and the balls were all over again."

A bittersweet episode occurred at the 1995 Ryder Cup, Ballesteros's final as a player. Out in the first singles match against Tom Lehman at Oak Hill Country Club, the once great but still proud Spaniard didn't hit a fairway and hit only two greens on the front nine but was still very much in the match against the American, who was playing well. Lehman won the match, 4 and 3, forever impressed at the will of Seve that day.

"His body language was the strongest of anybody, save Tiger in recent years," Lehman said. "It said, 'Hey, I may have hit a crappy shot, but if you miss this next one, you'll miss the greatest shot ever hit.' That's just the way he walked, the way he acted, the way he carried himself."

At the 1983 Ryder Cup, at a time when Ballesteros was revving up Europe's chances in the biennial matches, Zoeller had witnessed just what Lehman described. Three-up in his singles match against Zoeller after eleven holes, Ballesteros lost the advantage and they were all square playing the par-five eighteenth at PGA National Golf Club. Seve hit a lousy drive and a poor second shot into a fairway bunker about 245 yards from the green.

Watching Ballesteros take a three-wood into the sand, his opponent was shocked. "I was licking my chops, thinking, 'What the hell is he doing?'" Zoeller said. "I didn't think he could pull it off. It wasn't a shallow bunker—it was about four feet deep, and I would have parked a five-iron out in the fairway. But not Seve—that's just not the way he was."

The way Seve was, he swung that piece of persimmon and steel as if he were standing on the beach at Pedrena, aiming his hand-me-down three-iron at a cloud. He made crisp contact, hitting a high, slinging cut that cleared the bunker lip and finished up near the green. Ballesteros got his par and halved the match.

"He would try shots none of us had the guts to try," Curtis Strange, his old adversary, said. "It's called talent."

The tears flowed for that talent and the man who owned it. "When you look at your idol, how do you see him?" Miguel Angel Jiménez said. "I saw him as immense, huge. He couldn't get through the door."

May 16, 2011

I reported and wrote this story while in Alabama covering the 2011 Regions Tradition at Shoal Creek on the Champions Tour. Seve Ballesteros's death deeply moved these contemporaries of the Spanish star, whatever differences they had with him during his lifetime minimized upon his passing as they reflected on his genius golf talent and charisma. At the 2012 Ryder Cup, the first biennial matches to be played since Seve's death, a European team, captained by José María Olazábal and wearing Ballesteros's silhouette on their sleeves, scored a stunning, final-day comeback victory over the United States at Medinah Country Club outside Chicago. Seve would have loved it.

2

INSIDE THE ROPES

Courses and Competitions

CHAPTER ELEVEN

Changing the Course of History

Golf was a creaky and scratchy sport in 1913. Its clubs were shafted in wood and its players clothed in wool, and although the game was on the move in the United States, where it had been introduced about two decades earlier, no one was sure exactly where it was headed. As the U.S. Open commenced that September at The Country Club in Brookline, Massachusetts, near Boston, the best players were British, and so was its soul.

Golf could catch on, or it could remain a minor diversion for the gentry. Many Americans didn't understand the game, and many others didn't like it. But even before 162 competitors teed off in the Open qualifier, it was clear this curious, imported game was being interpreted differently in the United States. Course architects were putting new twists in their designs. Like many American male players, Francis Ouimet had begun to play without a jacket, the better to make a free turn. And when Americans turned up to watch a competition, they clapped heartily for strokes that would have produced only a curl of the lips overseas.

American-born professional John McDermott won the 1911 U.S. Open and successfully defended his title in 1912, but he didn't get much attention despite the fact that he was a confident 130-pounder willing to take on all comers. Pros had little status at the time. (In 1913 at The Country Club they used the stables if they needed to change.) To keep evolving in America, golf needed another catalyst, a homebred hero who could warm hearts. In one rainy week—of which there remain few photographs and scant moving pictures but ever-bolder newspaper headlines as the miracle played out—Ouimet became that person.

Scores of golfers have executed heroic shots and authored final-round comebacks, and a few have pulled off upsets that made people look twice, but when Ouimet won the 1913 U.S. Open he tugged his sport in a different direction, providing "an injection of romance into American golf," as Bobby Jones put it. There were about 350,000 golfers in America in 1913. Ten years later there were two million.

What Ouimet did was win a championship in which he didn't believe he was going to be able to play, on a course upon which he grew up caddieing (and which he would sneak on to practice), against competitors few gave him a prayer of beating. Rallying to tie British stars Harry Vardon and Edward Ray in the fourth round and then beating them in an eighteen-hole playoff the next day, the twenty-year-old amateur proved that Americans, wealthy or not, had a place in golf.

An international rivalry was born. "I never once expected that I would win," Ouimet said after his victory. "No one is more surprised than myself. I did the very best I could, and tried hard to keep the cup this side of the water. I am happy, indeed, that it stays." The British invented golf, but after Ouimet, they no longer owned it.

"The next thing I remember is sitting in my bedroom looking out on the rain and writing frantically," later wrote Bernard Darwin, the dean of British golf writing, who had marked Ouimet's scorecard and witnessed his countrymen's loss that fateful day. "I felt like a war correspondent on some stricken field, sending home news of the annihilation of the British Army. But the victory had been so glorious that no grudging of it was possible."

Ouimet was the son of a gardener who grew up across the street from The Country Club, at 246 Clyde Street. He caddied there and often slipped out before dawn to play as many shots as he could before the greenkeeper ran him off. Ouimet got his first club by trading in three-dozen balls he had scavenged. He had no birthright to golf, but on the sly and around the crude holes he and his brother fashioned in their family's backyard, Ouimet made the most of his circumstance.

"Had a pleasant young man from a good Park Avenue family or some stiff and staid professional defeated Vardon and Ray," Herbert Warren Wind wrote in *The Story of American Golf*, "it is really very doubtful if their victory would have been the wholesale therapeutic for American golf that was Ouimet's. Here was a person all of America, not just golfing America, could understand—the boy from the 'wrong side' of the street, the ex-caddie, the kid who worked during his summer vacations from high school—America's idea of the American hero."

The truth was sweeter than fiction. When Ouimet was nine, he found his first rubber-cored ball and played with it until he wore off all the paint. After putting on a fresh coat, he stuck the ball in the oven, alongside a loaf of bread his mother was baking, so that it could dry. The ball melted and made a mess of the oven, but Ouimet found more golf balls. He played on, joining his high school team. He attempted to qualify for the U.S. Amateur from 1910 through 1912 but failed to qualify by a stroke each time. He finally made the field in 1913, giving eventual champion Jerome Travers a tough match in the second round.

Ouimet's "breakthrough" came that summer, when he won the Massachusetts State Amateur and proved he was capable of explosive golf by playing the last six holes of his semifinal match in six under par.

His form had a modern hint about it. On full shots, Ouimet utilized a strong left-knee action on the backswing and a drive of the legs coming through the ball. Around impact, there was a resemblance to a young star who would hit the scene some sixty years later, Johnny Miller.

On the greens, Ouimet used more of an arms-and-shoulders stroke than many golfers of the day, and it was effective. As he demonstrated at Brookline, he was able to keep his wits about him under pressure. And long before it became the thing to do, Ouimet tried to keep his golf simple. "I am the type who enjoys a word or two with a friend while walking from the tee to my ball," he wrote in his 1932 autobiography, *A Game of Golf,* "but I want the chatter to be short and sweet, so that when I come to think over my shot I have not got a dozen other things to think of."

Ouimet thought he might not even get to play in the Open. He had taken a vacation from his job as a sporting-goods clerk to play in the U.S. Amateur and didn't have the nerve to ask for more time off. But when his boss saw in the newspaper that Ouimet was entered, he told him to go ahead. Ignoring a pair of 88s he shot in casual play a couple of days before, Ouimet qualified easily.

Vardon was making his second tour of the United States. He'd first come over in 1900, wowing Americans with his textbook technique in exhibition matches and hitting demonstrations in department stores. He was paid hundreds of dollars for his shows, and he seldom disappointed. From a very open stance on all shots, Vardon used a more upright swing than most of his contemporaries. In 1913, when he was forty-three and convinced Ray to accompany him on another American tour, Vardon had won five British Open titles (he would add his sixth the following year) and was still a titan. Going around the country, he noticed how much Americans had improved their golf since his first visit. Between his two tours of America, Vardon contracted tuberculosis. As he arrived in Boston, his putting wasn't what it used to be, and some thought the TB was a reason.

Like Vardon, Ray came from the Isle of Jersey but was seven years younger. While Vardon smoked a pipe only when things got tense on the course, Ray kept a pipe in his mouth all the while he

Inside the Ropes

played. Ray was over six feet and 200 pounds, and as the longest driver of the time he gave his shots a mighty clout. "Hit it a bloody sight harder, mate," Ray advised someone who wanted more distance. In contrast to Vardon, who nipped his iron shots cleanly, Ray was known to take lunch pail–size divots. But around the greens, Ray, the 1912 British Open champion, had a soft touch.

Ray was usually a genial man, but on the evening of the first day's play at The Country Club he was involved in what the newspapers reported as a "lively row" with countryman Wilfrid Reid over the British tax system. Ray punched the smaller Reid twice, bloodying his nose. Tied for the thirty-six-hole lead with Vardon, Reid's game disappeared after the fight. The next day he shot 85-86 and finished tied for sixteenth, clearing the way for Ouimet, Vardon, and Ray to intersect.

In 1913 the national championship was contested over two days, with competitors playing thirty-six holes each day. With a third-round 74, Ouimet moved into a tie for the lead with Vardon and Ray at 225. In the fourth round that afternoon, all three players struggled. Ray was in early with a 79 for 304. Vardon could do no better and matched his countryman. Ouimet, after a front-nine 43 and a double bogey 5 on the tenth hole, appeared to have blown any chance of winning. He needed to play the last six holes in two under just to tie. At No. 13 he chipped in for the first birdie. Word of his plight filtered to the clubhouse. Many doubted he would get another birdie. It was pouring rain. Travers, who had seen Ouimet firsthand at the Amateur, wasn't so sure. "Ice-water nerves," he said.

On the seventeenth, the hole he could see from his house and the place he'd hit many of those furtive shots before the sun came up, Ouimet faced a fifteen-foot downhill putt for birdie. Traffic was backing up on adjacent Clyde Street. Horns were honking. Ouimet ignored the tumult and caused some more when the putt dropped. A par at No. 18, thanks to a five-foot putt, put Ouimet in the playoff.

Incessant rain overnight turned the course into a quagmire the next morning, but thousands of fans showed up to root for the homebred. Ouimet hit his approach to the par-four fifth out of bounds but calmly knocked the next one on the green and salvaged a bogey. All three went out in 38. Then, on the short tenth, Vardon and Ray both three-putted to fall behind the young amateur, who parred. Ray began spraying shots way right and struggled in with a 78. Vardon was just one behind playing the seventeenth, but he drove left into a bunker and bogeyed. Ouimet finished birdie-par for a 72 while Vardon had a 77.

Vardon and Ray were gracious losers. "We have no excuses to make," said Vardon, "for we were defeated by high-class golf." Ray said, "I have no hesitation in saying that he played better golf the whole four days than any of us." Years later Vardon admitted surprise over his loss. "I had seen sufficient of [Ouimet's] golf on the previous day to realize how good he was," Vardon wrote, "but I did not think he would prove able to sustain that form in the playoff. I had made a mistake."

Ouimet's victory was made all the more storybook because of Eddie Lowery, the ten-year-old caddie who accompanied him into golf history. Ouimet's sidekick wasn't as tall as the clubs he carried. He recently had been in the hospital with a badly cut foot from stepping on a bottle, and it was still bandaged as he trudged around at Brookline. The money he earned he gave to his widowed mother to help pay the bills. The week of the U.S. Open, Lowery was in trouble with a truant officer for playing hooky, and as he toted his man's clubs to the first tee for the playoff, one of Ouimet's friends tried to take the bag. Lowery resisted, Ouimet backed him, and the little boy was there for the duration. He picked up about $150 when a hat was passed at the end of the day.

Lowery went on to become a state champion golfer in his own right (Massachusetts, 1927), built thriving Lincoln dealerships in San Francisco, and befriended champion golfers Ken Venturi and Harvie Ward on their way up. "It was his life, really," says Margaret Lowery, his widow, "because he was always known as Francis Ouimet's caddie. A lot of people wouldn't want to be known as somebody's caddie, but he did. It opened a lot of doors for him."

As the years turned into decades, until Ouimet's death from a heart attack in 1967 when he was seventy-four, the unlikely champion and his little imp of a caddie would talk about twice a week on the phone, separated by three thousand miles but linked forever by their rainy walk to glory. "Francis was sophisticated and quiet at times, then he could be the biggest needler I've ever seen," Margaret Lowery says. "He could really get at Eddie, and Eddie could really get at him."

To those who knew him, Ouimet was as modest as his feat was monumental. In *A Game of Golf,* he devoted just seventeen of 274 pages to the 1913 U.S. Open. He discussed more thoroughly his U.S. Amateur victories of 1914 and 1931, the latter coming when he was thirty-eight and, many thought, past his prime. Quick to remember a name but eager to stay in the background, Ouimet showed kindness in ways small (giving a couple of clubs to a paperboy who didn't have any) and large (establishing the Francis Ouimet Scholarship Fund, which has awarded more than $9 million since 1949).

"He never brought his golf home," says Ouimet's daughter, Barbara McLean. Her sister, Janice Salvi, says, "He was just one in a million that way. At dinner he'd never talk about golf—he'd ask us how we did at school. We'd pick up a newspaper and see that he'd won something."

Only once, Salvi remembers, did her father ever boast about anything having to do with golf. When Ouimet got word in 1951 that the Royal and Ancient Golf Club of St. Andrews was naming him captain, the first American to receive the distinction, he informed his wife, Stella, and their girls at the dinner table. "He said, 'I received the greatest honor of my life,'" Salvi says, "and he told us all about it. That was the one thing he raved about."

Later on that year, in a ceremony that traditionally marks the occasion, Ouimet drove off the first tee of the Old Course to the boom and smoke of a cannon and the applause of the British gallery. If the onlookers gathered in the Home of Golf clapped louder than usual, there was cause.

September 17, 1999

It was a shame that the 2013 U.S. Open couldn't have been contested at The Country Club. The championship was staged instead at Merion Golf Club near Philadelphia, another classic venue. Still, the centennial of Francis Ouimet's amazing accomplishment received its due. I again wrote about the 1913 U.S. Open for *Golf World*, among my research being a pleasant day in the Boston Public Library viewing newspaper microfilm, including all of Bernard Darwin's dispatches from Brookline as the wild week unfolded. Late in 2012 I was on a media panel in Boston as the Francis Ouimet Scholarship Fund—which has now given more than $25 million to deserving students for their college education—kicked off its year-long commemoration of Ouimet's win for the ages and promoted the substantial helping hand of the foundation. Besides getting a peek at Fenway Park, which I hadn't visited before, I got to chat for a few minutes with Eddie Lowery's daughter, Cynthia Wilcox. For a moment, 1913 didn't seem so far away.

CHAPTER TWELVE

The Streak

In 1945 professional golf was long on weeds, short on golf balls, and owned by Byron Nelson just as surely as if he had a deed. No one before or since has come close to doing what Nelson did fifty years ago, and it would still be hard to fathom were it not for the numbers, which leap out of the record book as if launched from a springboard.

Nelson entered thirty official events in 1945. He won eighteen and was second seven other times. Only twice did he finish out of the top five. His scoring average for medal events was 68.33, and in his final rounds he was even better, averaging 67.68. He had seventy-nine rounds in the 60s and ninety-three rounds under par in 112 rounds. Excluding two match-play events and two other tournaments in which he prevailed in playoffs, his average victory margin was slightly more than seven strokes. His worst score of the year was a 75. He won tournaments in more states (eleven) and provinces (two) in twelve months than most people even visit in a lifetime.

And there is, of course, the matter of The Streak.

These days, sport psychologists would say Nelson was "in the zone" or had great "flow-state concentration." He did, but in the middle of the most sustained period of golf dominance ever, Nelson simply said that he had the "hot hand." Did he ever.

From March through August, Nelson entered eleven tournaments. He won eleven tournaments. He won in Florida, North Carolina, and Georgia. He won in Quebec and Pennsylvania. He won in Illinois, Ohio, and Ontario. He won in the rain and in the heat. He won holding the lead, and he won coming from behind. He won holing a bunch of putts and won hitting approach shots so close to the hole that he barely needed to putt.

Finally, more than six months after he started winning, Nelson lost. He was vanquished by amateur Fred Haas Jr., who putted the lights out of the grainy common Bermuda greens at Chickasaw Country Club to win the Memphis Invitational.

Haas and Nelson were paired together in the final round, and Haas can still see most clearly Nelson's seven-iron tee shot on the sixth hole. Nelson, fighting back from a 73 on Friday, had pulled to within two strokes of Haas through five holes. As Nelson's ball arched skyward toward the green, tailing ever so slightly to the left as it lost altitude, as most of his shots did—not so much a draw as a gentle waver—Haas watched it strike the flagstick and try to bury in the hole before it bounced out and ran forty feet away across the green, like some squirrel hot for a nut. The Streak was going to be stopped.

It had all started back in early March. Franklin Roosevelt was still alive, and the Allies were moving decisively toward victory in Europe and making big strides on the Pacific front. Down in south Florida, the International Four-Ball tournament matched up two-man teams. Nelson's partner was Harold (Jug) McSpaden, a Kansas City native who, outside of Nelson's wife, Louise, knew him better than anyone.

They had traveled the circuit together since the mid-1930s, sharing many a mile along America's blue highways and railroad routes. As Nelson worked to refine his swing into a one-piece, less handsy move with lots of knee and foot action that would be the model for generations of golfers to follow, McSpaden provided a keen, observant eye.

When America was drawn into World War II late in 1941, Nelson and McSpaden discovered they shared something else: both would be rejected for military service on medical grounds. Nelson was a "free bleeder," his blood taking almost five times the normal two and a half minutes to clot. His condition improved with age, but at that time he dared not travel far without a supply of styptic powder in case of a shaving nick, and the dread of an accident at an isolated juncture in his tournament travels was never far from his mind, or Louise's.

But Nelson met his fate with equanimity, which wasn't too surprising given that he had been nearly given up for dead after a difficult birth and again eleven years later, when a stubborn case of typhoid fever ravaged his body for weeks, taking sixty pounds off his young frame before he finally recovered. Although Nelson always had a nervous stomach, it was clear to see why he might be able to keep golf in perspective better than others. He knew he was lucky to be around.

McSpaden's affliction wasn't life-threatening, but he was subject to severe bouts of hay fever and sinusitis, a problem that occasionally demanded that he wear tinted glasses when he played and once forced him to walk off the course at a Canadian tournament when a sneezing fit prompted a profuse nosebleed.

Both ruled 4-F for the war, Nelson and McSpaden began in late 1942 a marathon, two-year exhibition tour at military camps and hospitals and at war bond charity drives and USO and Red Cross shows. Sometimes they would hook up with entertainers such as Bing Crosby and Bob Hope and play the straight men. Their duty couldn't be compared with being overseas, but an arduous travel schedule and simply seeing all the scarred veterans added to the unease felt by these two outwardly healthy men. They got their share of dirty looks.

In 1945 Nelson and McSpaden still did plenty of charity for the military, and other pros did too, but by then the exhibitions were an adjunct to what was building back to a full circuit. As the pros got to Miami, they had already played nine events, starting in Los Angeles and working their way east. Nelson already had three victories in the young year, most recently in a playoff with McSpaden at New Orleans.

By the time they teamed up in Miami, Nelson and McSpaden were well known as the "Gold Dust Twins" for their propensity to take what sparsely available war bonds and cash existed during the war years, and they lived up to the nickname at Miami Springs. They were twenty-one up and never threatened in four matches. They walloped former New York Yankee Sam Byrd and Denny Shute, 8 and 6, in the scheduled thirty-six-hole final. In the second round, Nelson-McSpaden scored a 4-and-3 victory over Ed Dudley and a rusty Lt. Ben Hogan, who was playing in his first tournament in some time on a break from the Army Air Force.

The victory was particularly significant for McSpaden because he didn't win another event that year. While Nelson set a record for victories, McSpaden set one for placing second. McSpaden had thirteen runner-up finishes—seven times when Nelson won. "To be truthful," McSpaden says now, "he was more interested in winning than I was. I never played better, except he was playing even better than I was. He was just tuned to a little higher level in '45."

On the trip up for three consecutive tournaments in North Carolina, some of the pros stopped off for exhibitions in Aiken, South Carolina, and Augusta, Georgia, home of the Masters, which was not staged for the third straight year due to the war. Charlotte was first, followed by events in Greensboro and Durham.

The second notch in Nelson's skein, as sportswriters of the day called it, wouldn't have happened had Sam Snead—who had a three-tournament winning streak of his own stopped by Nelson at Miami—not had a loose finish in the final round of the Charlotte Open at Myers Park Country Club. Leading by one shot with two holes to play, Snead scrambled for a par on the 490-yard seventeenth hole after his two-wood second shot flew over the OB markers but hit a car on bordering Roswell Avenue and caromed

Inside the Ropes

back into play. But he wasn't so lucky on the eighteenth, a long par three. Snead's one-iron tee shot came up short, and he three-putted from fifty feet, dropping into a tie with Nelson.

Snead had beaten Nelson in one extra hole after they tied at Gulfport, Mississippi, a month earlier, but custom on the tour dictated an eighteen-hole playoff to settle a tie, with contestants sharing 50 percent of the playoff gate receipts, unless both agreed to sudden death. The two golfers battled for control in the playoff, with Snead getting an assist from Nelson's first double bogey in weeks—a 6 on the fourth hole—and taking a one-stroke lead as they came to the seventeenth. But again he battled to par the hole, allowing Nelson's routine birdie to square the score.

At the conclusion of eighteen playoff holes, Snead was in agreement with PGA officials to continue with extra holes, but Nelson balked. "None of those sudden-death finishes for me," he said, perhaps remembering his failure at Gulfport and his success at New Orleans, when he had beaten McSpaden in eighteen extra holes.

Even so, the second playoff almost didn't happen. That morning in the *Charlotte Observer*, sports columnist Jake Wade wrote about ongoing gossip that a gambling fix had been on—that Snead had deliberately bogeyed the seventy-second hole so that an extra day would be necessary and he would be able to claim a share of the extra day's receipts. Wade reported the gossip in order to refute it, but Snead was livid, and only a hotel meeting with Nelson and PGA director Fred Corcoran convinced him to play. A distracted Snead shot 73 and lost to Nelson's 69 in front of a grim, quiet gallery of 1,800 fans. It was the strangest backdrop to any of Nelson's triumphs in 1945.

Charlotte was also where veteran pro Willie Goggin, thirty-five years before the advent of the all-exempt tour, led more than thirty pros in petitioning for a 30 percent reduction in prize money for first through third place in order to ensure more money for the rank and file. Almost everyone except Nelson, Snead, McSpaden, and Byrd liked the idea, and it was to go into effect at the start of the summer tour in Montreal. But at least in one quarter, in the form of the *Charlotte News*'s Evangeline Davis, it was nothing short of communism on the course. "What about side purses for the laziest galleryite, or the greenest reporter, the most backward ticket-taker, the slowest caddie?" Davis wrote. "Where will this thing stop, short of links socialism?"

Unconcerned with the labor movement, Nelson went about his business at the Greater Greensboro Open, which already was known for large, lively crowds who loved to watch Snead. By the end of this edition, though, they were behind Nelson, whose 271 total was eight shots ahead of Byrd. Snead wasn't a factor.

After a Red Cross exhibition in Pinehurst, it was on to Hope Valley Country Club and the Durham Open. Hope Valley's turf, like all courses of the day, was a blend of weeds and grasses. Courses were full of dandelions, clover, buckhorn, and Hope Valley's weed du jour, chickweed. Herbicides had yet to be introduced, and superintendents resorted to measures such as injecting individual dandelion stems with sulfuric acid in an attempt to eradicate them.

"If it was green, we considered it grass," remembers Hope Valley member Brad Henderson, who was eighteen when he watched Nelson come from a shot back to shoot a five-under-par 65 in the final round and beat Toney Penna by five.

"The courses were pretty ragged," says Nelson contemporary Johnny Bulla. "For [Nelson] to score the way he did was something else. All of them were in bad shape."

It is impossible to quantify *how much* Nelson's technique—which brought the clubhead into the ball on a fairly level angle of attack, resulting in small divots and the freedom from too many squirting shots out of the weedy lies—helped him with the course conditions, but without question it did. The tour occasionally invoked winter rules during 1945, but rolling the ball over, when it did occur, didn't always help much.

In addition to his ability to pick the ball cleanly off bad lies, Nelson carried with him two other key advantages throughout

1945. He was superb with a two-wood, which made most par-fives birdie holes for him. And twenty years before the use of yardage books, Nelson was a keen judge of distance.

"He was the best two-wood player to the green that I ever saw," says McSpaden, his memory full of watching Nelson strike countless brassie shots toward his target. "If there were sixteen par-five holes in a tournament, you could bet he would be ten to twelve under par for those holes."

As for Nelson's ability to judge distances, which produced more stony iron shots than anyone other than Johnny Miller in his brief 1970s spurt, Nelson recalls being asked by an army colonel to assist his charges in their artillery training. Nelson was preparing to do so before failing his army physical. Because he so adeptly figured how far to hit his shots, he seldom played practice rounds. And as the year wore on, staying away from tournament sites an extra day paid off in a little more peace and quiet.

It was for all his skills that writer O. B. Keeler, who had chronicled Bobby Jones's career, tagged Nelson "The Great Precisionist" when he rolled over the field by nine strokes at the Iron Lung benefit tournament in Atlanta in early April, the last event on the winter tour. Nelson set the tone for his fifth straight win on the first day as he fired a 64 in cold, blustery conditions to take a five-stroke lead.

Nelson had a new nickname to take with him on hiatus from the circuit, because he already was being called "Big Byron Nelson," "Lord Byron," "The Mechanical Man," "Mr. Golf," "The Golfing Machine," and "The Umbrella Man," the last for his promotional role with Haas-Jordan, for whom he helped develop the golf umbrella.

Nelson played little golf on the two-month break from competition, but he showed no rust at Montreal as he opened quickly with a 63 at Islemere Country Club and ran away from the field with a ten-shot victory over McSpaden. The only person who took any attention away from Nelson's sixth straight title was Bing Crosby, who Friday shot a 37 for nine holes in between songs and gave a Saturday performance.

Crosby was also at Philadelphia the following week, where he sang and played at the Philadelphia Inquirer Invitational. Nelson claimed his seventh win in a row, and this one came squarely at the expense of McSpaden, who lived in the area and was hosting the Nelsons. McSpaden had such severe hay fever early in the week that he had to seek daylong refuge from the pollen in air-conditioned restaurants and movie theaters, but he came back with three 66s after an opening 73, and his 271 total was five clear of the field. Except for Nelson.

Trailing McSpaden and Bulla by one stroke starting Sunday's final round at Llanerch Country Club, Nelson made the turn at two under for the day. McSpaden was also playing well, Nelson found out, so he knew he had to answer. His reply was birdies on the thirteenth, fifteenth, sixteenth, seventeenth, and eighteenth holes. The finisher was a tap-in from two inches after a 300-yard drive and a wedge second shot. McSpaden was back on the fourteenth hole when he got word of Nelson's 63. He shook his head. Behind Llanerch's eighteenth green, many spectators moved in close on Nelson, eager for a handshake or an autograph. Police cleared a path for him to make the twenty-yard exit to the locker room, but he lingered to sign scorecards, albums, and scraps of blank paper. Some of the admirers were servicemen, admitted free of charge, as they were at most tournaments. Once inside, quenching his thirst with a glass of orange juice, Nelson called it "the greatest round I've ever played."

Next stop was the Chicago Victory National Open at Calumet Country Club, the wartime substitute for the U.S. Open. Nelson sprained his upper back in a Saturday driving contest, but he was hampered little in the thirty-six-hole Sunday finale. He closed with 68-70, and he had another runaway victory, this time seven ahead of a faltering McSpaden (76) and Ky Laffoon. Eight straight was secure.

With the PGA Championship up next and the season near the midpoint, Nelson and his fellow pros had the unique wartime worry of coming up with enough decent golf balls to use. With rubber earmarked strictly for the war effort, new balls hadn't been manufactured in about three years, and although some pros hoarded all they could when production ceased, even storing some in bank vaults, supplies were running low by the middle of 1945.

McSpaden, for instance, had purchased five hundred dozen new balls early in the war. He kept most to be sold at the pro shops he ran when he was off the tour, keeping a gross for himself. "Twelve dozen wasn't near enough," McSpaden says. "I ended up paying $60 a dozen for plenty of dozens around 1945."

When Bobby Jones invited Bulla to play at East Lake Country Club in Atlanta during the war years, he also got something in return. "Bobby Jones ran out of golf balls," Bulla remembers, "and I would give 'em to him." Out on the circuit, if a fan came up to a pro and offered the gift of a prewar ball, as occasionally happened, he would gratefully accept and put the present in play.

For the PGA Championship at Moraine Country Club in Dayton, Ohio, Nelson's ninth straight triumph, the record book shows he was comedalist at 138, then a total of thirty-seven under par for 204 holes for five rounds of match play, each scheduled for thirty-six holes. But in the second round against Mike Turnesa, Nelson nearly came up empty. He had his closest call since Snead's costly three-putt at Charlotte.

Turnesa, an easygoing member of the golf-loving Turnesa family of White Plains, New York, looked good when he built a one-up lead through the morning round and maintained his lead through twenty-seven holes. It was then that Nelson saw Turnesa's red-haired wife, Mary, in the crowd.

"He came over to me," Mary Turnesa remembers. "He had reddish hair himself, and he said, 'Let me pat your red head for good luck.' So I let him."

Bad move. It took several holes, but Nelson found his luck. With just four holes to play, Turnesa had increased his lead to two up, and he fired an iron to within ten feet on the par-three fifteenth. But Nelson countered with an even better shot, and when Turnesa barely missed his birdie putt—if it had trickled in, The Streak surely would have been over—Nelson made his to pull closer. He squared the match with a birdie on the tricky sixteenth hole. At the seventeenth, a par five, Nelson's long-hole superiority paid off as he holed a twenty-five-footer for eagle against Turnesa's birdie. All that remained was for Nelson to wiggle in a four-footer for par on the last hole. Nelson shot 68-66 for the day, Turnesa 68-69.

"I was seven under and still lost," Turnesa said after the match. "How the hell are you supposed to beat this man?"

When the tour went to St. Paul, Minnesota, for the next tournament, Nelson played two exhibitions in Iowa and Minnesota, then checked into the Mayo Clinic. He had gotten through the PGA thanks to nightly heat and massage treatments on his aching body. After three days of exams, the doctors gave him a very uncomplicated, unscientific diagnosis. They told him his muscles were too tense. They told him to relax.

That was a tall order, given the attention Nelson was receiving by now. But the aches may have actually helped deflect his worries. His expectations may have been lower too. When he rejoined the tour a week later in Chicago for the Tam O'Shanter All American, the richest event of the year ($60,000 in war bonds), Nelson didn't miss a beat. He handled Tam O'Shanter's clover-laden fairways with customary aplomb, finishing nineteen under par, a full eleven strokes ahead of second-place Hogan, who was now out of the service.

"I sweated plenty winning this one," Nelson said. "For the first time, I started a tournament fast, which put me under more pressure than ever. People forget that I worry about beating par as much as the next fellow, and that I'm only human."

Beating par was the last thing Canadian Open organizers wanted

Nelson to do to Thornhill Country Club in Toronto. His scoring blitz in Montreal had seen to that. So Thornhill was stretched out as long as possible, and par was reduced from 71 to 70. Nelson topped a shot during both the first and second rounds, and while his seventy-two-hole score of even par was as high as any since the start of the season at Riviera Country Club, he still won by four over Herman Barron. Eleven in a row.

En route to Memphis, Nelson and many of the other pros stopped off in Spring Lake, New Jersey, for the thirty-six-hole Spring Lake Pro-Member Invitational. In addition to being only thirty-six holes, the official purse was only $2,500, $500 less than the required $3,000. But this was only a fraction of the available pot at Spring Lake, which had the richest and perhaps most raucous Calcutta, or auction pool, then on the pro scene (a practice banned months later by the United States Golf Association). In 1945 Spring Lake's Calcutta was worth $73,500, and Nelson was certain to have pocketed part of that in addition to the $2,100 he won outright when Barron missed a sixteen-inch putt to tie on the thirty-sixth hole.

"I met Nelson once," says Bill King, now the Spring Lake head pro. "I told him where I was from and he laughed, 'I won more money there than I did at any of the other eleven.' And he did."

World War II ended two days before the Memphis Invitational began, and it soon was apparent that things were also changing in golf. Nelson dug too great a hole on Friday when he shot a 73. That put him nine shots behind amateur Bob Cochran, an insurance man from St. Louis, who passed the amateur baton to another insurance salesman, thirty-year-old Fred Haas Jr., who had stormed into the lead Saturday with a 64. Despite a third-round 66 of his own, Nelson trailed by four, and when he didn't catch a break on his near-ace early in Sunday's going, Haas had the breathing room he needed.

"I think he was a cinch to catch me," Haas says, "but he got the toughest break in the world on the sixth. If that shot goes in the hole, I think he would have won."

The Streak was ending. Haas, who was recruited to play golf for Louisiana State by no less than Huey Long himself, had become the first amateur to prevail over a field of pros since Ken Black's victory at the 1936 Vancouver Open. He has also become the answer to a rather prominent trivia question.

Nelson could feel his muscles slacken. The next day he traveled across Tennessee for that week's tournament in Knoxville. En route he and McSpaden stopped in Jackson for an exhibition against Haas and another amateur, Billy Gilbert.

"It wasn't even close," Haas says. "I think we lost 5 and 4. It was like he was saying, 'You haven't got a chance.'"

Afterward Nelson got in the car and went to Knoxville. He won by ten.

January 20, 1995

My view, and I'm certainly not alone, is that Byron Nelson's 1945 season will never be matched or eclipsed. The odds of a Major League hitter batting .400 (which hasn't happened since 1941) or a pitcher winning thirty games (last achieved in 1968) are a lot better. Not surprisingly, given the dominant hold he has had on his era, Tiger Woods has come the closest to Nelson's record, winning seven consecutive PGA Tour events between July 2006 and January 2007. Woods also has streaks of six (August 1999–February 2000) and five (September 2007–March 2008) straight victories. As for challenging eighteen wins in a calendar year, Ben Hogan, with thirteen titles in 1946, is the nearest any man has come to Lord Byron.

Inside the Ropes

CHAPTER THIRTEEN

He Went Down Swinging

Before he teed off on the tenth hole during the final round of the 1954 Masters tournament, Billy Joe Patton paused. He had made a hole-in-one and two birdies in his last four holes, and suddenly the thirty-one-year-old amateur was right back in the hunt. The Masters belonged as much to him as to Sam Snead, who already was down in Amen Corner, or Ben Hogan, who was still playing the front nine.

Much of the gallery had gathered around Patton hoping for a miracle, so much so that he now had several Pinkertons escorting him from green to tee. Roars and yelps filled the air, dim sounds compared to the explosion of noise that erupted when he aced the sixth, but loud still. Patton tried to gather himself.

This was the moment for which he had yearned most of his life. It was why he had beaten so many balls in the North Carolina winter after he got his invitation to play back in January, on the very day his youngest child was born. Patton sold lumber when he wasn't playing golf for fun, and the question was really this: Was he like the cheap stuff that ended up under upholstered chairs and sofas, or was he like the fine wood that became sideboards and dining tables for all to see?

He had just birdied the ninth for the fourth day in a row. He assumed that his mother and father, Margaret and Nollie Patton, were at the ninth green as they had been for the first three rounds. But the new First Methodist Church back in Morganton was being dedicated on this day, and after Patton slipped back Saturday with a 75 to fall five strokes behind Hogan and two back of Snead, his parents figured Billy Joe was off his game. There might be other Masters for Billy Joe. They decided to drive home. Forty years later one can only hope it was a good sermon, because their son would never have another Masters quite like this.

Patton had been lucky just to receive an invitation. He had come to Augusta as a result of being an alternate on the 1953 U.S. Walker Cup team—a qualification long since discarded by the Masters committee. But at the time, Cliff Roberts and Bob Jones liked the idea of a large amateur contingent, and Patton was one of twenty amateurs in the 1954 field. He had played some nationally but was known mostly in the Southeast. His biggest wins prior to his Masters appearance were victories in the Carolinas Amateur in 1947 and the Carolinas Open in 1950 and 1951.

Anyone who saw Patton play didn't easily forget him. He squeezed everything he could out of his unorthodox game, like juice out of a lemon. He had a strong grip, and his backswing was a blur of speed. From the top, Patton quickly and decisively cleared his left hip, and he often cut off his follow-through at chest level. His right foot would remain planted on the ground, and at the end of a swing he could look more like someone hitting a single than a tee shot.

"Billy Joe was what some people would call a slasher, or a hitter," remembers Byron Nelson, who was paired with Patton for the second round at Augusta in 1954. "He just took it back and swung through all out. There was no pause at the top. But he hit the ball rather well."

"He looked to me more like a baseball player than a golfer," recalls Harvie Ward, an amateur rival of Patton's. "But Billy Joe did everything fast back then. Talked fast. Everything. And it fed into his golf swing."

Inside the Ropes

More than anything else, though, Patton was strong. "He was built like a halfback, and he had powerful hands," says Bill Campbell, another amateur peer. Campbell remembered one transatlantic trip on the ss *America* to Great Britain for a Walker Cup Match. He brought along a twenty-six-ounce practice club to stay limber on the long voyage. "Billy Joe was the only one of us who could actually hit balls with that club," Campbell says.

Patton had been content with his unorthodox method except for a brief period after he returned from three years of navy service in World War II. He thought the time was right to learn a more classic action, one that allowed him to drive the ball straighter. "The first couple of weeks I was home, I tried to work on a more classic swing, something that was slow and had a different timing to it," Patton says. "But I got so discouraged that I decided to go ahead and play the way I wanted to play. A week after that decision, I went to the 1946 Carolinas Amateur and lost in the thirty-six-hole final. I figured my swing couldn't be all bad."

Above everything else, though, Patton could do two things: he could putt with the best of them, and he was a Houdini getting out of trouble.

"Billy Joe had a lot of guts," says another amateur rival, Jim Ferree, "and he was awfully good at scrambling. A lot of folks hit a wild drive and then get embarrassed or upset. But Billy Joe would just go find his ball, grit his teeth, and find a way to get out. It wasn't a discouraging thing, it was a challenge for him."

Ted Bishop, who lost to Patton in the 1951 U.S. Amateur, once said, "He's the worst best player I've ever seen. He's a tough golfer to beat, but he can beat himself."

As soon as Patton opened the envelope containing his invitation on January 3, 1954, he started getting ready for the Masters. His job at the Huffman Lumber Company afforded him plenty of time to play during golf season, but this was winter in the foothills of the Blue Ridge Mountains.

"It's pretty damn cold in Morganton in January," Patton says, "but I didn't want to embarrass myself. I hit balls on my lunch break, and hit a few more balls on Saturdays and Sundays. When the days got a little longer, and it got a little warmer, I'd hit a few balls after work. By the time I got ready to go, I knew I was ready." Tears interrupt Patton's memory now as he recalls what he did next.

"I went downtown and bought a white sports coat," he says. "And the reason I got it was, in the event that I was called on, I just wanted to look presentable. I was confident."

Patton got a confidence boost on Masters Wednesday, the day before the tournament began. In those postwar Masters, an instructional clinic and long-drive contest were held on the practice area to the left of the eighteenth fairway. Trick-shot specialist Paul Hahn, who had visited Morganton several weeks earlier to give an exhibition, was concluding his show when Patton arrived.

"Wasn't anything out there but red clay with a little grass on it," Patton says of the area where the contest was held. He had expected the balls to be provided by the club, so he didn't bring any. But he asked Hahn if he could borrow a couple from him.

"I asked Paul to give me three balls out of his shag bag. I picked what looked like the best one, then I hit it. I hit it pretty good, and I heard someone with a foghorn call back, 'Three, three, eight.'" Patton tossed the other two balls back to Hahn's caddie and stood on his first, and only, shot—a 338-yard poke.

"That shot won the contest," Patton says. "There wasn't an irrigation system, there wasn't much grass, but everybody was hitting on the same damn ground. Looking back, that was a big part of the week. I looked on Augusta as being a long golf course, and winning that contest made me feel like I had a little advantage off the tee. I knew I could putt as well as anyone there, and if I was a long hitter as well as a good putter, I felt I almost belonged."

Joe Cheves, the pro at Patton's home course, Mimosa Hills Country Club, drove down that Wednesday to film some footage of Hogan and also to check out Billy Joe. He remembered that Patton "looked like he was ready to play. You could see the look in his eyes."

Thursday dawned cool and cloudy. Heavy rains would hit Augusta later that day and last into the night, but Patton, out at 10:48 a.m. with fellow amateur James Jackson, had the good fortune of getting done before the worst of the weather hit. He went out in 32, came home in 38, and with a 70 tied for the first-round lead with veteran Dutch Harrison. In addition to the blustery weather, Masters officials had heard about some low scores during practice, and some of the pros complained that the holes had been tucked in tough places for the first round. The Augusta National greens also had become afflicted by Poa annua. Such things were nothing for an amateur like Patton to get worked up about, but he downplayed his chances after his hot first round.

"Just a minute, boys," Patton told sportswriters. "Hold on a minute. I may shoot an 80 tomorrow. Let's don't go too strong on this thing."

But he didn't shoot an 80. In cool and windy conditions Friday, Patton wasn't hot and cold as he had been in round one, but steady. Playing with Nelson, Patton was even par through the first sixteen holes before bogeying the seventeenth and eighteenth. But scores were high—Peter Thomson's 72 was low round of the day—and Patton's 74 gave him the lead at 144, a stroke ahead of Hogan, two better than Bob Rosburg and Lloyd Mangrum. Snead was another stroke back at 147. It was the highest score to ever lead the Masters through thirty-six holes, and not everyone was convinced Patton would hold up.

"If this guy wins the Masters, he'll set golf back fifty years," Cary Middlecoff said, referring to Patton's extraordinary action.

Back in Morganton, news of Patton's exploits had the town's six thousand residents in a frenzy. Betsy Patton tried to keep up with what was going on as well as she could by listening to radio reports and getting calls from friends who had been to Augusta and come home. She would stay at home with the children over the weekend, but plenty of Patton's fellow Tar Heels would make the drive down to watch. An amateur had never led a round outright at Augusta, much less won the whole show. Their bespectacled, short-haired Billy Joe had accomplished the former. It was too big to think about the rest of it, but they did anyhow. At $7.50 a head for the weekend rounds, the Billy Joe Show was a bargain.

"They piled in their cars and came down," says sports columnist Furman Bisher, who was covering the event for the *Atlanta Constitution*. "They were whooping and hollering—shrieking. It was like nothing the Masters had ever seen."

But the additional rooters didn't advance Patton's game Saturday. Paired with the hard-nosed veteran Lloyd Mangrum, whom he outdrove by as much as fifty yards on some holes, Patton excited his fans but struggled to score. His 75 dropped him five strokes behind Hogan, who had a 69 for 214. Snead's 70 put him at 217. Patton was at 219, three over, tied with Middlecoff and Tommy Bolt. Five strokes.

Patton was spending the week at one of the trailers the club brought on the property so the amateurs could save a buck. As he retired for the night, he wouldn't let himself get down. After all, he hadn't brought his new coat for nothing.

As he had a lunch of vegetable soup with Bisher late Sunday morning, Patton seemed raring to go. "These folks thought they saw something the first two days," he told Bisher. "I'm going to show them something else today." This was a time of big, shiny cars, and Patton was going to prove his game had fins.

Patton had a 12:30 starting time with Jimmy Demaret. Snead was off at noon with Nelson. Hogan and Jack Burke Jr. had a one o'clock time. The inclement weather had abated. Whoever was going to prevail had the best weather of the week to do so.

There was nothing auspicious in Patton's first five holes. He made a birdie at the easy, par-five second, but had a bogey at the fourth. He was even for the day, still three over par for the tournament, as he got to the tee of the 190-yard sixth. The hole was cut in a tough spot—front-left of the green, not far beyond a bunker.

　　　　　　　　　　　　　　　Inside the Ropes

There were a few thousand people around the hole. Some were there to see Patton, but most were waiting for Hogan to arrive.

Then, with one home-cooked Patton swing, all hell broke loose.

Patton selected a five-iron for the downhill shot but wasn't comfortable with where he had set his peg in the ground. He re-teed the Spalding Tournament ball, then let it fly. The ball arched toward the target, on line all the way. As it came to earth, it slammed into the hole, lodging between the right side of the cup and the flagstick, which was thicker than those used today.

Cheers erupted through the tall pines, and fans who weren't at the sixth scurried like ants at a picnic to get there. Bill Campbell was at the clubhouse, having finished his final round. "Sounded like an explosion down there," he recalls. In his cabin along the tenth fairway, Bob Jones saw framed photographs rattle on the wall. "I'm willing to bet," Jones told a visitor, "that Billy Joe Patton has done something unusual."

With all the delirium on the sixth hole, referee Joe Dey had the good sense to tell Patton to be careful when he removed the flagstick. He was, amid roars nearly as loud as when the ball had flown into the cup. Most of the fifteen thousand fans were moving toward Patton now. He was back in the hunt, and Hogan knew what the commotion was about.

Patton birdied the eighth. Another birdie at the ninth—the hole he had owned all week—pulled him even with Hogan. He parred No. 10. At the eleventh, he got up and down from just over the green. About the same time, Hogan was bogeying the short seventh. Patton was leading the Masters.

Patton bogeyed the twelfth after overshooting the green but was still in good shape as he drove at the 470-yard thirteenth. He hit a mediocre drive, slightly pushed, finishing in what passed for rough at Augusta, just off the right side of the fairway. The rye-grass overseed didn't hold the ball's weight, and it settled slightly.

"He didn't have a very good lie," recalls Harvie Ward, who had gone out with buddy Ferree to watch Patton finish his round and said he was within twenty-five feet of Patton as he decided what to do with his second shot. "The ball was sitting down a bit. To me, it was a questionable lie. He put his hand on a wood club, and glanced over at Jim and myself. We shook our heads—no. Then he touched an iron, and the crowd yelled, 'Go, Joe, Go, Joe.'"

Patton remembers none of that. He says he and his caddie, Freeman Harris, debated whether to "burn" a two-iron or hit a four-wood, because there was a "puff" of wind in his face. In those days, golfers played by feel, without yardage books, but Patton figures he was around 205 to 210 yards from the hole, which was cut in the rear-right portion of the green, protected on the front and the right side by Rae's Creek. Others insist Patton was farther from the hole than that. On Friday, Patton had been twenty to thirty yards farther from the green, ripped a two-wood, and just missed clearing the creek. But he had saved par.

Patton decided to hit a four-wood. The shot flew straight off the Bobby Jones Autograph clubhead, but it tailed near the end of its flight. The ball cleared the hazard and landed on the fringe before kicking to the right and down into the hazard, which was then a weedy mess, not the tidy graveyard it is now. Before you knew it, Patton had stripped off his shoes and socks and was down in the water surveying his options.

"The ball was just barely covered, and at first I thought I could splash water, ball and all on the green," says Patton. "But I got down in there and saw that the bank in front of the ball was so steep that I couldn't have gotten it out."

Still barefoot, Patton noticed the pairing behind waiting in the fairway. He took his drop behind the creek and pitched to the hole. He cleared the water but came up short, in the fringe. On his fifth shot, he chipped five feet past, then missed the comebacker for bogey. "Looking back, missing that putt was important," Patton says. "I don't remember missing a putt of that length all week up to then."

Stunned but aware he could still win after his double-bogey disaster, Patton walked to the fourteenth tee and uttered something to the disappointed fans who had grown silent. "Let's smile again," he said, heading to the tee. That statement would earn Patton international praise for his good-natured sportsmanship—and he did have plenty of that—but those weren't totally selfless words. Patton had fed off his fans, and he didn't want them to wilt just when he needed them most.

Within minutes Patton had them roaring again. This time it was because he nearly holed his eight-iron approach and had a tap-in birdie at the fourteenth. Hogan, unsettled by all the noise coming from Patton's problems at the thirteenth, had double-bogeyed the eleventh. As improbable as it seemed, heat from Patton was melting the Wee Ice Mon.

Patton, however, would seal his own fate at the par-five fifteenth. He rope-hooked his drive far to the left of the fairway, and his ball finished up on a patch of hard, bare ground. He was 240 yards or more from the water-fronted green, and the odds weren't with the shot he chose—a go-for-broke two-wood. He skulled the ball off the difficult lie, and it bounded along the ground for a long while before disappearing into the pond in front of the green.

"The one at 15 was the stupid shot," Patton says today. "I probably couldn't hit that green one out of fifty tries from that lie."

About the time Patton was making the bogey that would kill his hopes, Snead was at the eighteenth finishing off a 72 for 289. Patton parred the last three holes to shoot 71 and complete play at 290. Hogan, in part because he failed to convert a four-footer at the seventeenth for birdie, settled for a 75 and a tie with Snead, who would defeat him in a playoff the next day. [The 289 total, matched by Jack Burke Jr. in 1956 and Zach Johnson in 2007, remains the highest winning score in Masters history.]

Patton got to wear his white coat later on Sunday at an awards ceremony for the low amateur (he beat Dick Chapman by five). He got his trophy and medal from Bob Jones and posed with Hogan and Snead, who told him, "Billy Joe, you nearly got the whole turkey."

But the crowd howled with approval after Patton told them, "I don't feel bad about that 6 at 15, and I don't feel bad about that 7 at 13. And I don't want my rooters to feel bad about them. I made up my mind I was going to go for the pin 72 times if I had the opportunity. I told myself that I wasn't going around after the tournament thinking I could have saved a stroke if I could have played bold. So I played it bold. And the way I made those birdies is the same way I got that 6 and that 7." His words were broadcast over the radio, so the folks back home got to hear them too.

Patton stayed around to watch the playoff and attend a lumber convention that happened to be held in Augusta. He returned home midweek to the adulation of the folks in Morganton, who had reveled in his success, much as they would local son Sam Ervin's appointment to the U.S. Senate later that year. As the *News-Herald* editorialized, Patton's exploits had gotten the attention of people "who don't know a putter from a 'possum." Soon Patton was honored at a baked ham supper, and he received an oversized key to the city.

The weekend after the Masters, he was invited back to Augusta to play golf with President Dwight Eisenhower. Before long, he would be invited to join Augusta National, and he is a member today. He would play in twelve more Masters tournaments, with eighth-place finishes in 1958 and 1959 being his best efforts. (Ironically, in his last competitive round at Augusta National, the second day of the 1966 Masters, Patton went for the green on his second shot at No. 13 and came up short—and wet.) Patton was a force in amateur golf throughout the 1950s. At the U.S. Open at Baltusrol Golf Club in 1954, he led after the first round and eventually finished tied for sixth, gaining low amateur honors. He was also low amateur in the 1957 U.S. Open at Inverness Club. Patton was a member of five Walker Cup teams.

He never thought life as a tour pro would suit him but admits that had he won the Masters in 1954, the money might have been too great a temptation.

"I got to test my game against the best," Patton says. "I played six to ten events a year, full-bore, full-guts all the time. The pro golfers were playing twenty to thirty events a year. That wouldn't have suited me."

Says Campbell, "He put such tension into his game. While he might be physically strong, he would get nervously worn out. I don't think he would have liked it or responded well to it had he turned professional. Billy Joe was the ultimate amateur. He played golf because he wanted to."

Except for a six-week escape to south Florida each winter, Patton still lives in Morganton. Now seventy-one and retired from his own lucrative lumber business, slowed some by a 1984 heart attack, he still plays golf three to five times a week, by all accounts with most of the zest he took to the course four decades ago when he broke on the scene at Augusta.

"He is the same guy now that he was then, a terrific guy," says Joe Cheves. "He really loves golf deep down. He's fun to play with. He has had some physical problems that cut his length, but he can still pull off those shots."

Patton returns to the Masters each year and, like many Augusta National members, serves as a rules official. Sometimes duty takes him to the thirteenth hole, leading to incidents that have further layered his legend. When Ben Crenshaw won the Masters in 1984—thanks in part to a conservative, avoid-disaster lay-up at the thirteenth on Sunday—he claimed that having seen Patton on the hole that week convinced him to learn from history.

And the following year, as Curtis Strange seemed to be heading toward victory on Sunday, Patton was working rules at the thirteenth green and saw Strange pay a visit to Rae's Creek with his second shot. Then, after Patton's duty was up and he was walking back to the clubhouse, he paused at No. 15 long enough to see Strange find the pond with his second shot. Like Patton thirty-one years before, the disasters cost Strange a green jacket.

"He did a double, in the water both places, just like me," Patton says. "I was sorry to see him put it in the water, but that was about the end of it."

Patton does not like to dwell on the past. There isn't much evidence at his Morganton home that he ever played in a Masters, much less was the star of one. One recent inspection couldn't immediately locate the silver cup he received for being low amateur in 1954. It wasn't in Patton's den, or in a china cabinet that housed a lot of his other amateur trophies. He suspected it was up in the attic, but he didn't want to search for it. The gold medal he also received for being low amateur was stolen in a burglary at his office about ten years ago. He claims that he had the ball with which he aced the sixth hole mounted once upon a time, but he is not sure what became of it.

"All I ever wanted was the memories," Patton says. Those, he can find.

April 1, 1994

Billy Joe Patton lived a long time after I visited him when putting together this story. After a period of declining health, he passed away January 1, 2011, in his hometown of Morganton at age eighty-eight, further winnowing the great generation of American amateur golfers—men who played for pride, not pay. I have covered every Masters but one since 1985, and I can't wander down to the par-five thirteenth hole without looking at the landing area and thinking about Billy Joe, four-wood in his strong hands, going for broke all those years ago. It invariably makes me smile.

CHAPTER FOURTEEN

Homero Blancas's 55

The weeds, wild blackberries, and overgrown trees exist with a mystery spawned by an abandoned place. The shuttered buildings, cracked pavement, and rusting tanks suggest how long it has been since this location on the outskirts of Longview, in east Texas, was a working oil refinery surrounded by a nine-hole golf course where men laughed and gambled and invented shots to tame its quirks, and where one man, Homero Blancas, once had a day of golf like no other.

In addition to the course, time has claimed the scorecard and the trophy and attached an asterisk to the achievement. Blancas knows what some people contend—that the events of August 19, 1962, unfolded in a county fair of a tournament on a cupcake of a course—and it bothers him not at all.

For years Blancas's feat was listed in the *Guinness Book of Records*, but it was purged when the record keepers limited their low golf scores to those shot on courses of at least 6,561 yards in length, and at 5,002 yards, the funky, claustrophobic par-seventy Premier Golf Club—on which two slightly different sets of tees formulated eighteen holes fraught with out-of-bounds stakes and creeks—didn't qualify. But if you're the man who had the 55, the lowest competitive score any golfer has ever shot, there is nothing but beauty in the details.

How many golfers ever made "Ripley's Believe It or Not"? How many other players have made thirteen birdies and an eagle, totaled 27 for one nine and 28 for the other, hit seventeen greens in regulation, and required only twenty putts? "And the thing is," says Blancas, "I shot 62 in the morning. That might be the most amazing thing."

He was twenty-four and competing in the Premier Invitational, part of a cluster of amateur tournaments that thrived in towns such as Longview, Center, and Kilgore from the 1940s into the 1960s. The events, also known as the "East Texas Tour" or the "Barbeque Circuit," were a breeding ground for a couple of generations of Texas golfers, from Jackie Burke to Marty Fleckman. Longview was home to the eight Cupit brothers. Jacky Cupit, the youngest, who would lose the 1963 U.S. Open in a playoff, finally did something his brothers couldn't do when he won the Premier in 1959 and 1960. "It was a real short course, but there were no bailouts," says Cupit. "You had to be as straight as an arrow." Until Blancas, Cupit held the course record: 60.

The course was built in 1938 by Sylvester Dayson, a native of France who had been a World War I aviator before getting into the oil business and immigrating to the United States in the 1920s. By the mid-1930s, he had started the Premier Oil Company. "He was a fanatic about golf, but he had a skeet-shooting course first," says Dayson's daughter, Suzette Shelmire. Dayson held a skeet shoot to raise money for a local hospital, but with World War II came an ammunition shortage, so golf took its place.

Competition was keen, scores were low, and interest—spiked by Calcutta betting pools that could bulge with more than $50,000, a "monster Calcutta," according to former Texas A&M golfer Jim Fetters—was high. "The world was a different place back then," says Fred Marti, Blancas's teammate at the University of Houston and a central character in his epic day. "Those tournaments were big deals in those towns. There weren't a lot of entertainment options."

On the eve of the final day at Premier, Marti, Blancas, and a couple of others drove over the border to Bossier City, Louisiana, to sample a night that wasn't so still. Driving back Sunday near dawn, they missed a turn. "We skidded through a gas station but missed the pumps," says Blancas. "We were lucky we didn't get killed." Blancas napped briefly before trying to make up a seven-shot deficit to Marti with thirty-six holes left. "I was a little groggy," he says. "Maybe my instincts just took over."

The son of a Mexican immigrant who was a greenkeeper at Houston's exclusive River Oaks Country Club, Blancas grew up in modest quarters on the grounds and began caddieing when he was eight years old. Not big enough to tote larger bags, he looped for younger golfers with small bags and good games. Conditioned to believe everybody played well, Blancas wore out his hand-me-down clubs practicing to become like those players. "I would absorb their talent," Blancas says. "All I saw were good swings, guys shooting in the 70s. And all I wanted to do was hit golf shots. I'd play three holes or five holes at dusk. The first or second time I played eighteen holes, when I was about ten, I shot an 89."

He turned into a birdie machine, firing at flagsticks regardless of their position or his. "Homer never saw anything but the flag," says Frank Beard, who became one of Blancas's best friends on the PGA Tour. "When he was off, he never knew how to play to the safe side. But when he was on, he went low."

As far back as his high school days, Blancas always had good luck against Marti, but with eighteen holes left at Premier he still trailed him by five strokes—which was quite a working margin at Premier. "Some of the greens were so tiny you could hop across 'em," says Marti, "and you could hardly get around without penalty strokes." Roy Pace, a Longview golfer who played at Louisiana Tech and who was the defending champion, stood between them, four shots off the lead. "The greens were built up, like big anthills," says Pace. "It was tricky."

Blancas's final-round heroics were an intersection of crisp shots and good bounces. He began with a birdie at No. 1. At the par-five second, he skulled a chip, but the ball clanged off the flagstick and dropped for an eagle. After two more birdies, he missed a three-foot birdie attempt at No. 5, then came back with two straight birdies. Another birdie at No. 9 put him eight under for the day. "I really was thinking one shot at a time," Blancas says. "It was, 'Got to put it in the fairway, got to hit it close, got to make a putt, got to catch Fred.'"

The back nine was a blur of birdies and hooting from a growing gallery that found out what was going on. Blancas was an implacable force in the middle of it all. "He just looked so loose," recalls T. C. Hamilton, who witnessed the round. "No jumping around, just a lot of smiles." But by the seventeenth hole, thirteen under for the day and having overtaken Marti, Blancas got nervous. He hit a forty-five-foot birdie putt much too hard, but it banged the hole, popped six inches into the air and fell in. At No. 18, a five-hundred-yard par five, he pushed his drive, but it hit a tree and bounced safely back into play. After pitching his third shot to four feet, Blancas managed to sneak in his final birdie. "I was feeling it the last two holes," he says. "I hit that sucker as hard as I could, and it barely rolled in."

Dan Jenkins chronicled the round two weeks later in *Sports Illustrated*, bringing Blancas national attention and giving him a bigger sense of achievement. After a couple of years in the army, Blancas started a good but not great pro career: four PGA Tour victories, one Senior PGA Tour win, $1.9 million in career earnings. He was partial to his kids and a good time more than he was to Hoganesque practice sessions. "Homero didn't log a lot of time on the practice tee, but I didn't, either," says Jacky Cupit, now sixty-three. "We weren't lazy, but we just didn't have that desire."

When recalling Blancas, it is common for peers to note his all-or-nothing style and how often he was hurt. Blancas's eleventh surgery, a partial replacement of his right knee, occurred on February 26. He recently played his first round of golf since the procedure, and he is pain-free for the first time in years. If his recovery continues well, he hopes to play a couple of senior events next year. Now sixty-three, he gives lessons at Glennloch Farms Golf Club in Spring, a Houston suburb.

One of his most loyal pupils is Dr. Fred Hansen, a Houston dentist who won the gold medal in the pole vault at the 1964 Tokyo Olympics. Hansen, sixty, has made it to the finals of Senior PGA Tour qualifying three times, including last year, when he missed his card by five strokes. "I've never been with a guy so knowledgeable about golf," says Hansen. "He talks about moments that every great player has in his swing." Blancas's go-low karma has rubbed off on Hansen, who has shot a 62 himself.

Blancas and his wife, Noel, have two sons, Tommy, thirty-three, a club pro at Greatwood Golf Club near Houston, and Jerry, thirty-one, a replay producer for the Houston Astros' telecasts. When golfers encounter Tommy, his last name often rustles the recall of his customers. "They think he shot a 59," Tommy says. The son will offer a gentle correction. "He's told me some stories about the 55," says Tommy, "but he's very modest. I think he's very proud that it happened, and he knows part of it was luck."

But there is the part that wasn't luck too, and that is the way Blancas let the birdies keep flowing, undammed by limits or expectations golfers usually burden themselves with, the comfort zones sport psychologists now try to shake them out of. "Nine out of ten golfers would have put the brakes on when they got to the 60 level," says Beard. "Call it choking or feeling like a deer in the headlights, or whatever you want, but it would have happened. People talk about it being a little country course, but I don't give a darn where it was, it was remarkable, miraculous golf."

Setting foot on the property for the first time since he departed it nearly forty years ago, Blancas gazes around like someone going back to an old neighborhood where the house is long gone. Squinting through the years and the pines, he sees a green, places a fairway, envisions some of the many OB stakes. Pace, who recently left Wee Burn Country Club in Connecticut to return to his hometown to run a practice range, contributes his mental compass, sketching a configuration of the layout. They agree that the oddest hole was the three-hundred-yard seventh, a dogleg par four that dared a player to try to drive the green with a tee shot that flew or skidded atop a huge oil storage tank. Blancas played it safe in 1962, but Fetters pumped four drives OB in the third round and walked in.

Longview still loves its golf. Pace's lesson book is full. At Longview Country Club, where a couple of working wells recall the boom days when the city gushed with oil and money, a regular gang throws a few dollars in the pot and tees off every afternoon at one o'clock. One of the favorites is the course's owner, seventy-three-year-old Buster Cupit, who regularly shoots in the 60s on his 5,497-yard layout, and holds the course record, 58, which is noted in the shop on the type of bulletin board that often denotes a sermon or a daily special.

The day Blancas visited Longview, the Ladies Day prizes were about to be distributed and lunch was on the counter in the banquet room, steaming in metal trays. Blancas is invited to help himself to the barbequed chicken, corn, and rolls before the ladies begin to fill the room with chat and giggles. The food is down-home tasty, and the fare and the banter take Blancas back to the meals he shared at the bustling Cupit household when he was just a young golfer stoking up to see how good he could become. "We'd usually stay with people in homes near the courses," Blancas says. "We met a lot of nice people." As the only minority in his elementary school, Blancas was an outcast, but his golf talent helped him assimilate into the white culture. At college, where the cutthroat competition sharpened Blancas's shotmaking, teammates tried to soften any racial slants. "If I couldn't get into a movie," he says, "they wouldn't go."

Not far from the old Premier course there is a historical marker at a Longview city-limits sign. It has not been erected to honor

Blancas, but its presence in the vicinity makes him smile none-theless. And with not an asterisk in sight or mind, he happily poses for a picture. He doesn't have much to mark the occasion of his 55. He didn't think to keep the golf ball he used. The score-card and trophy were destroyed by a fire at his parents' house in the mid-1960s.

Blancas can live with those who believe his record doesn't stack up to more famous rounds shot by more famous golfers. Although sub-60 scores are more common now, many hall-of-famers haven't done it. Just last year Tom Watson was saying one of the few regrets of his career is that he never shot in the 50s. Blancas couldn't really explain how the magic happened then, and he can't now, but when he watches NBA star Vince Carter make the hoop look like an oil drum and light up an arena with an easy 50 points, he can relate as few can. "You get in a zone," Blancas says, "and to some extent I never felt like I did during the 55, ever again."

He didn't get rich and famous from his 55. Blancas won't say how much money he made that day in addition to the $125 he got for selling the set of irons given to the winner, a common prac-tice then. This is not surprising, since he did not turn pro until 1965, about the time the NCAA and USGA were cracking down on the appearance of high-profile amateurs in the big-money Calcut-tas. "But in our day," says Marti, "everybody knew what was going on. Some of the college coaches would be there. Walker Cup play-ers would be there. Everybody knew, and they didn't do anything."

It was customary then for the winner of the Calcutta pool to share 5 to 10 percent of his windfall with the golfer who made it possible. According to the handwritten notes on a mimeographed breakdown that Pace's father has had tucked away all these years, Homero Blancas was bought for $1,875 and the pot totaled $10,875. The winner's take was 31 percent of the championship-flight pot, so Blancas likely pocketed a couple of hundred bucks, and for a boy who grew up in a barn, that must have seemed like the world.

From the men who competed against him that day and saw him do the impossible, though, he earned something else—something he still has. Surveying the remains of the old course as a hot wind blows, he doesn't feel like a footnote.

August 3, 2001

Homero Blancas got some company in the "55 Club" after I wrote about his amazing feat, but neither occurred in a tournament. Steve Gilley shot a sixteen-under 55 at Lynwood Golf and Country Club in Martinsville, Virginia, in May 2004. Another professional, twenty-six-year-old Australian Rhein Gibson, shot a sixteen-under 55 in May 2012 at River Oaks Golf Club in Edmond, Oklahoma. Those were two fantastic scores, but to me, Homero's 55 on that long-gone funky course remains one of golf's neatest tales.

Inside the Ropes

CHAPTER FIFTEEN

Lost and Found

At certain times of the day, at certain spots on The Olympic Club's Lake Course in San Francisco, enormous trees—pine, cedar, fir, eucalyptus—segregate the light, turning the fairways and greens into a Rorschach test. The strong light and the deep shade make it possible to imagine many things: success and failure, risk and caution, the possible and the lost. And forever and always at The Olympic Club, it is impossible to look into the sunlight and the shadows and not see Arnold Palmer and Billy Casper, one losing a lead as big as the Mississippi and the other there to find it, in the fourth round of the 1966 U.S. Open.

It remains one of the most captivating major championships of all time. Never have two of the best players of their time—of all time—been caught up in such a stunning reversal of fortune in the glare of a major championship. The Greg Norman–Nick Faldo 1996 Masters was one for the books, but compared to the 1966 U.S. Open, it was near-drama. Norman led by six strokes as the final round began; Palmer led Casper by seven with only nine holes to play. More, Palmer and Casper weren't so much competitors as contrasts.

Palmer played golf like a man desperately trying to find daylight from the middle of a kudzu patch. Not for nothing did he title his autobiography *Go for Broke*. Right from the days when Palmer was at play at home in Latrobe, Pennsylvania, earning nickels for hitting drives over creeks for the female members, golf was strictly pass-fail. As far as the soldiers in Arnie's Army were concerned, either outcome was a good show.

Casper, on the other hand, was enamored of the detached style of Ben Hogan. He always thought—still does—that if you threw caution to the wind, Willie Mays would always be there to catch it. As a result, he played cautiously and seriously, with little regard for the fans on the other side of the rope. The most exotic he ever got was a diet he tried in the mid-1960s to lose weight and combat allergies, which included game such as elk, hippopotamus, and the bear meat he had for breakfast on the day he ate Palmer's lunch. But when he was on the course, he ordered off the menu.

Palmer and Casper arrived in San Francisco for the 1966 Open with one national championship apiece, each accomplished in inimitable fashion. When Palmer stormed from behind in the final round to win at Cherry Hills in 1960, he drove the first hole, a par four. When Casper won at Winged Foot in 1959, he laid up each day on the third hole, a par three.

Palmer turned the key and went. Casper called AAA first.

It is not Arnold Palmer's favorite subject. "He doesn't want to talk about it," warns his longtime assistant, Doc Giffin. "He's tired of talking about it. He's talked about it since 1966."

But in a parking lot at the Home Depot senior tournament in Charlotte, North Carolina, Palmer does talk about it. Looking robust again, seemingly fully recovered from his prostate cancer surgery of last year, the sixty-eight-year-old is standing by his white Cadillac. There is a pro shop's worth of irons in the trunk. Palmer, who probably has fiddled with more clubs than any man alive, is trimming the butt ends of the red graphite shafts with the serrated saw-blade on a Leatherman tool, and he is wrapping on new leather grips. He doesn't have a vise, and he doesn't need

Inside the Ropes

one. Palmer has his hands—steely mitts still, hands that he relied on to muscle his way out of almost any trouble.

The questions aren't new, and neither are the answers. What happened to Palmer at the 1966 U.S. Open is the most spectacular failure in a career full of Everest highs and Death Valley lows. Sure, he's thought about it, at the controls of his jet or with a beer in his hand, but Palmer always has been in motion, always has moved on.

"It's obvious that I made some serious mistakes on that back nine," Palmer says, looking up from his regripping. "Your adrenaline is flowing. You don't know how fast, but it is. I never thought anything like that could happen, but it did. But I don't wallow in my blood. That's done, gone."

He goes on. "There's nothing greater than winning, but don't think that a loss in the right situation can't be of some help to everyone. Golf is a humiliating game. If you don't think it is, have a good look at it. Just when you think you're beyond it, a loss can bring you back to earth, make you a real person again."

When Palmer got to the tenth tee that fateful Sunday afternoon at Olympic, he was a real person about to get in as much real trouble as one can find on a golf course. He forgot about beating Casper, the man beside him, and started thinking about Ben Hogan—or, more to the point, about Hogan's then–U.S. Open scoring record of 276 set in 1948. Palmer needed only to shoot a one-over 36 on the back nine to break it.

"Unfortunately, I thought about the record," Palmer says. "One of the things my father always taught me was to get the real job done and then worry about the extras."

Billy Casper is at play in the Pacific Ocean, sixty miles offshore from San Diego, but he is careful. He doesn't put just any sardine on his hook. The twenty fishermen around him on the eighty-five-foot *Pacific Queen* are hurrying lines into the water at the prospect of a yellowtail, which are mostly swimming by someone else's boat this day, but Casper takes his time at the bait hold, looking for a little fish that is just the right size, has the proper sheen, and makes the right moves.

An eight-inch sardine selected, Casper casts his line and with the drag off lets the bait drift away from the boat. Soon the line he is nursing in his chubby fingers goes out more quickly. "He's getting excited," Casper says. "Something's chasing him."

Casper gets one yellowtail early, but for most of the twenty-two hours he is on board, he is just one of the frustrated fishermen, killing time between stops when the skipper believes the ship's sonar might have spotted something. Casper, a portly sixty-six-year-old with eleven children and twelve grandchildren, fishes as much as he can these days. His fifty-one PGA Tour victories place him fifth on the all-time list, but his fellow fishermen on the *Pacific Queen* haven't a clue what Casper accomplished in golf. "The skipper knows, the cook knows, a deck hand knows," Casper says. "Nobody else." To the rest he is just the grandfatherly presence in Sansabelt jeans, a meticulous figure with a rod and reel.

"I just enjoy being one of the group," Casper says later, enjoying a perch on the top deck en route to another fishing stop. "Isn't it nice being up here looking down on everything? It's like being in a movie, particularly when the water is calm."

Whether Casper is talking about fishing, his family, the way he played golf, or how he beat Palmer, the tone of his voice doesn't change. "My primary purpose was making a living for my family," Casper says of his playing career. "I got myself into almost a hypnotic state when I was on the course, and I was extremely successful doing it. I disciplined myself so I wouldn't get involved emotionally with a good shot or a bad shot. I don't know whether I could have played the other way or not. But what fits one doesn't necessarily fit another."

Casper had been hooked on Hogan since the day, at age fourteen, he watched Hogan play at San Diego Country Club, negotiating the course the way an accountant does a spreadsheet, even though it was only an exhibition. From that day on, Casper began to emulate him. "I was a course manager," he says. "I'd go for a shot at the right time if I had the feeling, but if I didn't have the feeling, I wouldn't try it. I used to analyze every course, and there *were* certain places I didn't want to hit the ball. I figured I could hit away from trouble and still get up and down."

Sometimes it's a good idea to trust the man with the map.

The 1966 U.S. Open was a full deck. It had the protagonists from eleven years earlier, upset winner Jack Fleck and the icon he beat, Hogan. Fleck was back at Olympic as a qualifier. Hogan returned thanks to a special exemption, the first ever given for the U.S. Open by the United States Golf Association. Fellow player Jay Hebert had suggested the idea that spring at the Masters, and the USGA Executive Committee agreed. Hogan, who was fifty-four and last played in the U.S. Open in 1961, was pleased but surprised to be included.

"I think he got a bit of a shock out of it," remembers Australian Bruce Devlin, then a young man who traveled to Olympic with Hogan and practiced with him before the championship began. "He was a pretty humble man. You never heard Hogan tell anybody how good he was."

Devlin tried to spend as much time as he could around Hogan. Sometimes he and the late Canadian pro George Knudsen would travel to Texas and sit by Hogan's knee as he practiced. As Hogan prepared for another go at Olympic, Devlin was with him. When they got to the sixth hole one day in practice, Devlin noticed a fairway bunker guarding the left side of the hole, the only fairway sand on the course.

"Is it in play?" Devlin asked.

"No," Hogan said. "You just hit to the right of it."

Off the course, Hogan relaxed downtown at the Fairmont Hotel. "It took him two nights—Monday and Tuesday—to tell us what happened about his accident," Devlin says. "People say that he didn't talk much, but he went into the most minute details, the psychological side and the physical side of the comeback." One thing Hogan didn't talk much about, though, was the heartbreak of 1955.

Johnny Miller, a nineteen-year-old Olympic Club member and sophomore at Brigham Young University, was brash enough to believe he could win the Open, even though he had gotten the one spot available at local qualifying in Salt Lake City by chipping in on the first playoff hole. After breezing through sectional qualifying (among the other qualifiers was a Mexican American named Lee Trevino, making his first appearance at the national level), Miller tuned up at Olympic with Jack Nicklaus. One day Miller saw Hogan up close for the first time.

"Hogan was at the lunch table, and I was five feet away from him," Miller remembers. "It was the first time I ever heard him speak. He declined a young boy's autograph request. He said, 'Excuse me, I'm eating my soup.' He didn't even look up. But he said it nicely."

Preparing for his first Open, Miller was trying to think like Hogan. The rough wasn't the jungle it had been in 1955, especially after USGA chief Joseph C. Dey pulled rank on course superintendent Al Caputa and ordered it trimmed from six to four inches late Wednesday afternoon. Still, it could be punishing.

"The rough was the perfect height in 1966," Miller says. "You could hit out of it sometimes with a five-wood, but most of the time you just had to use an eight- or nine-iron. I decided I would be super conservative off the tee, more than I ever had before, so I could keep the ball out of that stuff."

Casper adhered to the same rule at Olympic as he did anywhere else: "If I didn't like a lie and I didn't think I could hit a four-wood," he says, "I'd drop down to the five-iron. Always."

Palmer, who had played in the 1955 Open as the reigning U.S. Amateur champion, settled into the home of Ed Douglas, a Pennzoil executive and one of his good friends. Palmer's main motivation was to put a major title in his pocket, something he hadn't done since the 1964 Masters. There were whispers that, at thirty-six, his prime was behind him. But he also wanted to win so Douglas, who had never witnessed one of his victories in person, could enjoy it. A month earlier Palmer had been nearly brought to his knees with lower-back pain after a hard swing in New Orleans. Palmer's back wasn't 100 percent, but, as he showed during several practice rounds with Dave Marr, he was confident.

"Arnold said, 'I think they'll break 280 here,'" said Marr, recalling the moment before his death last year. "He said, 'Tell you what, I'll bet you $10 that I break 280.' I said, 'You've got it.'"

Casper made no such prediction. His body was in good shape (thanks to the diet, he had lost fifty pounds and six inches off his waist in the previous two years) and so was his mind (a February trip to cheer U.S. troops serving in Vietnam had boosted his morale as well). He was refreshed from a couple of weeks off the tour, but he prepared the way he always did: he found out where he *didn't* want his ball to go. Casper was a gifted player, able to shape his woods one way and his irons the other, and he was a genius on the greens. He putted with a tapping stroke of his right hand, as if driving in a barn nail. Not only would Casper make many putts, but his lag efforts usually left him gimmes. "Billy Casper could really play," says Jack Nicklaus. "I can describe his game as very efficient."

Casper's efficiency carried over to how he played practice rounds. He preferred to go out alone and early. If it rained in the morning, he always had the afternoon.

It became the Palmer-Casper U.S. Open on Friday. By then first-day leader Al Mengert, a club pro from Spokane, Washington, had fallen back. Rives McBee bolted into contention with a 64. But Palmer, with a 66, and Casper, with a 68, shared the thirty-six-hole lead at 137. McBee and Phil Rodgers were at 140. Nicklaus and Miller were at 142. Nicklaus was in the news more for his reaction to being tailed by USGA officials for slow play. "It's not easy being followed by a police force," said Nicklaus, who bogeyed Nos. 7 through 10 after being warned.

Slow play had been the subject of a *Golf Digest* cover story the previous year, and, for the first time, pokey tour pros were being indicted as bad role models for recreational golfers. Before the 1966 Open, the USGA adopted another measure designed to speed up play: continuous putting, which meant that a golfer could mark and clean his ball only once per green and had to putt out once he started, except in cases where he would be standing in another player's line.

Palmer outplayed Casper on Saturday, shooting an even-par 70 to the latter's 73, and took a three-shot lead into the final round. But even with the end to his major drought in sight, Palmer was cautious. "I've lost some in this position," he said, and he was right. He had thrown away the 1961 Masters by making a double bogey from the middle of the seventy-second fairway after accepting premature congratulations from a friend. In both 1962 and 1963 he had lost U.S. Open playoffs, first to Nicklaus, then to Julius Boros.

In fact when asked after fifty-four holes at Olympic about the prospects, however slim, of another Open playoff, Palmer said, "I'd just as soon not be in one."

For most of Sunday it appeared certain that Palmer, Arnie's Army, Ed Douglas, and everybody else who was rooting for the most popular figure in golf would get what they wanted. Miller, who would finish eighth, and Hogan, who would be twelfth, were great stories, but mere window dressing for another coronation. Casper would have another high finish, earn another good check, 10 percent of which would go to the Mormon Church that he had joined earlier that year.

Palmer played the front nine in 32, Casper in 36, and now Palmer led by seven. Hogan's record was in his sights now that Casper was just two shots clear of Nicklaus, and he needed some of Palmer's magic to rub off if he was going to get to the clubhouse as runner-up.

There was little conversation that day between Palmer and Casper, but an exchange for the ages took place as they walked to the tenth tee.

"Arnie," said Casper, "looks like I'm going to have to work some to finish second."

"Don't worry, Bill," Palmer replied. "If you need some help, I'll help you."

"I should have never thought about the record," Palmer says now, "and I should have never listened to Bill."

Whenever leads begin to disappear, the shrinking starts innocently enough—$10 checks written by someone with a million-dollar balance. So it was when Palmer bogeyed the tenth. The lead was still six. Palmer and Casper parred No. 11. At 12, they matched birdies. A par might have been better for Palmer, who viewed the birdie as enhancing his opportunity to better Hogan's record.

Palmer bogeyed the par-three thirteenth but still led by five. "It's Palmer against the record right now," Jim McKay said as he described the action on the fourteenth hole, the first shown on the ABC broadcast. Palmer lipped out a thirty-footer for birdie. The lead was still five.

Then all turnaround broke loose. Casper hit first on the par-three fifteenth, drawing a sensible, useful shot into the center of the green, twenty feet long and left of the hole, well clear of the deep bunker that guarded the front of the putting surface. The same shot would have served Palmer just fine, but he shot for pins the way monkeys climb trees. He couldn't help himself, then or ever.

"I was trying to play the perfect shot—going for the record, not just the title," Palmer wrote in *Go for Broke*. His ball landed short and in the sand. "That was a big mistake," he says. "That was the place you didn't want to hit it."

Palmer bogeyed. Casper birdied. The lead was three, and the Army's mood changed from exuberant confidence to something else. The "animal-like cheers" that McKay described on the air minutes earlier gave way to panic.

Casper was there now, as steadfast as granite but still believing it was Palmer's championship. "I had played with Arnold many times in Ryder Cup matches, and he never showed any signs of the pressure," Casper says. "Until the last few holes, I didn't think I had a chance. When someone has a three-shot lead with three holes to go, he usually wins. Until that point, though, he never thought he could lose the Open. He was thinking about the scoring record. Then the fat kid crept up on him."

Casper played safely down the right side of the fairway on the par-five sixteenth. As on the previous hole, a conservative shot—say, a one-iron down the fairway—would have been the prudent play for Palmer. "I just couldn't pull it out of the bag," Palmer says. "It was an obvious mistake. I thought I could get away with it anyway, but I didn't."

Palmer hit his driver. The ball hooked viciously into a tree only 150 yards off the tee and settled in a nasty lie. The cagey Casper or even the young Miller would have taken an eight-iron. Palmer chose a three-iron. "I should have pitched it out," he says now. After two hacks, he was still 280 yards from the green. But he lashed his fourth shot into a greenside bunker, one hundred feet from the hole, and got up and down for what would have been, in other circumstances, a spectacular bogey. But when Casper, after playing a five-iron third shot, rolled in a fifteen-footer for a textbook birdie, Palmer's once-vast lead had been whittled to a solitary stroke.

Palmer hit another poor drive at the demanding par-four seventeenth, then scrambled his way to the green, where he faced an eight-footer for par. Palmer rarely was timid on the greens, but now, putting in the shadows, his ball stopped an inch short. Casper, scrambling too, holed a four-footer for par. The lead was gone, and the gallery began to move wildly, like extras in a Godzilla movie. "We could hear the sounds, the sounds of disbelief," recalls Chris Schenkel, who was anchoring the ABC telecast from the eighteenth-hole tower.

Inside the Ropes

Eight holes, seven strokes gone like a duck hook. Caution had caught Risk.

On the eighteenth tee, Casper had one of his intuitions. Instead of the iron he had played in three previous rounds, he chose his driver and struck a confident shot down the heart of the narrow fairway. Palmer, thinking now not about Hogan's Open record but his loss to Fleck, finally pulled out his one-iron. But it was a quick and ugly swing, like the others that had found trouble.

Palmer was left with only 120 yards to the green, but his lie was so tangled in the left rough that at first he thought his black-smith's strength could move the ball only halfway there. He fooled himself by gouging a nine-iron all the way to the green. "It was a hell of a shot," Palmer says.

But he still faced a treacherous downhill twenty-five-footer, and again he came up short—four feet short. Because of the continuous putting rule, Palmer had to putt again before Casper attempted his eighteen-footer. "That [par] putt—sidehill, sliding right—was one of the hardest putts I ever had," Palmer says. But he made it. Casper, the last man to try something foolish, coolly two-putted. Palmer had broken 280, as he predicted he would, but so had Casper. With Casper closing in three-under-par 32 and Palmer in 39, they were tied at 278. Dave Marr never paid Palmer that $10. "I never had the heart to go up to him," Marr said.

If ever a playoff was anticlimactic, it was the Casper-Palmer showdown the next day. Palmer led by two strokes through nine holes, but Casper holed a long putt at the eleventh and another at the thirteenth for birdies. Palmer bogeyed the eleventh, four-teenth, and fifteenth and made a double bogey on the sixteenth. The playoff scores were eerily similar to the fourth round: Casper, 35-34-69; Palmer, 33-40-73.

When it was over, the two rivals walked off the green together. Casper said, "I'm sorry, Arnold," and put an arm around his shoulder. "I felt a great feeling for him and what he had gone through," Casper says today. "I could really relate to Faldo hugging Norman at the Masters [in 1996]. Beating someone by a shot is not the same as being there when they kick it away."

Palmer doesn't reminisce much about days that didn't go his way, but friends say when the talk does turn to such disappointments, it is the 1961 Masters, not the 1966 U.S. Open, that comes up. Perhaps the suddenness of that blowup lingers most vividly, so that he can still feel the hand he shook before it was time. Perhaps Palmer, who basked in the love of a legion of fans that Casper's plain manner never brought him, knows that if Casper hadn't been ready to seize on his errors, he still would have won.

"Had I gone conservative that day, I would have probably gotten away with it," Palmer says. "But hell, I made a birdie on the twelfth hole, and I still lost seven shots. That's pretty dramatic."

Blowing that lead didn't keep Palmer from hitching his pants or shooting at pins. "I probably got worse after that," he says of his bold approach. "It's still a game."

Palmer and Casper met in another playoff of note, the 1981 U.S. Senior Open at Oakland Hills, and that day the scenario was reversed: Casper hit a shot in the water on the sixteenth hole, and Palmer prevailed. But after Olympic, Palmer never won another major, though he was close several times. "It might have had a little effect mentally," says Nicklaus of Palmer's Olympic experience, "but I don't think it was any big deal. Arnold came back and played a lot of good tournaments. He just didn't happen to win another major."

"People who are close to him and close to me say he was never the same after that," says Casper, "that he never totally recovered."

Casper, on the other hand, did win another major, the 1970 Masters, and enjoyed nearly another decade of fine golf before his game deserted him in the late 1970s. He won at least one tournament a year from 1956 through 1971, an accomplishment bettered only by Nicklaus and Palmer. Casper doesn't mind being linked for eternity with Palmer's grand collapse, for two reasons. It is an inescapable position. Plus, he won.

"It's like Walter Hagen said," Casper says. "You're lucky if you win one Open. But if you win more than one, it's not luck."

The day he picked Palmer's pocket, Casper was good and lucky, but most of all aware that at Olympic, what is light will soon be shadow.

June 12, 1998

The Olympic Club was the scene of more back-nine-on-Sunday drama when it hosted the 2012 U.S. Open. As it had been for Arnold Palmer in 1966, the par-five sixteenth hole was pivotal and costly. Former U.S. Open champions Ernie Els and Jim Furyk were each tripped up on No. 16, Els when he needed two shots to get back to the putting surface after missing the green long and left, and Furyk when, like Palmer forty-six years earlier, he yanked his tee shot left into trouble. The championship went to a golfer doing a nice impression of steady Billy Casper, Webb Simpson, who parred the last eight holes on the difficult course to win his first major.

CHAPTER SIXTEEN

A Champion's Last Hurrah

As was his custom, Ben Hogan arrived early for the 1967 Masters, more than a week before he would suffuse the emerald stage with uncommon drama. It had been years since Hogan was a favorite—Jack Nicklaus would be shooting for his third straight green jacket—but he was still Hogan, not quite a man in full but full of intrigue. He came with his flat linen caps and his cigarettes, his shoes with their extra spike, a suitcase full of gray, and a golf bag clanking with the extra-stiff-shafted clubs he still commanded like a drill sergeant barking to a hapless private.

"It's hard to remember specifics of playing with Hogan because he always hit it perfectly," says Deane Beman, who was paired with him in the first round at Augusta National Golf Club that week. "He hit almost every fairway, put it right where he wanted to. He played to the middle of the greens and always left himself uphill putts. He seldom hit a shot that short-sided himself. There wasn't anything remarkable about the way he played, except he played remarkably."

Hogan was a bit thicker through the middle than the Hawk of peak flight, the gritty bantam who ruled the sport in the late 1940s and early 1950s, his slightly relaxed waistline befitting a fifty-four-year-old man who spent as much time behind a desk as on a golf course. Having subsisted on oranges when he was a poor young golfer hooking his way to nowhere, the graying icon liked to lunch on fruit plates to try to drop a few pounds in preparation for Augusta's sharp hills, slopes that could wear out a younger man, much less someone north of fifty with suspect wheels.

He tuned up for the Masters, as he had forever, at Seminole Golf Club in North Palm Beach, but this spring training wasn't as vigorous owing to a bothersome left shoulder, one of the residuals from the horrific 1949 car crash that nearly killed him. "An indication of the Hogan sharpness for the 1967 Masters is given by his suntan," reporter Jim Martin observed in a pre- tournament story for the *Augusta Chronicle*. "It isn't as deep as last year."

In fact Hogan's shoulder, plagued with bursitis, scar tissue, and calcium deposits, had nearly kept him away from the major championship he had won in 1951 and 1953. "I developed some trouble last year, and it [hurt] all year," Hogan told reporters in Augusta. "So I decided it needed some work. But I got two shots of cortisone two consecutive mornings and have had 15 shots since then that helped it."

The injections—more of them than a doctor likely would allow today—lessened the inflammation and quieted the pain. Hogan knew another surgery would be necessary, but the scalpel could wait. He had competed in every Masters but two (1949 because of the crash and 1963 after a shoulder operation) since his first appearance in 1938. Bobby Jones wanted him in Augusta, and Hogan wanted to be there. The Masters was golf, and Hogan was a golfer.

Hogan was the antithesis of tournament tough when he got to Georgia, his last competition being the 1966 U.S. Open at Olympic Club, where, playing on a special exemption from the United States Golf Association, he finished twelfth. But inactivity didn't equal rust for Hogan. "He hits the irons so good, he's cheating," one of his protégés, Gardner Dickinson, told the *Chronicle* after a

Sunday practice round. "He hits it three feet from the hole at No. 6, and the pin was right on top of Old Smokey [the right knoll]."

The distinctive sound of Hogan's crisp shotmaking had become part of golf lore, but Bruce Devlin judged him with another of his senses. "He had the best control of the elevation of the ball of anybody that I ever played with," says Devlin, who as a young pro in the 1960s traveled with fellow pro George Knudson to Fort Worth to watch Hogan hit balls and was Hogan's frequent practice-round partner in his last tour appearances. Standing behind the legend as he hit drivers, Devlin would hold up his fingers, like a Hollywood director envisioning a scene, and see ball after ball soar through the same frame. "He had fantastic control. They all looked the same when they went off the club—no real low ones, no real high ones."

A cadre of pros usually took advantage of a rare Hogan sighting on tour to watch him practice—the range was far from "Misery Hill," as World War II–era pros called it—but average golfers craved a look too. On Tuesday morning at Augusta in 1967, Clem Darracott, a forty-one-year-old freight-line salesman from Atlanta who had attended the Masters for several years, approached Hogan as he exited the clubhouse heading for the practice tee and asked if he could film his swing with an eight-millimeter home-movie camera.

As detailed by Curt Sampson in *Hogan*, the Hawk wasn't a fan of movie cameras in his prime, likening their buzzing sounds to those of rattlesnakes that frightened him so as a boy. Hogan rebuffed CBS's attempt to capture extensive images of his swing at Augusta one year but had allowed LPGA legend Mickey Wright to shoot eight-millimeter movies of him in 1965.

"I had watched Hogan so much [at the Masters] that I had the feeling he was aware I had been a fan of his," recalls Darracott. "They had publicized it in the Atlanta papers that it would be the last time he would play [the Masters]. I think that was one of the reasons he allowed me to film. He thought, 'This guy's a

Inside the Ropes

fan. He's got a home-movie camera. I'll probably never see him again. Why not?'"

Hogan invited Darracott onto the range. From the side and down the line, he filmed Hogan as he worked through his bag while his jumpsuited caddie shagged the balls in the distance. Hogan's setup is without tension; on many swings his shoulders rotate beneath a lit cigarette. The action is dynamic and fluid, differing from his younger swing only in how he moved through impact—with a bit less stress on a more relaxed left side. "In those days it was a battle with those knees of his," says Devlin, "particularly the left knee. He just couldn't drive up onto his left side the way he used to, yet he found a way to make it work."

Later Hogan welcomed Darracott to follow his practice round: Hogan and Devlin played against Jay Hebert and Jackie Burke Jr. "I understood it to be $100 a hole," Darracott remembers, "and Hogan was taking their money right and left. He hit so many shots up close to the hole you couldn't believe it."

Darracott got a sense of Hogan's precise expectations on the seventeenth hole, where he watched the group's approach shots land on the green. "He walked over and asked me where his ball hit," Darracott says. "[I told him], and he grunted and said, 'It should have hit three feet back here.'"

New bunkers in the landing areas at Nos. 2 and 18 were a hot topic before the tournament. Some players were grousing about them, but not Hogan, who dismissed the added hazards with characteristic bluntness. "I don't care where they put the bunkers," he said. "You shouldn't be in the bunkers or the woods." Similarly he refused to join the chorus of complainers about the fairways, whose rye overseed was causing some jumpy lies. Said Hogan, "I see nothing wrong with the course at all."

But the no-fuss, no-excuses, no-doubt-it-was-going-to-be-a-good-swing legend turned mortal once he walked on a green. "My putting impediment" was Hogan's description. It didn't happen on every putt, but when it did, it was ugly—as if a fine, purring engine suddenly coughed and refused to turn over. Especially in contrast to his still-graceful long game, Hogan's putting often was a jerky, messy, labored ordeal that didn't seem like it could belong to golf royalty. "Once I put the putter back of the ball," he explained, "sometimes I can move and sometimes I can't."

Once one of the game's surest putters, Hogan never knew when the paralyzing tentativeness would crop up. Dan Yates, an eighty-eight-year-old Augusta National member who has been to every Masters tournament, remembers one moment of an older Hogan. "I never will forget watching him on No. 11, standing over about a three-foot putt," Yates says. "I timed it—it was a couple of minutes before he could draw the putter back."

During the 1966 U.S. Open Hogan locked up over a putt so severely he walked away toward fellow competitor Ken Venturi. "He was looking at me without seeing me. He said, 'I can't draw it back,'" Venturi recalls. "I said, 'Who gives a damn? You've beaten people long enough.' And his eyes opened and he damn near made [the putt]."

As he teed off in his twenty-fifth Masters, Hogan knew he could connect with the dime-size sweet spot in his Hogan irons until Augusta's azaleas lost their blossoms and bloomed anew, and he would still be battling his putter. Nothing in his first two rounds certainly changed his mind. He opened with 74-73, workmanlike scores by a hardworking man, good for a tie for twenty-third, seven strokes behind leader Bert Yancey.

Hogan fared much better than Nicklaus, who blew to a second-round 79 to miss the cut by one shot (one of only two times he didn't play the final thirty-six holes at the Masters from 1960 to 1993). Nicklaus stuck around for the weekend to award the green jacket to the winner, and after sleeping in Saturday, he went to the course and watched some golf on a cart with club cofounder Clifford Roberts. The gallery acknowledged Nicklaus's presence on the second nine with applause, but it would make more noise for someone else.

The third round was played on a good Coppertone day, the temperature reaching 77 degrees. The larger world was busting open over war and race in the 1960s, but golf spectators generally minded their manners, didn't hoot and holler. "In those days," says Venturi, "there was no yelling and screaming, there was just applause." Fans simply put their hands together, louder for some players than others, rising to their feet if the moment called for it, and the afternoon of April 8, 1967, was one of those times.

Hogan, "the little champion of another era," as the Associated Press called him, teed off at 12:24 p.m. with thirty-two-year-old Harold Henning, one of the golfing Henning brothers from South Africa. The first nine was as low key as the first thirty-six holes, Hogan turning in even-par 36 after escaping with a 5 on the par-five eighth, where missed eighteen-inch putts had led to double bogeys Thursday and Friday.

Taking the bit of better karma with him toward Amen Corner, Hogan began to peel away the years. A strong drive at the tenth set up a seven-iron to seven feet. Birdie. Another good tee shot on No. 11 left him with a six-iron that he drew to a foot. Birdie. He chose the six-iron again on the par-three twelfth, hitting it to twelve feet. Birdie.

"I putted better than I have in a long time," he said later that day. "I'm still embarrassed to get before people in a tournament and pretty embarrassed on a putting green alone. The only way I can beat the thing is to play in a tournament. But I conquered it out there today."

Often Hogan liked to pitch-and-putt his way to success on Augusta's par fives, but on the thirteenth a four-wood approach left him within fifteen feet, where he two-putted for his fourth straight birdie. "What happens with someone like that, your body goes back in time," says Venturi. "He was no longer that [fifty-four-year-old] person. He was back in the early 1950s playing golf. He was in a zone."

Frank Chirkinian was directing a CBS broadcast that was being done with substitutes calling the action because the talent and the technicians were on strike. "I had all the management guys on towers as announcers," says Chirkinian. "One of our guys identified Tommy Aaron as 'Tommy Walker, a member of the Aaron Cup team.'"

Hogan was subjected to no misidentifications. A par at the fourteenth was followed by another two-putt birdie at No. 15 after another pure four-wood second shot. As he strung the shots together, orderly as the laundry of a neatnik housewife, Hogan remained his implacable self on the outside. "I remember Dad saying [Hogan] never acknowledged anything that he said to him," says Hanley Henning, whose father died in 2004. "Every time he hit a good shot and Dad acknowledged it with 'Nice shot,' he never uttered a word. Not a thank you."

In Hogan's immediate wake, in the 12:32 pairing, were Doug Sanders and Chi Chi Rodriguez, Technicolor counterparts to the taciturn Hawk, with a trailing view they still remember. "If you weren't playing with Ben Hogan, it was a privilege to play in front of or behind him because you could watch the whole thing," says Rodriguez. "Hogan was such an icon," says Sanders. "Just to be in his presence and breathe the same air was very unusual because you didn't see him that much."

There were standing ovations at every green, and necks craned to see Hogan's name on the leader boards. "Naturally the atmosphere was charged," says Dan Jenkins, a longtime Hogan chronicler who was covering the Masters for *Sports Illustrated*. "Chirkinian claims he was crying in the truck when Ben came up the eighteenth fairway. I believe it. A lot of us teared up. But we didn't let [crusty Pittsburgh writer Bob] Drum see us."

Chirkinian's cameras caught Hogan on No. 18, wearily making his way to the elevated green. "He was really struggling to get up the hill," says Chirkinian. "They were slow and deliberate steps, and it wasn't because he was looking for applause, I'll tell you that." Hogan vowed after three-putting No. 18 to lose the 1946 Masters to Herman Keiser that he never would leave his approach above the hole, but he had, twenty-five feet away. Still he sank the putt to come home in 30 for a 66 and trail 54-hole leaders Yancey, Julius Boros, and Bobby Nichols by two shots.

"Usually, when a long tournament day is over, the galleries plod for the exits tired in eye and limb, but there were no weary steps that evening," Herbert Warren Wind wrote in the *New Yorker* a couple of weeks later. "Hogan sent us home as exhilarated as schoolboys."

The protagonist wasn't feeling too bad himself. "I saw him upstairs after the round," says Venturi. "He wasn't one to jump around, but you could see the twinkle in his eyes and the satisfaction he had. He said, 'That's not something I dreamed I could do.'"

Addressing reporters, Hogan sounded like the realist he had always been. "As for chances of winning," he said, "a lot of fellows are going to have to fall dead for me to win. But I'll tell you one thing: I'll be playing as hard as I ever have in my life." His wife, Valerie, told the *New York Times* on Sunday she would "consider it a miracle if Ben won."

Says Jenkins, "I knew 66 would be his last hurrah. I remember Drum and I putting his over-under number on the final round at 75."

Hogan began his final round with a par, but the euphoria of the previous day evaporated quickly with bogeys on the second, third, and fourth holes. He was wary of all the tight hole locations and three-putted four times en route to a 77 that dropped him into a tie for tenth place, ten strokes behind Gay Brewer Jr., who closed with a 67 to edge Nichols by a stroke.

The gallery masked its disappointment, standing and clapping at every green, appreciation for the body of work and the man. "What a phenomenal day it was," says Joe Black, who was on the rules committee. "In the last round Ben got a standing ovation on every hole. It was almost chilling."

Hogan visited the pressroom Quonset hut for the second straight day for an interview. "You fellows must be gluttons for punishment," he told the reporters, "asking me to come down here and describe my round. Jeepers, creepers, it was awful."

He would not return to the Masters, not even to attend the Champions dinner he helped start in 1952. He continued to make rare tournament appearances until 1971, when his bad knee forced him to make an ignominious withdrawal from an event in Houston.

Everyone had a Hogan story, but he owned the memories.

"You talk about something running up and down your spine," Hogan told Furman Bisher in *The Masters* in 1976, recalling that special Saturday in 1967. "I'd felt those things before. I'd had standing ovations before. But not nine holes in a row. It's hard to control your emotions. I think I played the best golf of my life on those last nine holes. I don't think I came close to missing a shot."

In 1995 Clem Darracott's movie of Hogan was marketed as a video, twenty-three minutes of a maestro tuning up for his last virtuoso performance. After receiving a copy, Valerie Hogan invited Darracott to Fort Worth. She told him "it was the first time Mr. Hogan had seen himself swing."

Until his death at sixty-nine, Harold Henning liked to look at a framed newspaper clipping that had a prominent spot in the den of his Miami Beach home. It hangs there still, the front page of the April 9, 1967, *Augusta Chronicle-Herald*. The focus of the page is a four-column photo of Henning standing over the man who wouldn't talk to him, helping him check his scorecard, signing off on a day that really wasn't about numbers at all.

March 30, 2007

Ben Hogan's third-round 66 in the 1967 Masters remains one of the great days for an old warrior at Augusta National. Equipment and conditioning keep more veteran stars in the fray longer these days than in Hogan's, no icon having a finer spotlight encore than

Inside the Ropes

the tenacious Tom Watson who, at fifty-nine years old, had the lead going to the seventy-second hole of the 2009 British Open at Turnberry before making a bogey and then losing a playoff to Stewart Cink. As Hogan and Watson and other aging stars have shown, it's very special when someone digs deep one more time, rediscovering and displaying the skills that made them legendary.

CHAPTER SEVENTEEN

Surround Sound

When I was growing up in small-town North Carolina in the 1960s and 1970s, life was a routine punctuated every now and then by a bolt of the unexpected. Supper time featured a rotation as predictable as that of my beloved Baltimore Orioles. It was fish one night, spaghetti the next, roast after that, followed by chicken, shaken up with flour in a grocery bag then pan-fried by my father. Occasionally, though, just when I could envision one of the familiar tastes on the table, a surprise: chow mein.

Against the background of the roar of stock car racing and the chirp of golf, the same pattern was repeated. Many a Sunday afternoon, my father and I would go outside to our Ford wagon, turn on the Philco radio, and tune in to the broadcast from Rockingham or Darlington or whatever spot below the Mason-Dixon line they were going round and round that week. From their various positions around the track, the radio voices, over the roar of the cars, would report the race. Lap after lap, despite their best efforts, sameness. Then drama: screeching brakes and a crash, or a lead change off a dramatic pass. Race over, Dad and I would grab the five-iron and putter we shared and turn our attention to the sunken can in the backyard. Just when we thought we were hopeless, a thirty-footer would tinkle the aluminum, surprising us and keeping us at it until the mosquitoes came out.

A kid has difficulty identifying the bait that hooks him on the game; he just wants to come back for more. For the virtuoso and the hack, it's the same two-piece ball: wait, then surprise. But Jack Nicklaus, from puberty to middle age, worked off a different equation. His was one of predictable dominance, the reality advanced by the saying that sounded like Yogi Berra gone to logic class: *He knows he's going to win. We know he's going to win. And he knows we know he's going to win.*

Yet by the time Nicklaus came to Georgia for the 1986 Masters Tournament, the equation had changed. He had amassed a record that would stand up forever, but he was now forty-six years old and had last enjoyed a victory on the PGA Tour at his own Memorial Tournament in 1984. Playing in seven PGA Tour events prior to the 1986 Masters, Nicklaus missed three cuts and stood a woeful 160th on the money list. He wouldn't be a favorite among the azaleas this time. Right there in the Atlanta newspaper, Sunday before the Masters, it said as much. The game now belonged to the next generation: Seve Ballesteros, Greg Norman, Tom Watson, Curtis Strange. Forty-six? The Masters Tournament is a young man's playground.

All this, however, only put Nicklaus in position to become one of sport's sweetest things: a familiar surprise. A champion, long loved and dominant, diminishes just enough that he can slip through the back door and rouse everyone when he does, the memory of past accomplishment melding with the miracle of current.

Nicklaus's victory would be especially sweet to me. I was only twenty-six and had been too young to appreciate what he did at his peak. It was like Willie Mays: I'd seen him play, but only after age had made him just another baseball player trying to bounce a single through the infield.

Like others of my generation, I thought I had been born too late to be able to actually be present when Nicklaus entered the record book again—if he did. When he came oh-so-close in the 1982 U.S. Open at Pebble Beach before Watson drew into a straight flush to beat him, I peeked at the action inside a Sears store in Athens, Georgia, not far from the youth soccer tournament I was supposed to be covering. Growing up, I had settled for the accounts in the newspaper tossed into our yard each morning, the *Greensboro Daily News,* a small daily with some of the longest datelines in the business. Whether the contest was being played indoors or out, I knew exactly where sports editor Smith Barrier was. REYNOLDS COLISEUM, RALEIGH. KENAN STADIUM, CHAPEL HILL. PINEHURST COUNTRY CLUB, PINEHURST. AUGUSTA NATIONAL GOLF CLUB, AUGUSTA GA.

By 1986 Nicklaus had captured seventeen professional majors plus two U.S. Amateur titles. He needed one more for a nice, even total that surely would never be matched as long as golfers waggle. But he was searching. After tying for sixth place in the 1985 Masters, he missed the cut in both the U.S. and British Opens for the first time in his career. Much of his time was spent with a burgeoning golf-course design business, at which he seemed intent on becoming as dominant and successful as he was with a club in his hands. In a sense, Nicklaus seemed to want to establish himself as a premier architect because those works would stand time with more durability than his name etched on so many trophies. Yet unless the game or its practitioners mutated into some other form, it was hard to believe his résumé in the majors could be assailed.

Nicklaus's most enjoyable experience on the golf course in 1985, for that matter, had been the final round of the North and South Amateur Championship in Pinehurst, North Carolina, the day his oldest son, Jack II, won the title as his father had done in 1959. That summer, Nicklaus, always tempted by food, especially ice cream, went on a diet and lost a considerable amount of weight. He looked nearly gaunt.

By the following April, though, Nicklaus had regained enough weight that a minor-league paunch threatened his beltless slacks. With his ever-present blond shock, thinning now, Nicklaus again

Inside the Ropes

had the presence of a younger man. Early in the week, for the first time since he wore a crew cut, Nicklaus wasn't asked to the old Quonset hut for a pre-tournament Masters press interview. But perhaps Nicklaus's mother, Helen, knew something: She was coming to the Masters for the first time in many years.

A decade can be an awkward measurement; sometimes styles change and wrinkles set, and sometimes they don't. Two decades or a generation is a more predictable yardstick. But 1986 was ten years ago. Don't believe it? Let's go to the videotape. There's Gary McCord without a quip, Ben Wright without a care, Greg Norman without a hat. Many of the golfers are dressed to kill: hard collars that would cut, slick slacks, few belts. We dress better now. On the tee: real woods. In the fairway: mostly forged irons still, looking like scale models compared to what's favored today. All clubs still shafted with steel, glinting in the Georgia sun. And this: "You the man" is nowhere to be shouted, its creators still blessedly off somewhere learning the words.

I was there, photographing my second Masters. You can't do justice to Augusta National's elevation changes with still or video cameras, but the flowers, white sand bunkers, tightly cut green expanses, mottled shade cast by the huge pines, and the inevitable tension wrung from the same stage each spring make photographs taken at the Masters stand out from those made elsewhere.

As I would come to better understand later, after attending several of each, the U.S. Open is marked by images of golfers surviving—escaping from tall grass and scrambling to save par. The British Open is beating the elements against a neutral hue. And memorable photographs from the Masters, more often than not, picture golfers in a triumphant pose after having figured out the heart, soul, and defense of Augusta National, its lubricious greens. Nicklaus certainly had done that, five times already as he began play in 1986, only now he showed up using a putter with an oversize head, novel for the day, which looked like it might be used to weed tomatoes, brand cattle, or both.

Nicklaus, on rounds of 74-71-69-214, was lurking as the final round began. He trailed Norman, the third-round leader, by four strokes. Given Nicklaus's theory that it's not the number of strokes behind but the number of golfers in front of him that figure into his chances on the final day of a major tournament, the fact that, including Norman, only eight players stood between him and the lead was good news. But the bad news was that the small group included golfers with exceptional pedigrees, all with younger legs. Nick Price, who had blistered the course with a record 63 on Saturday, was there, along with former champions Ballesteros, Watson, and Bernhard Langer, plus Tom Kite, still waiting to win a major. When I photographed Nicklaus and his fellow competitor Sandy Lyle as they hit their tee shots on the second hole—a good, early spot to shoot the contenders—on Sunday afternoon, I didn't expect to see him very much the rest of the day.

On the cbs telecast it was nearly half an hour before Nicklaus was shown—on tape-delay—making a birdie at the ninth hole. Nicklaus discussed the fifteen-foot downhill putt with his son, Jack, who was caddieing for him. Two loud roars, the sound of eagles, came from the direction of the green at the par-five eighth hole. Nicklaus knew that they meant threes on the hole for both Ballesteros and Kite, two groups behind him. Then, in an unusual move even for a golfer such as Nicklaus, who doesn't grind his way around a course but goes in and out of intense spurts of concentration, he said something to his gallery. "Okay, let's see if we can get a little yell of our own going here." A faux cheer was followed by the real thing, more robust now, when Nicklaus made the putt.

I was by then en route to the photographers' tower behind the tenth green. Nicklaus faced a twenty-footer up the hill out of the familiar dappled sunlight that is the trademark of pictures taken of that green. Sensing the putt was going to fall, Nicklaus raised his putter in the air, sword-like, then ran away from the hole when the ball disappeared—a milder version of his reaction on the sixteenth green on Sunday in 1975, when his monster putt there had been the key to his fifth Masters victory. He rolled home another twenty-footer for birdie at the eleventh to pull within three strokes of the lead.

We didn't know it at the time, but those efforts might not have counted for much had Nicklaus not gotten a lucky break back on the eighth hole. Having pushed his tee shot to the right behind some trees, he attempted to fade a three-wood shot around a tree. Instead of the cut he desired, he pushed the ball. But instead of ricocheting off a pine—to who knows where, and making him just another golfer playing the final round—the ball scooted through a small gap.

Nicklaus has never claimed to have been anything but fortunate. He was stricken with polio as a child, but it was a mild case. There was no lasting grip to keep him from becoming strong and sturdy. He still had fullback-strong thighs that stretched the surface of his plaid slacks, and as he put together his spurt that afternoon, his stride grew even quicker, more resolute, as that of a child walking to view the ocean for the first time.

"You're probably not as fresh as you used to be," Nicklaus says, "not as good as you used to be. But your memory and your past skills of what you used to do make up for a lot of that." He always got nervous, yes, but the swirling emotions of pressure, which could disable the rest, enabled him. "Down into the tournament stretch," he says, "for some reason I have been able to keep myself together. My attention span gets more acute, my focus is better." He was about to test his recall.

Nicklaus's momentum waned when he bogeyed the twelfth after overshooting the green, but he followed that up with a two-putt birdie on the par-five thirteenth that for the moment brought him to within two strokes of Ballesteros. I photographed him there and remained to document Ballesteros. The Spaniard hit a magnificent second shot to within eight feet and holed the eagle putt. The fact that Ballesteros was now nine under, ahead of Kite by two strokes and Nicklaus by four, caused me to follow his group instead of making for the grandstand beside the green at the par-five fifteenth and wait for the play to come to me at a spot where big things could, and often did, happen. I also ignored the over-zealous celebration back in the thirteenth fairway between Ballesteros and his caddie and brother, Vicente, who clasped hands like it was already a lock when his second shot snuggled close.

Remaining with Ballesteros instead of Nicklaus was a bad decision on my part, as the overpowering sound carrying back up the hill from the fifteenth hole soon told me. The noise wasn't the kind you hear from people who are liquored up or prompted by cue cards. These shouts came from within, joined with the clapping and carried toward the blue sky, reverberating off pines.

The thunder was summoned by a vintage Nicklaus four-iron shot, a towering stroke that sent chills through the young man in the white coveralls carrying his bag. Nicklaus's shots never sounded different—the way Ben Hogan's admirers waxed on about his—but they looked different. Nicklaus's strokes were both long and high, an enormous perfecta. His long-iron shots had such a distinctive quality that they have sent scores of golf writers to their thesauruses looking for descriptive help. Alfred Wright might have done the best job, once observing at a Masters that a ball launched off a Nicklaus long iron came to earth as if delivered by a friendly robin. So it did here.

When Nicklaus sank the twelve-footer for eagle on the fifteenth to again pull within two strokes of Ballesteros, the sound was so loud it was like being in an arena with tall trees to the rafters. When his five-iron tee shot at the sixteenth hole then very nearly went into the hole, the eruption enveloped in noise all who were there. Dave Musgrove, Lyle's caddie, later recalled that from the sixteenth tee, all he could see were legs—the legs of the people, fairly jumping with glee out of their green folding chairs around the green.

By then I had scrambled up to the top row of the grandstand beside the fifteenth, determined to see what Ballesteros, who still led the tournament but now by only one shot over Nicklaus, would do on the hole. Nicklaus's eagle was the latest in a spate of them at the fifteenth, and Ballesteros could follow suit. But Ballesteros's second shot, with a four-iron, was not far in the air when a growing murmur spread among the spectators. Even before the ball splashed into the dyed-blue water in the pond short of the green, I was making my way back down the stairs and toward the seventeenth green to catch Nicklaus. Could his wait—my wait—be over?

Over at the seventeenth hole Nicklaus realized what had happened. Part of the appraisal of his diminished status had been conventional and not unfounded wisdom that, whatever the shape of his game, he no longer intimidated the competition as he once did. Ballesteros's dunking suggested that Nicklaus still did; before playing from the fifteenth fairway, Seve had heard the cacophony with everyone else.

He knows he's going to win. We know he's going to win. And he knows we know he's going to win.

Now tied for the lead with Ballesteros, Nicklaus got away with a poor tee shot pulled to the left at 17. If he still smoked on the course, as he once did, how deep a drag he might have taken now. But he had a clear opening and hit a wedge to within eleven feet. Not only was it a good shot, but it positioned him such that he was putting toward the setting sun, convenient for the phalanx of photographers now among the crowd opposite him.

Nicklaus could taste the result before the ball disappeared. As he raised his putter with his left arm, he stuck his tongue out like Michael Jordan soaring toward the basket. Then he raised both arms skyward. Later on, despite the drama of the resulting photographs, I heard some people thought the Jordanesque tongue out of character. They said that it didn't look like Jack. But Nicklaus, for all he had done before, had never done this.

A familiar surprise. It was the only thing that could have coaxed the sound that then came out of the people lining the eighteenth hole, rows of human insulation now but chilled by the prospect of watching a page from a book pull off the impossible.

Two putts from fifty feet and par left Nicklaus at nine under par. He hugged his son and went to see if his lead would hold up. In my spot beside the eighteenth green, I wiped away a tear and rewound the film in the camera with which I shot Nicklaus's long approach putt. To my horror I discovered I had loaded the wrong speed film. Those pictures would be unusable. Later some writers told me that the pressure of trying to capture the enormity of Nicklaus's accomplishment had caused them to choke over their keyboards that night. I could sympathize. This time it was the journalists who had choked. The golfer—Nicklaus—didn't.

It's February 1996. Via a long-distance telephone hookup, I am listening in on Nicklaus as he talks about the 1986 Masters to an audience of reporters near his Florida home and office. The connection has gone dead once already. Nicklaus is fifty-six. On the telecast of a senior tournament a few weeks before, he still looked blond and fit, but he isn't cheating the years as he once did. There is no mistaking the passage of ten years since he worked his magic.

Anniversary stories being as much a part of the sports pages as box scores, Nicklaus has been besieged by writers wanting to get his recollections on what happened that day at Augusta. The details come matter-of-factly, as they always have from Nicklaus. He is talking as briskly as he strode Augusta National's hills that hot, sunny Sunday. A couple of times he can't recall exactly which club he used.

Nicklaus has always moved on with his life, better at plotting tomorrow than recalling yesterday, even one so sweet. Maybe that's why his tomorrows were better than most. But I can't help remembering the first time I saw him in the flesh, in 1972, at a short-lived tour stop in North Carolina. He was the trim, fashionable model by then. The gallery wasn't too large, and on pro-am day it was easy for a kid to snap some Instamatic pictures and collect autographs. The latter pursuit had not become so popular or sophisticated. Golfers signed somewhere in your tournament program with a ballpoint pen, the signatures invariably lacking letters at points where the ink didn't take to the paper stock. Nicklaus began his first and last names with a big-letter flourish that made it pretty easy for me to mimic.

Those were the days when Nicklaus was in his prime, expected to win. The 1986 Masters had been much different. "It was at a point in my career when nobody expected me to win, including myself," he said. "And most of my career at Augusta, most people expected me to win—the players, the press, the fans, and myself. And I don't think anybody did in 1986. It was very special, probably the most special win that I ever had." Maybe part of it is not being in the same room with Nicklaus, but his words seem insufficient, too clinical for what transpired that dramatic day.

Nicklaus is bowing out of both the U.S. Open and British Open, he says, a concession to his game's losing fight with time. But he will continue to play in the Masters, seeing if he can find the friendly robins, waiting for a surprise. Imagine what he must hear there, even now, ten years since the sound was all around.

April 18, 1996

Amazingly in 1998, a dozen years after his stunning Masters victory, at fifty-eight and with a gimpy left hip that would soon be replaced by an artificial joint, Jack Nicklaus turned back the clock on another Sunday in Augusta. A win wasn't in the cards, but a closing 68, and tie for sixth place, was the Golden Bear's last hurrah at the Masters. In 2011, on the twenty-fifth anniversary of Nicklaus winning a green jacket for the sixth time, I wrote about the reason he wore a yellow shirt that fateful day. It was in honor of a young Ohio boy, Craig Smith, a friend of the Nicklaus family who died of bone cancer in 1971 at age thirteen. When Craig was battling the disease, a yellow shirt worn by Nicklaus on tournament Sundays was his special way of saying hello to Craig. At the 1986 Masters, it was a tribute to his late pal. I've heard lots of roars at Augusta since that sentimental yellow shirt brought Nicklaus so much good luck, but none louder than those the Golden Bear caused that glorious afternoon in 1986.

CHAPTER EIGHTEEN

Devil's Island

Take a listen some afternoon around the seventeenth hole of the Stadium Course at the Tournament Players Club at Sawgrass, in Ponte Vedra Beach, Florida, and it doesn't take long to hear a cacophony of failure. The sad plunk of the foozled hit that gets wet before it gets airborne. The loud thwack of the low liner that strikes the wooden bulkhead before drowning. The inevitable plop of the Texas Leaguer that never has a chance. The arresting splash-skip-gurgle of the solid, straight ball that looks good until it carries a tad too far, misses land, and wiggles like a sick fish to the murky bottom.

You bet accidents happen at No. 17, emergency rooms full of them, which makes all the more sense when you realize the hole was never supposed to have an island green. It wasn't supposed to make tour pros and tourists alike squirm, sweat, and swear. It wasn't supposed to become the most feared 132 yards of real estate in golf, a measly short-iron shot that can seem like you're trying to hit a buoy in the Gulf of Mexico—or worse when the wind blows. If there hadn't been so much good dirt once upon a time at No. 17, there wouldn't be so much water there now.

Course architect Pete Dye had envisioned a green guarded only by a lake on the right, no pushover but a fairly buttoned-down par three that wouldn't make golfers go apoplectic. When Dye got around to actually creating the hole, however, he encountered a problem: all the sand on that part of the property had been excavated to form other fairways. "I go back to build the par three," Dye says, "and there ain't nothing there. I had dug it all up. There was nothing there but a gargantuan hole where I'd taken all the sand."

Alice Dye, his wife and collaborator, had an idea. "I said, 'Why don't you just make an island out of it?'" she recalls. "We weren't trying to be innovative and do something that hadn't been done before. It just looked like such a neat idea."

Many sixes, eights, and Xs later, the Stadium Course has evolved into a severe yet manicured layout, its greens softened several times after player pouting. Areas off the fairways have been tidied up nicer than a suburban neighborhood. It is a stark contrast to the swampy, snaky site the Dyes started with twenty years ago. The seventeenth hole, though, has gone basically unchanged.

If it's not the most famous hole in golf, it may be the most notorious. It's certainly not as charming as the seventh at Pebble Beach, as mysterious as the twelfth at Augusta National, nor is it as beautiful and brawny as the sixteenth at Cypress Point. *Golf Digest* recently named it the thirty-third-best par three in America. What No. 17 does have is the ability to make people notice. Since the Tournament Players Club (TPC) at Sawgrass opened in late 1980, and the Players Championship moved there two years later, the seventeenth has been the postcard that can make you sick.

"Oh my goodness, that hole gets your attention," says Roger Maltbie, the NBC golf announcer and former tour player. "You don't make too many swings in golf that are all or nothing. If you make four threes there in a tournament, you're doing fine, just fine." During the second round at the 1990 Players, Maltbie wasn't doing so well. He popped three balls in the lake, made a nine, signed for an 85 a hole later, and withdrew, citing a "forty-five-minute virus."

The first time Jim Colbert came to the seventeenth hole, during a practice round for the 1982 Players, he handed an iron to his caddie, Willie Miller, and said, "You do it." Before the start of each Players Championship held at the TPC, Colbert would try to vaccinate himself against disaster at No. 17 by tossing four balls into the water. "I wanted to pay my dues," he says, "and I never did hit it in the water."

The hole has had scores from 1 to 66, helped move course architecture into another realm, spawned hundreds of imitations, turned golf pros into praying men, given the Players more attention than it ever could have bought, and done more for the profit margins of ball manufacturers than a slice that wants to live in the next county. Each year divers retrieve about 120,000 balls from the bottom of the four-foot deep lake at 17—an average of three per paying customer. A local rule asks golfers to move to the drop area after dunking two balls, but unless play is clogged up, rangers look the other way. After all, the green fee in high season is $190.

"A lot of these guys won't get off the tee until they get one on," says TPC locker room attendant Joe Schmalzried. "A guy I was in the Marines with was playing about two months ago. Did not get on. He put six in the water, moved up to the drop area, and put in three more. His son finally hit it on for him."

There is a tendency in golf to praise the subtleties of some rusty, revered course even though it features bunkers deep enough to hide an NBA center on a stepladder. When Dye was finished cooking up what former PGA Tour commissioner Deane Beman had ordered for the Stadium Course—a visually dramatic, penal design in which the best players in the world would be required to walk a tightrope—there was no such confusion.

"There was a period of time in the 1950s and '60s when golf courses started getting pretty doggone bland," Dye says. "Now maybe we've started overdoing it, but the TPC sure changed the perspective of what a golf course should look like." Says course architect Mike Hurdzan, "Everybody was doing plain vanilla, and all of a sudden Pete's doing a chunky, rocky road, swirl kind of thing."

Rocky road would be an apt description. Early on, Jack Nicklaus remarked, "You want controversy? Okay, let's have controversy. A lot of guys would like to put a bomb under that thing." A golf ball hit from the seventeenth tee has few career options. It goes in the water, stops on the green, settles into a tiny doormat of fringe, or catches a litter box of a bunker short-right. Like the earth and the people who live on it, the hole is mostly water.

"That's what the hole is all about—the penalty," says Len Mattiace. "You're a little antsy. If you're not, you're not in touch with yourself."

Mattiace was in touch with the lead at the Players last year, just one stroke behind Justin Leonard, when he reached the penultimate hole in the final round. Mattiace, who lives nearby and practices often at the TPC, had reeled off eight birdies through the first sixteen holes. Victory would be the sweetest of presents for his gravely ill mother, Joyce, who, though confined to a wheelchair, was watching from the gallery. It would also take him, at age thirty-one, to a new level.

The cup was cut where it always is on Sunday, in the right-rear portion of the four-thousand-square-foot putting surface, beyond a swale. "I'd played that hole a hundred times in my head before the tournament," Mattiace says. "I told myself I'd go ten feet short and ten feet left of the hole. I wasn't going at the hole. There's a little crown. I saw the ball hitting it and rolling down the swale." Debating between a hard pitching wedge and an easy nine-iron, Mattiace chose the longer club and tried to smooth it. But with his adrenaline pumping, he flushed it, and the ball sailed over the green without so much as a bounce on land. From the drop area, an eighty-yard shot, he pushed an L-wedge into the sand. His next shot also went long and got wet. Splashes turned to groans. Mattiace made an eight.

During the first couple of years of the Players Championship, Dye would settle into the gallery at No. 17 for long stretches, like an artist looking on as others assess his brushstrokes. "I just begged everybody to get across the first couple of years," Dye says. "I didn't want to get shot right off the bat." Several years he played in the pro-am. Once, he needed to finish par-par for 72. He dunked one ball, then another. "There went my 72," he says. Last year Dye was watching on television. "I always feel sorry for someone when they get in a mess like that," he says of Mattiace's waterloo. "I don't want to try to torture somebody. But that's what's out there. A bunker used to be a hazard. Now the only hazard golf professionals have is H2O."

Besides, the seventeenth wasn't the first hole in golf—or even the first in its own neighborhood, for that matter—with an island green. Only a couple of miles away is the ninth hole at the Ponte Vedra Inn & Club. Architect Herbert Strong's 1932 design was 161 yards long, but the island was big enough to include several bunkers and palm trees. And even that wasn't the game's first island green. The first one is believed to have been built in 1904, on the 330-yard tenth at the original layout at Baltusrol Golf Club in Springfield, New Jersey. The green was surrounded by a moat, but members found it too tough, so in 1918 the hole was redone. William S. Flynn's 1923 design of Cherry Hills Country Club in Englewood, Colorado, included a green encircled by a stream on the par-five seventeenth, a hazard best known for sucking up Ben Hogan's third shot (and his last chance for a fifth U.S. Open) in 1960. And Robert Trent Jones's Golden Horseshoe Golf Club in Williamsburg, Virginia, featured an island green on the par-three sixteenth when it opened in 1964.

Other island greens also preceded No. 17, and many others would follow, including versions shaped like the jaws of a shark and an apple. From the moment of Alice Dye's inspiration, though, the hole had a singular voice, hitting a note the imitations did not. "I think 17 confirmed what Alister MacKenzie thought a good short hole must be: short," says Hurdzan. "It's totally psychological. The best players in the world can be intimidated by it."

The first time the pros played the Stadium Course, in 1982, winner Jerry Pate birdied the seventeenth three days out of four.

The hole played slightly over par the first two years, but in 1984's first round, a blustery day with winds gusting to 40 miles per hour, No. 17 got nasty. The stroke average for the day was 3.79, and sixty-four balls got wet, including one by John Mahaffey, who called it "one of the easiest par fives on the course." That week No. 17 averaged 3.368 strokes, the hardest it has ever played.

When Jodie Mudd won the 1990 Players Championship, he pulled a nine-iron into the water in the rain-delayed finish of the third round Sunday morning. That afternoon, holding a one-stroke lead, he aimed for the middle of the green and pushed his nine-iron within six feet of the tucked pin. "I got away with it," Mudd said. Others weren't so lucky that year. In addition to Maltbie's nine, Tom Watson was in contention when he hit two balls in the water in the third round and made an eight. Phil Blackmar made a ten in the second round when he dunked three.

Robert Gamez, then a tour rookie, was just three strokes off the lead with two holes left in the third round. His tee shot, an eight-iron, splashed long over the green. His L-wedge from the drop area spun back into the water. He repeated the error with a sand wedge. Another sand wedge went too far. His next one finally found the green, and Gamez got your basic two-putt eleven, the *Titanic* of seventeenth-hole sinkings. "We were attacked by aliens," joked Gamez's brother and caddie, Randy. "The first was a good shot, but the wind died," Gamez says now. "The next three were just bad swings. I didn't get mad. You live and learn. The next week I won at Bay Hill."

Angelo Spagnolo also survived the seventeenth hole, though he had to putt around the lake and up the footpath to the green, carding a 66, in *Golf Digest*'s World's Worst Avid Golfer competition in 1985. So did Jeff Sluman, who was getting ready for a six-foot birdie putt to beat Sandy Lyle in a 1987 TPC playoff when a spectator acting on a $250 dare jumped in the water and caused a commotion. Sluman missed the putt and Lyle won on the next hole. In 1997 Davis Love III hit his tee shot to four feet but accidentally brushed the ball with the toe of his putter on a practice stroke. He then failed to replace the ball in its original spot, signed an incorrect scorecard, and was disqualified, an error that cost him at least $73,000.

In the seventeen Players Championships, No. 17 has dealt far more pars (4,827) than anything else, but the number of bogeys (733), double bogeys (453), and others (91) adds up to 1,277, more than the 1,036 birdies. There have been only three holes-in-one at 17 during the tournament: Brad Fabel in 1986, Brian Claar in 1991, and the loudest, when Fred Couples jarred a nine-iron in the fourth round in 1997. "To tell you the truth," says Couples's caddie, Joe LaCava, "I was happier when he just got it on land when he won in '96. It's a scary shot."

Larry Denton, who worked on the construction of the course, made the first ace on November 10, 1980. Ninety-eight aces have followed, at least thirty-one more than on any of the Stadium's other three par threes, including one on January 15, 1998, by a Harold Putt, who didn't have to.

Those are the stories with a happy ending. But next week, before the Players Championship begins, if you see a dark-haired man, name of Mattiace, tossing four golf balls into the lake at 17, you won't have to ask why.

March 19, 1999

I revisited this topic during the 2008 Players Championship by spending most of the week at the pesky seventeenth hole for a long piece as part of *Golf World*'s coverage, and the 132-yarder didn't disappoint when it came to drama. Hitting first in a sudden-death playoff against Sergio Garcia that began on the perilous one-shotter, Paul Goydos struck a pitching wedge that got caught in a headwind and splashed a few feet short of the bulkhead at the front of the green. Garcia followed with a spectacular tee shot to three feet to sew up his most important victory to date.

CHAPTER NINETEEN

Fortunate Son

The conclusion to the ninety-seventh PGA Championship was soggy and sweet, like strawberries and sponge cake. As quickly as the late-afternoon rain had come on Sunday to Winged Foot Golf Club in Mamaroneck, New York, it stopped, and the sun peeked through an angry sky. Two rainbows arched over the course at just the right moment, as if scripted by Frank Capra himself, and for Davis Love III, there wasn't a burden in sight.

For Love, this was news. No longer was he the skinny kid with a turn by Gumby who attracted gawkers because he could bust a golf ball into orbit. He wasn't the young pro whose game sputtered while he struggled to cope with the death of his teaching-pro father in a 1988 plane crash. No more was he the talented, amiable tour veteran who could deliver good quotes and win regular titles but who suffered only heartbreak and disappointment in major championships.

Finally, at age thirty-three, Love achieved what so many people—including his own slender-shouldered self—had long expected. "I'm thrilled beyond belief," Love said after a five-stroke victory over Justin Leonard on Winged Foot's rugged West Course. "So many times I felt like I should have won and didn't. There was a lot going on in my head today."

But in setting aside his emotions and shooting eleven-under 269 on the stingy, tree-lined layout, Love not only proved he could come through in the clutch but could do so in stunning style. His seventy-two-hole total, which included 66s on Thursday, Saturday, and Sunday, bettered by seven shots the Winged Foot tournament record established by Fuzzy Zoeller and Greg Norman in the 1984 U.S. Open. Other than Love and Leonard, only third-place finisher Jeff Maggert, who joined Love in securing a spot on the U.S. Ryder Cup team with his four-under 276, and Lee Janzen, who shot 279 to finish fourth and became one of U.S. captain Tom Kite's two wild-card picks Monday, broke par.

While Winged Foot didn't deliver the spanking it did during the 1974 U.S. Open, which Hale Irwin won with a seven-over 287 total, dense rough made it play tougher than it did in 1984. "I catch fish in water that is more shallow than the rough is here," said Phil Blackmar, who tied for sixth at 281.

Officially the rough was listed at five inches, but it wasn't cut during the week, and patches could be taller. John Daly, the surprise first-day coleader with Love, said he tore a blade from one particularly gnarly spot and estimated it at nine inches. Larry Nelson, who believed Winged Foot's hay was almost a match for the notorious Oakmont rough he triumphed over at the 1983 U.S. Open, had to hit one shot Friday with the end of his putter because his lie was so poor. "Using L-wedges doesn't even make a difference in this," Nelson said. "The size of your wrists might make a difference."

But powerful U.S. Open champion Ernie Els, who joined Leonard and Tiger Woods in a marquee pairing the first two days, measured his frustration in the eight yards he hit a seven-iron out of the tall stuff on the eighth hole during the first round. "I just made a complete mess of it," said Els. "That hasn't happened to me too often. It was quite embarrassing, to say the least."

Woods must hope his frequent trips to Winged Foot's trouble spots turn out to be illuminating as well as embarrassing. As at

Congressional and Troon earlier this summer, Woods showed a tendency to rack up too many big numbers, and he got close to enough pine, oak, and spruce trees last week to apprentice as a tree surgeon. He escaped from a bare lie between two oaks on the sixteenth on Saturday with a soaring, fading six-iron shot that set up a birdie and got him within three shots of the lead. But he limped literally (bad ankle, which he originally hurt while vacationing in France after last month's British Open) and figuratively (double bogey-bogey finish) to the clubhouse, closing the book on a major championship campaign that didn't quite fulfill expectations.

After his runaway Masters victory in April, Woods and his followers entertained visions of a multiple major performance in his first full year as a pro. Those dreams were ultimately replaced by sightings of him in awkward stances trying to pull off nearly impossible recovery shots. "You can't afford to hit the shots that far off line," Woods said Thursday, describing his seven on the par-five twelfth hole, "and in a major, you should get penalized like I have been."

There was a time when young Love hit the ball almost as far as Woods does now. In fact when he turned pro in 1986, Love's length was considered unprecedented and his technique dissected and analyzed, much the way Woods's is today. Love enjoyed the benefits of that length but hated being a curiosity, and early in his career, if he thought people were coming to watch him smash tee shots, he would pull out a one-iron until they went away. Groomed by his dad to be a complete player, Love found his progress as a pro slowed when his father was killed. "It definitely set me back," he said. "It was not a lot of fun for a couple of years." Except to his family and close friends, he kept many of his emotions to himself, and he was conflicted by the different critiques he received.

"A lot of people said that I had to get tougher or stronger or meaner," said Love, whose squinting on-course countenance at times disguises his good nature. "At the same time, a lot of people were saying, 'You've got to smile more, got to wave to the fans more.' Well, which did they want me to do?"

Love does acknowledge a possible cathartic effect from writing a memoir of life with his dad, *Every Shot I Take*, which was published earlier this year. "I think I can be a little bit more comfortable with the way people perceive me and why I might do the things that I do," he said.

On the course Love's career progression was as smooth as his tempo. He captured the MCI Heritage Classic in 1987, just his second year on tour, then won three times (including the Players Championship) in a whirlwind stretch in 1992, during which he and Fred Couples battled for the supremacy of American golf. But he was never at ease in the spotlight and got his comeuppance in the majors. "When I [turned pro] I honestly thought the majors would be the easiest tournaments for me to contend in," he explained. "I hit the ball long. I was a strong player. I thought putting wasn't as important in the majors. I obviously learned that it's the most important thing."

Unbelievably, it took Love ten seasons—and twenty-eight attempts—to notch his first top-ten finish in a major, a second place to Ben Crenshaw at the 1995 Masters. That barrier finally broken, he began a stretch of strong major performances that were soured by his efforts on the greens. Poor putting cost Love at the 1995 U.S. Open at Shinnecock Hills, where he tied for fourth place. His shocking three-putt on the seventy-second hole at Oakland Hills in last year's U.S. Open cost him a possible spot in a play-off. "He hadn't ever gotten negative about his putting," observed his brother and caddie, Mark, "but he had been frustrated."

Even before those disappointments, though, Love already had rededicated himself. Late in 1994 he huddled with his instructor, Jack Lumpkin, intent on fulfilling his promise. "He told me, 'I really want to do whatever it takes to be a good player,'" Lumpkin said Sunday from his Sea Island, Georgia, home. "He said, 'I don't think I've worked very hard, certainly not as hard as I need to. Tell me what I need to do.'" Lumpkin, an assistant pro at Winged Foot in 1960–61, began priming Love to succeed in this year's PGA, weakening his grip on sand and pitch shots so he could hit high, soft shots from the deep, troublesome lies encountered on the A. W. Tillinghast design.

Throughout this year Lumpkin had also been working with Love to quiet his foot action, especially his right foot on the downswing, and to extend through his shots. Even as Love was enduring a winless spring and summer and slipping from second to tenth in the Ryder Cup standings, they felt they were making progress. He missed the cut at the Buick Open two weeks ago but was at Winged Foot last Monday, hitting flat-footed eight-irons for a couple of hours to ingrain the feeling, and by Thursday he was ready. "I don't think I've ever felt this good about my swing," Love said after his 66 in the storm-interrupted third round.

By then Love's only worry was Leonard, who, having managed a 68 in the first round off some tenacious scrambling, broke the competitive course record with a 65 on Saturday, giving the two good friends the fifty-four-hole lead at seven-under-par 203, seven strokes ahead of Janzen and Kite. On a day when Winged Foot was at its thorniest (only eight golfers broke par), Leonard hit fourteen fairways and fifteen greens. Evidence of Love's improved putting was sprinkled about his scorecard, including twelve-footers for par at the sixteenth and seventeenth holes and a ten-footer for birdie at the 448-yard eighteenth in the gloaming after a late-afternoon storm. "If you're thinking you're going to make them and you're being patient, you can make some of them," Love observed of his par saves. "I don't want to have to scramble like that tomorrow."

It wasn't exactly Watson and Nicklaus at Turnberry in 1977, but forty years after the PGA Championship abandoned the match-play format, it had rediscovered an informal version in the Love-Leonard showdown. On Saturday night Love tried not to dwell on what was ahead, pausing during a steak dinner with his wife, Robin, and CBS-TV golf producer Lance Barrow only to worry that he and Leonard, who endorse the same clothing line, might show up on Sunday wearing the same outfit. They didn't, but Sunday morning, killing time prior to his 2:05 p.m. tee time, Love admitted, "[I] ironed my shirt four or five times and packed my suitcase as neatly as I've ever packed it."

The final round was played in sweltering heat and humidity, but Love's play was as precise as his packing job. He shot a front-nine 32 and, with Leonard posting an uneven 37, led by five as he stepped to the tenth tee. But that didn't put Love's mother, Penta, at ease. "I wish we didn't have to play the back side," she said.

Three holes later Love's lead had been trimmed to three strokes, and his four-iron tee shot at the 212-yard thirteenth had finished long and left, on a so-so lie on top of some matted rough. With Leonard waiting to putt a fifteen-footer for birdie, Love nearly holed his wedge shot, softly lobbing his ball off the flagstick for a tap-in par. "I think that saved the tournament for me," he said. "That gave me the confidence that I could get up and down from anywhere. I could handle anything."

And for the first time in a major championship, Love did just that. When the downpour struck while the final pairing played the sixteenth, Love made a textbook par. "He never, never let up," said Leonard. "He hit the ball solid all the way around. And even though he missed a couple of fairways by three or four yards, he's strong enough to put the ball on the green."

After playing 312 tour events, after so many bad fittings for formal wear, this major fit. Love, who with Leonard was one of the last tour pros to switch from a persimmon-headed driver to one with a metal head and graphite shaft, drove beautifully and hit six iron shots within twelve feet of the hole. His putter never got balky, and he didn't force the outcome. "I didn't try too hard," Love said. "I tried to enjoy it. I tried to have fun. I tried to let my game come out. And I knew that on this course if I played my game, I could win."

In 1960 his father had come to Winged Foot to play in a U.S. Open sectional qualifier with six stitches in his right hand, suturing a wound suffered when he rescued a woman who'd been trapped in a car accident. Doctors, worried that he would tear the

Inside the Ropes

stitches taking divots, urged Love not to play. Instead he cobbled together a makeshift set that included nine woods, improvised a slow-motion swing designed to sweep the ball off the grass, and qualified in a playoff, parring the first hole with a driver, three-wood, nine-wood, and putter.

Thirty-seven years later, as his son maneuvered his way through Winged Foot's dark and stormy final stretch, his biggest worry wasn't dry grips but dry eyes. "The last six or seven holes I was choked up," he said. Sitting by his TV in Georgia, Lumpkin was tearing up. And there beyond Winged Foot's final green, where Love faced a twelve-foot birdie putt with victory already certain, the clouds finally parted, revealing those two colored arches painted in the sky that he could scarcely make himself glimpse.

Rainbows? They resembled nothing if not the lines Davis Love Jr. often used to paint on the ground when he was giving a golf lesson.

"He knew his dad was with him," Penta Love said later. "When it was over and he hugged me, I said, 'Dad knows.' And he said, 'Yes, I'm sure he does.'"

August 22, 1997

Davis Love III, who will turn fifty on April 13, 2014, has not won another major championship since his wonderful week at Winged Foot, a second-place finish at the 1999 Masters being his best result. In 2008, though, Love won his twentieth career PGA Tour title, a mark bettered by only thirty-two players. That may not be quite the bounty many observers expected when the precocious Love arrived on the scene in the mid-1980s with the power and sound game few golfers had possessed, but it is a fine career. As the legendary Dan Jenkins says, writers root for "the story," but at the 2012 Ryder Cup, having known Davis as long as I have, I was rooting, inwardly, for the Love-captained U.S. side. Unfortunately the Americans were overtaken on the final day at Medinah Country Club by an inspired European team, but Love, as ever, was classy in defeat.

CHAPTER TWENTY

Thoughts from Augusta

Doug Ford, who won the 1957 Masters tournament and is eighty-five years old, has enjoyed a long golf life, from Otey Crisman to Scotty Cameron, if you want to mark time with famous putter designers of yesterday and today. When you've been around the game as long as Ford, you've seen it all on the greens: monster putts made and itty-bitty ones missed and as many kinds of strokes as types of grass. "George Low was the greatest putter I ever saw outside of Tiger Woods," Ford said before returning to Augusta National Golf Club last week. "George could putt with his foot better than most guys could with their putter. That's the truth. I saw him beat a guy in Havana for $35,000 putting with his foot."

Low was one of the great characters of twentieth-century golf. As Dan Jenkins described him in *The Dogged Victims of Inexorable Fate*, "He is, all at once, America's guest, underground comedian, consultant, inventor of the overlapping grip for a beer can, and, more importantly, a man who has conquered the two hardest things in life—how to putt better than anyone ever, and how to live lavishly without an income."

While Low's father, a Scot named George Sr., was a formidable competitor—a tie for second place in the 1899 U.S. Open is among his accomplishments—the younger Low preferred money games on a putting clock to the grind of competition, although he was low pro in the 1945 Memphis Open when Byron Nelson's win streak was stopped at eleven by amateur Fred Haas. Regardless, his savant-like skills with a putter—along with the largesse of his friends—kept him afloat. Low was the rare golfer of his day who bragged about his ability to putt. Back then, when wristy strokes on hairy greens were the rule, outward pride in one's short game was the exception even though the best players always knew how critical putting was.

"Putting—a game within a game—might justly be said to be the most important part of golf," Bobby Jones wrote in *Bobby Jones on Golf*. "In almost every championship, or even in friendly matches, if the competitors are anything like evenly matched, the man who will win will be the one enjoying a definite superiority on and around the greens. . . . Among first-class competitors, it is hardly ever possible to gain enough in the long game to offset the least bit of loss in putting."

Although Low never played in the Masters, he was a friend and sometimes putting mentor of four-time champion Arnold Palmer, who gave Low some credit after finishing birdie-birdie to win his second green jacket in 1960. "The only thing I did on those putts," Palmer said at the time, "was keep thinking what my old friend George Low always says: 'Keep your head down and don't move.'" More infamously, Low called Palmer over to congratulate him on the eighteenth fairway during the final round in 1961 shortly before Palmer made a sloppy double bogey to hand the title to Gary Player, who just happened to be using a George Low signature putter manufactured after Palmer's win.

From the first Augusta National Invitation Tournament in 1934 (although "The Masters" was cofounder Clifford Roberts's first choice, Jones didn't let it become the official name until 1939), it was evident that Alister MacKenzie's large, rolling greens were a key element in the overall design. In an article in The *Ameri-*

can Golfer previewing the 1935 event, Grantland Rice described the difficulty of a player solving the layout's challenges: "Practice rounds and pressure under fire are two different matters over a course that calls for such delicate short-game stroking as the Augusta National demands."

The greens were Bermuda overseeded with ryegrass. Comparing the turf conditions of the 1940s and 1950s to today is like contrasting the golf balls of the different periods (inconsistent quality control then versus perfect-by-the-dozen now, for one big difference). Suffice it to say, Augusta National's greens were quicker than most places the pros played. As Jenkins, who grew up in Texas, where greens were coarse common Bermuda, says, "They were faster than anything back home."

And their shapes and slopes were more intriguing than almost any in America, where greens tended to be circular and, if anything, tilted uniformly back to front. Viewed from above today, Augusta National's greens have the outline of peanuts, hearts, kidneys, part of an exclamation point (No. 8), a flying saucer (No. 4), and a square drawn by a drunk (No. 17). All of them are about as flat as the existing tax code, with hard-to-discern movement between the sizable slopes.

"They were nowhere near as intimidating as they are now," said Vinny Giles, a career amateur who competed in nine Masters between 1968 and 1977. "When I first played, they had Poa annua in the greens; if you played late, they got bumpy. A couple of years ago I played here, and on the first green I told someone you could putt it off the green if you weren't careful. I was putting back toward the fairway and putted it right off the green after having warned somebody about it. I think they are the most fun greens I've ever seen because they are so challenging. But you never get cocky on them."

Raymond Floyd, who won the green jacket in 1976, played in his first Masters in 1965, and last week, at age sixty-five, shot 80-74 in his forty-fourth appearance. "Well, relatively they haven't changed," he said of the putting surfaces. "More or less, they were the firmest and fastest greens that we played in the 1960s. They're still almost that way with the evolution with agronomy. It's tough if you get on the wrong side of the hole. I three-putted the second hole Thursday from three feet. You see that on these greens. But that's what makes it what it is."

Brad Faxon, one of the best putters of the past couple of generations, grew up in New England, home of some of the keenest greens in the country. But after he gained an exemption to the Masters for the first time and a member invited him for a practice round, the reality of Augusta's putting surfaces surprised him. "All you hear about is the greens and the speed and the breaks," Faxon said. "Most of the time when something gets hyped up so much, it never lives up to the expectation. This surpassed it. If Augusta National is the barometer for what every other course strives to be, none of them reaches it. I still have never hit putts as softly as I've had to there. You feel like you have to caress a putt more so there than any other place I've ever been."

Yet, says Faxon, who played in twelve Masters between 1992 and 2004, "if you get fearful there, you're cooked. If you go there with an attitude of trying to avoid a three-putt, you have no chance of success. I try to say, 'Let's keep having fun out there.'" When the tournament lore includes five-putts and other assorted disasters, that is easier said than done. "You're going to hit some great putts there that do a power lip," said Faxon, "and all of a sudden you have a five- or six-footer left, and you go 'Holy smoke.'" Or, as Seve Ballesteros once said after four-putting the sixteenth green, "I miss, I miss, I miss, I make."

Beyond anecdotal proof, there are some statistics to contrast how the greens putted before and after they were converted to bent grass prior to the 1981 Masters. Philadelphia reporter Fred Byrod kept track of the putting statistics, and *Golf Digest* published them in 1973, detailing the total putts by Masters champions from 1961 through 1972. They ranged from a low of 118 putts for Gary Player (1961) and Billy Casper (1970) to a high of 135 for Jack Nicklaus (1972). Winners in this twelve-year period averaged 126 putts.

The putting surfaces were particularly bumpy in 1966 (Nicklaus, 133 putts) and 1972, evidenced not only in the Golden Bear's totals but in his three-putts, eight in 1966 and seven in 1972. "I've never seen greens so slow here," Arnold Palmer said in 1966. "I think they cut them with fairway mowers." Casper, whose distinctive "pop" stroke produced some of the best ever results (fifty-one PGA Tour victories), was the only winner to go seventy-two holes without three-putting during this period.

The figures from 1961 to 1972 contrast starkly with putting statistics from 1987 through 2008, the bulk of the bent-grass era. In those twenty-two years there was a variance from 104 putts by Mike Weir (2003) to 124 by Vijay Singh in 2000. The average for winners was 112.54 putts for seventy-two holes, nearly fourteen putts fewer than in the measured Bermuda/rye period—or three and a half shots per round. Of the twenty-two winners in the measured bent-grass period, sixteen ranked in the top ten in total putts for the week; only Singh (T-38, 2000) and Woods (T-37, 2001) ranked outside the top thirty.

Nicklaus, Tom Watson, and Ballesteros are the only golfers to have won a Masters on both Bermuda and bent grass. But according to Watson, there has always been a constant. "You've got to have touch," he said. "Nicklaus put it right: you've got to have a young man's nerves to play this golf course."

No one has seemed more at home on Augusta National's greens than two-time champion Ben Crenshaw, who was competing in his thirty-seventh Masters last week. With his flowing stroke and exquisite feel, it can seem as if Crenshaw is using a different kind of brush and paints no one else can buy. "I played a lot of practice rounds with Ben in the early '70s and used to love to watch him putt these greens because he had a different approach to it," said Giles. "Let's say I played a putt to break three feet from right

Inside the Ropes

to left. He might play it to break twelve feet from right to left. He lined it up differently. He 'felt' it to the hole differently. I always thought I was a good putter when I was younger, but I couldn't feel what he seemed to feel."

The object of Giles's admiration was standing under the large oak tree behind the clubhouse one afternoon last week talking about Augusta's greens, one of his favorite subjects. "They're the darndest set of greens," Crenshaw said. "The slopes and how they work—they escape your eye because a lot of them are barely convex." At this point Crenshaw made a wavy motion with his right hand. "They go this way and they go that way then they go this way. That's why you miss your pace a lot; that's why speed is so critical."

Crenshaw, whose still-silky putting motion belies his age (fifty-six), thinks his Masters putting strategy came out of necessity. "I thought it was the safest way, but it's not the boldest way, by any means," he said. "I tried to picture the highest line. I think that has served me real well on approach putting, but from the standpoint of being bold and having a real good chance at making one, I'm a little timid sometimes. That's the flip side. Line is vital, but pace is even more vital, to picture the ball rolling out at a certain speed. That's what everybody is trying to do. That's what's hard to do."

Golfers have gone to great lengths to prepare for Augusta National's greens, to become accustomed to their pace and aware of their nuances. No one has been more meticulous than the late Bert Yancey, whose fascination with the Masters turned into an obsession. Yancey played in eight Masters between 1967 and 1975; on his first trip to Augusta he constructed Play-Doh models of the greens on a plywood board so he could better understand what he faced.

Yancey had two top-three finishes at the Masters, and he hasn't been the only golfer to take unorthodox measures to meet the unique challenge. Ian Woosnam, perhaps because he is only

5-feet-4½, said he practiced putting on a snooker table before winning the 1991 Masters. Before his second Masters, in 1997, Paul Stankowski tried putting on the concrete floor of the garage at his Texas home. In his Thursday round at Augusta, on a day when the greens were wickedly firm and fast and some of the hole locations bordered on goofy, Stankowski shot a 68. The same afternoon, putting maestro Loren Roberts shot an 85 with forty putts.

Before he came to Georgia for the 1995 Masters as the reigning U.S. Amateur champion, Tiger Woods practiced on the basketball court at Maples Pavilion at Stanford. The preparation didn't pay off on the first hole, when Woods stroked his twenty-foot birdie a little too hard, and it scooted off the green. "Next thing I know," Woods recalled last week, "I'm chipping for my next shot."

But Woods was a quick study, going seventy-two holes without a three-putt en route to a record twelve-stroke victory in 1997. "Even though they have probably gotten faster over the years, I guess through experience they slow down to you," Woods said. "[The course] is playing a lot more penal off the tee, but the greens are still the same. The greens are still just as penal."

There were no reports last week of any golfer having tuned up on a gym floor, but Brandt Snedeker and Zach Johnson practiced at the Frederica Club in St. Simons Island, Georgia, two weeks ago on a green that was rolling at least as fast as Augusta's surfaces. Johnson has learned a lot about the greens since his first Masters in 2005. "I remember someone telling me after that week was over, 'You don't try to make putts at Augusta—you try to see your line and hit it down your line, and if it gets to the hole, great,'" Johnson said last Saturday after shooting 68. "That's usually the way you go about it. My second putt on 18 today was all of eight feet, and [the way I stroked] that ball on most greens it probably would have rolled about two feet."

"It's hard to imagine you hit it that softly, and it goes that far past," CBS's David Feherty observed Sunday as Phil Mickelson's downhill thirty-five-footer rolled fifteen feet long on No. 4.

Inside the Ropes

Bermuda or bent, there has always been some complaining about the severity of Augusta National's greens. Not everyone had as good a time putting as Casper in 1970. "They sure are saving on the water bill on the greens because they black-topped them last night," quipped Dave Marr. In the final round that year on the dipsy-doodle sixth green, seventeen consecutive players three-putted. The severity of that putting surface at No. 6 was reinforced last week in the second round when Snedeker chipped in from the back-right portion of the green over a steep slope to the back-left hole location, a tactic that fellow competitor Tom Watson thought showed the twenty-seven-year-old's imagination. "He was dead with the putter in his hand," Watson said, "and lo and behold he chipped it in the hole. The best he was going to make [putting it] was four or maybe five, and he chips it in."

In each of the first three rounds last week, ten cups were located five yards or less from the edge of a green; on Sunday eight were situated that tight. Watson thought the hole location at the par-four third Friday was too severe, although his criticism was much milder than Nicklaus's was during the 1982 Masters. "The cup at 18 must have been cut at midnight," the Golden Bear said after five three-putts and a second-round 77. "These pin positions are asking you to make an ass of yourself."

For decades players thought Masters officials prepared the greens one way for practice rounds and another way once the tournament began. "You could spend hours on that practice putting green," said Faxon, "but I always thought they had some magic dust they sprinkled Wednesday night on the course. It was a little bit quicker than the practice green. It was a little bit harder. A pin placement might be in a little different spot than you thought it would be."

The tournament's inclination for fast greens probably reached its peak in the late-1980s with the arrival of superintendent Paul Latshaw from Oakmont Country Club, which is known for having some of the quickest, meanest putting surfaces in all of golf.

Augusta's greens were triple-cut daily during tournament week for the first time in 1987 and were just as firm and lightning-fast in 1988. "If you've got a downhill putt, you're just touching the ball and hoping you can make the ten-footer coming back," Fuzzy Zoeller said. "If that's golf, I'm in the wrong damn league."

By that point in Augusta National's history, flippy putting methods had gone the way of walk-up ticket sales for the Masters. It was essential to have a putting stroke with a "fascinating absence of hurry," as O. B. Keeler described the technique of French star Arnaud Massy in 1926 during Massy's exhibition tour of the United States. In *The Master of Putting*, his 1983 instruction book, Low wrote, "As far as I'm concerned, in putting, speed of stroke definitely kills."

Many decades before mowers and grasses got so good, Ed Stimpson thought excessive speed of greens was detrimental to the game. A couple of months after the 1935 Masters was won by Gene Sarazen, the U.S. Open was played at Oakmont. Stimpson was struck by reports of how difficult the club's fast and undulating greens were. An unheralded local pro named Sam Parks, who had played the course dozens of times and knew it better than anyone, won with an eleven-over 299, but the devilish putting surfaces gave everyone else fits. "That year I got the impression that the greens at the Open were too fast," Stimpson told the *New York Times* in 1983. "On one hole that year, Gene Sarazen putted off the green and into a bunker. He had two putts on that green, but they were not in succession."

Stimpson, who won the Massachusetts Amateur title in 1935 but had been intrigued by putting since missing an eighteen-inch putt to lose the 1926 New England Amateur, got to work figuring out how to measure the speed of a green, designing a thirty-inch wooden device with an indentation for a golf ball twelve inches from the end closest to the ground. When raised 15 degrees off the ground, the ball rolled away, and Stimpson noted how many

Inside the Ropes

inches the ball traveled. He repeated the process in the opposite direction and averaged the two numbers to come up with a green speed in inches, or "stimps."

In October 1936 Stimpson took delivery of twenty-five "Stimp Meters" produced by Charlton-Johnson Manufacturers of Boston. They cost $1 apiece. Stimpson explained his invention in an article in *Golfdom* the next year, noting the variables his putting research revealed. "In general," Stimpson wrote, "these experiments proved conclusively that great accuracy is necessary in the force of the blow in sinking putts on curved surfaces, and that wide variation is possible in the line on any one putt provided the force of the putt is properly correlated to the line chosen."

It would be decades before Stimpson would see his "golf level" utilized the way he had initially hoped. He gauged the greens at The Country Club in Brookline, Massachusetts, during the 1963 U.S. Open and found they measured thirty-two "stimps," or 8.9 feet, by what would become the current standard. United States Golf Association senior technical director Frank Thomas modified Stimpson's design in the 1970s, creating a thirty-six-inch aluminum "Speedstick" that released the ball thirty inches from the end when it was lifted 20 degrees. Because the ball rolled farther on greens that were faster, measurements were taken in feet instead of inches. The USGA began selling "Stimpmeters" to golf course superintendents and others in the industry in 1978. One costs $54 plus shipping today.

For many years Stimpson was an interested, long-distance observer of the Masters. "From his original work with the Stimpmeter, he knew how fast a ball rolled and how much friction was needed to slow the ball down," Edward Stimpson III said recently from his home in Massachusetts. "He did a lot of experiments where he timed a ball rolling off his Stimpmeter. He would watch the Masters on TV with a stopwatch, calculating how fast the greens were based on how long it took the ball to roll to its destination. He would watch the Masters and think the greens were too fast.

Then he would write [the Masters chairman] and say, 'I calculate the greens were such and such.' He wouldn't hear for a while, then he'd finally get a very clipped letter back: 'Dear Mr. Stimpson, we don't measure our greens.'"

Then, one year, a friend of Stimpson who knew someone on the Masters committee got a look at a report sent out after the tournament. "It had a table," recalled Stimpson III, "that showed every day from Sunday before the tournament through the final round with details from morning and night—green speed and notes as to what should be done: double-cut this one, water and slow this one. It was clear the Stimpmeter was being used."

The week of the 1981 Masters, chairman Hord Hardin said Augusta National's greens were 9.9 on the Stimpmeter and he desired to get them to 10, but in subsequent years the club has treated the speed of the greens as it does gallery size and tournament merchandise sales: as state secrets. "I would say they were [running] about 13 today," Crenshaw's longtime Masters caddie, Carl Jackson, said last Thursday. "They were quick, but we like 'em crazy-quick."

Jackson learned his craft from Willie (Pappy) Stokes, who carried for the Masters champion five times from 1938 to 1956, including Ben Hogan's two victories. Stokes walked Augusta National from his days as a boy bringing water to construction crews in the early 1930s. "When the greens were Bermuda, they were tricky," said Jackson. "Now they're true. Ninety percent of the putts, everybody in the gallery knows which way they're going to break. It's when you get on that fall line, you've got to know what to lean on." Jackson relies on the influence of a "hot spot" he learned from Stokes, and it's more involved, he says, than simply Rae's Creek or the lowest spot on the property. "Pappy taught it to me, and the only other person that knows it now is that man [Crenshaw]."

Rest assured Crenshaw has never gotten a read like John Mahaffey got once from a club caddie on No. 16. "I had a four-footer for birdie," Mahaffey said. "Some of these greens have optical illusions in them. I was a little confused and asked my caddie to have a look. I said 'What do you think?' He said, 'Outside the hole.' I said, 'Which side?' He said, 'Pick one.'"

Phil Mickelson's caddie, Jim Mackay, has been working the Masters for nearly two decades. Because Mickelson knows the course so well, Mackay reads fewer putts at Augusta National than at any other venue. Televised highlights reinforce the way certain putts break. Despite the familiarity, though, Mackay said, "It's one of those places where you know exactly what you've got in front of you, yet you still find yourself scratching your head a lot on the greens."

A few years ago Mackay got to play a round at Augusta National. "As a caddie, you sit there when your guy has a twenty-five-footer and think it isn't that tough," he said. "The one time I got to play it, I was like 'Oh, my goodness.' It just gave me so much more respect for the difficulty the guys have to deal with."

The most amazing putt Mackay has witnessed at the Masters came in the final round in 2003. After spraying his tee shot left into a hazard on the par-five second hole, Mickelson took a drop, then hit a driver 285 yards onto the front-left edge of the green. The pin was back right. "He made it from 110 feet as the crow flies for the most incredible four," Mackay said. "But the ball probably traveled 150 feet because he had to putt it up to the back fringe and have it come back to the cup."

Trevor Immelman didn't sink anything quite that dramatic on Sunday at Augusta National in winning his first major championship, but he made enough putts for the week, eight fewer (112) than runner-up Woods. Putting gets a lot more respect than it once did, but some things don't change. On the eve of the final round, Player left Immelman a voice mail that included a putting tip. He told him to keep his head still. Somewhere in the great beyond of great putters, George Low might be looking for his cut.

April 18, 2008

Because of agronomic advances, it is easier for golf courses to have and maintain slick, smooth putting surfaces. Augusta National's, though, still offer a singular challenge. Whoever wins the Masters each spring will have putted well. Ben Crenshaw hasn't been in contention at the Masters in years, but the sight of him with that simple blade putter in his hands, still divining those maddening slopes with aplomb, is not to be taken for granted. In 2013, at age sixty-one, Crenshaw played in his forty-second consecutive Masters. Much younger men would love to have his touch on those confounding greens.

3

MORE THAN A SCORE

The Characters

CHAPTER TWENTY-ONE

Shades of Greatness

There is more talent than you can count in professional golf these days, but not so many characters. This is a reflection of the times as much as the people. With the corporations crowding in and the money stacking up, there is less gin and more juice, more stock quotes and fewer memorable quotes. Golfers do their curls in a fitness trailer, are in bed before *Letterman*, and never have to wonder what their swings look like because of the video camera they tote with them, along with the multivitamins, magnets, and laptop computer. If he were coming along now, the forces would conspire against Jimmy Demaret being who he was, but no doubt he would make it a good fight, taken late into the night with a big smile, a cold drink, and likely, if he were in the mood, a song.

"Get out and live," he said once. "You're dead for an awful long time."

By all accounts, Demaret took his own advice. Although 2000 is the ninetieth anniversary of Demaret's birth and marks fifty years since he became the first man to win the Masters tournament three times, those who knew him well don't need to be prompted by the calendar to remember. Talk to someone about Demaret—someone who heard the jokes, was warmed by the grin, or saw him shimmy into his narrow stance and create a best-selling fiction of a shot that did a fox trot upon landing—and the joy seems as fresh as today's paper.

Demaret, who died of a heart attack in 1983 when he was seventy-three, wasn't the game's first showman and he won't be the last—in so much as the species can exist at all in these perfect turf, exact yardage, courtesy-car times—but the multitalented Texan carved a singular niche. "He was a wonderful guy, a happy-go-lucky devil," says Sam Snead. "I never met one person who said they didn't like Jimmy Demaret."

He made his mark by combining a winning game with a congenial personality that bulged with generosity and humor. He was a nightclub-quality singer, at ease and not needing many shots when he was alongside Bing Crosby, as he often was. And he was smart, despite having had to drop out of school before he got to junior high to help his disabled father support a family of nine children. "Many people don't know how unbelievably bright he was," says Jack Burke Jr., Demaret's longtime friend and business partner at Champions Golf Club in Houston, which the pair built in the late 1950s. "He had a mind like a Swiss watch, a tremendous mind. He became a pilot, and he could handle boats with big engines. He had a great memory. I don't think people know how complicated he was."

From 1938 through 1957—a lengthy span of success few golfers have achieved—Demaret won thirty-one PGA Tour events (tied for sixteenth place in career victories through the 2013 season). Runner-up in the 1948 U.S. Open, he finished one stroke out of the playoff in the national championship in 1957 when he was forty-seven years old. At fifty-one, in the 1962 Masters, he finished fifth. And when he was fifty-three, he nearly became the oldest-ever winner of a tour event, losing a playoff to twenty-eight-year-old Tommy Jacobs at the 1964 Palm Springs Classic.

"Tommy's a good boy and it was nice he could win," Demaret deadpanned afterward. "After all, I've got a lot of years left, and he's about through." Demaret had more wins than Lee Trevino,

Johnny Miller, or Gary Player, despite the fact that from 1951 forward he played the tour part-time while spending much of each year tending to his duties as a club pro. Demaret's prime was also interrupted by World War II, which he spent in the navy stationed at Corpus Christi, Texas, playing not an insignificant amount of golf.

"Every war has a slogan," Demaret said. "'Remember the Alamo,' or 'Remember Pearl Harbor.' Mine was, 'That'll play, admiral.'"

Demaret struck the ball low so it wouldn't be affected by the wind ("You could hang laundry on the one-irons he hit," says a friend, Bernie Riviere), but no one was unaffected upon meeting Demaret. That long list would include Bob Hope, who borrowed jokes, and Ben Hogan, who learned shots from him. "He was the most underrated golfer in history," Hogan said. "This man played shots I haven't even dreamed of. I learned them. But it was Jimmy who showed them to me first."

In the khaki and gray days during and following World War II, Demaret was an Easter parade of color in custom-tailored clothes that could brighten Juneau in January. "Everybody looked like pallbearers," he observed of the monochromatic circuit he joined. "I learned early that color puts life into things." Demaret got a sense of color from watching his father, John, a painter and handyman, mix paints. In time he married the red-haired Idella Adams, and he turned into a rainbow. "Just before he would step on the first tee," recalls the Demarets' only child, Peggy, "everybody in the gallery would say, 'I wonder what he's going to have on today?'"

Demaret might pair a dusty rose cardigan with an electric blue shirt and green suede shoes. Or he could choose garments of flaming scarlet, peach, purple, tangerine, burgundy, canary yellow, or vermillion topped with a showy tam crocheted by his mother-in-law, Ethel. It was a 64-Crayola collection that set a vivid standard for peacocks such as Doug Sanders and Payne Stewart who followed. Snead remembers arriving at a hotel in South America once with Demaret to play some exhibitions, and as soon as his friend got out of the car, necks craned and traffic stopped.

"When he got out of that car," Snead says, "it was like everybody stopped breathing."

He was paying for clothes what people were putting down on a house: in 1954 he counted seventy-one pairs of slacks, fifty-five shirts, thirty-nine sport coats, and twenty sweaters. Over the years he accumulated hundreds of pairs of shoes, most with a brightly covered saddle, and when he got older, he'd let friends go up in his attic and pick out a pair to take home. Decades before Forrest Fezler slipped on a pair of shorts during the 1974 U.S. Open, Demaret defied authority and bared his legs during a hot tournament in Chicago.

While people noticed what he wore, they remembered what he said. In an era when most pros worried much more about keeping their shag bag full of golf balls than filling reporters' notebooks, Demaret was full of witty observations, one-liners usually, that often had him laughing before he finished his delivery. "He could put people down without being mean, and he told jokes on himself," says former tour pro Bob Goalby. "He acted like he knew you even if he didn't. He made you feel good about yourself."

A gas siphon hose was an "Oklahoma credit card." Lew Worsham, the 1947 U.S. Open champion who had a prominent chin, was "the only guy in the world with a built-in bib." When Sam Snead started putting with a side-saddle style, Demaret said, "He looks like he's basting a turkey." At the Crosby one year, everyone awoke Sunday morning—some after less sleep than others—to see Pebble Beach coated with snow. "I know I got loaded last night, but how did I wind up in Squaw Valley?" Demaret said. Of Bob Hope, Demaret quipped, "He has a wonderful short game. Unfortunately it's off the tee."

Demaret's humor could pop up at any time, prompted by almost anything. "He had the freshest, sharpest wit," says Riviere. "He could respond to any situation with something funny, and it was always his—he didn't steal material from anybody. We always felt if he kidded you, he liked you."

Riviere, his brother, Jay, and Dave Marr—a trio Demaret had taken under his wing—headed out on the 1959 winter tour without much success. "The Crosby was about the fourth tournament of the year and Jimmy shows up," Riviere says. "He said, 'I wasn't coming out this early, but I was worried about you. I thought you might have been killed.'"

Johnny Bulla remembers one Masters in the early 1950s when Frank Stranahan, the buff amateur, showed up after an off-season of working on a swing that looked much different than it used to. Demaret, waiting to tee off at the first hole, peeped, "I thought Hogan was the one who had the accident." Johnny Carson was a foil for Demaret on an appearance on *The Tonight Show* in the 1960s. Carson swung a club and asked Demaret what he thought. Demaret, shifting positions to get a different view, asked him to swing again. And again. "Tell you what, John," he finally said. "If I were you, I'd lay off for a couple of weeks." Demaret paused—Cary Middlecoff at the top of his backswing—and told Carson, "And then I'd quit."

Demaret came from grinding poverty, a family of nine children who often wondered how their plates were going to get filled. Some of the children lived for periods in other homes so life wouldn't be so hard. "We were a very poor family," says the youngest of the Demaret children, Mahlon, who was thirteen years Jimmy's junior. "He had quit school and was caddieing and shining shoes by the time I came along." The circumstance of his youth, according to his daughter, forged his outlook later. "If you struggle hard when you're growing up," says Peggy Jackson, "never knowing where you'll get your next meal, you treasure the things you have."

By the time he was sixteen, Demaret was working as an assistant pro to Jack Burke Sr. at the exclusive River Oaks Country Club in Houston. Occasionally he would babysit the young Jackie Burke, who was three when Demaret started at River Oaks, but he spent most of his time sanding wooden shafts, building clubs, and then polishing clubheads when they rusted. The labor strengthened Demaret's large hands and inflated his forearms, giving him a blacksmith's power.

A few years later he became a pro at the municipal course in Galveston, hard by the Gulf of Mexico, where an ever-present wind punished shots that weren't spanked underneath it. Demaret honed a left-to-right game that would become the envy of his peers. Owing to his four-year apprenticeship on the shore, most of Demaret's shots were low, solid darts with a slight fade—no one, it is widely thought, has ever been better in a breeze. If his wind cheaters needed to bounce or check quickly, he could make it happen.

"He had a simple move," says Burke. "He knew where the face of the club was at all times. The club broke [cocked] the same way every time. He didn't really have to practice." The taciturn Hogan loved being around the loquacious Demaret but may have gotten his greatest pleasure from watching Demaret strike shots when they teamed in the Inverness Four-Ball in Toledo, Ohio. Hogan noticed how well Demaret's bread-and-butter fade stayed in play and made the style his own, scaling the heights once he did so. "Ben copied Jimmy's game," Burke says bluntly. "Jimmy was a left-to-right player, and Hogan didn't carve a career for himself until he started moving the ball left to right."

Demaret, stocky at five feet ten and about 200 pounds, had the build of an offensive guard from the days when boys got strong working on the farm. "Nobody was stronger than Demaret," Burke says. But his sturdy buttocks, thighs, and calves carried him along lightly. As historian Al Barkow described in *Golf's Golden Grind*, Demaret "had technique and mannerisms that were the stuff of pantomime. He walked with a short, quick, rhythmic step, like someone treading over a fairway of unbroken eggs, his buttocks shimmying from side to side."

A majorette would have been proud of the way Demaret twirled the club as he approached his ball. Even as he settled into his

More Than a Score

narrow stance, everything was in motion, fluid movements of someone who knew how to keep a beat. To keep his golf muscles supple, Demaret often swung a weighted club. His balance was extraordinary. A foursome of golfers at Champions once found out just how good it was one day in the early 1960s. Crowing to Demaret about how well they had played, the men presently found themselves back out on the course in a match against him, four against one. There was a twist: for the first four holes, Demaret played every shot standing only on his left leg; he played the next four holes standing on his right leg. When they reached the ninth tee, Demaret was even par and the men were hundreds of dollars down. At that point Demaret's mercy matched the fun he was having. He gave them enough shots and presses on the last hole so their wallets didn't blow away.

Another time, when Demaret was in his early fifties, he got to the eighth hole of the Cypress Creek course at Champions in a friendly match with some members. The hole was playing about 140 yards, all carry over a lake. "I hit an eight-iron to about ten feet," recalls Joe Scardino, "then Jimmy hits a seven-iron inside of that. Another fellow in the group—people at Champions will know who he is—said, 'Gee, Jimmy, you won the Masters three times and you had to hit more club than Joe.'"

Now Demaret could run to daylight better than Gale Sayers, and he saw his opening. He took the putter out of his bag, and a bet was made that he could hit the green with the thirteen remaining clubs, $100 riding on each shot. Demaret went to work—hooding a sand wedge, feathering a three-iron, bunting a driver—and was successful every time. "Unbelievable," says Scardino. "It was the most amazing thing."

Like Walter Hagen before him, Demaret cultivated the image that grew out of the laughs and the late nights. "Jimmy let people think he partied all the time," Al Besselink, who shared some of those evenings with him, once observed. In a 1956 interview Demaret addressed his lifestyle. "You can't drink—that is all the time, be an alcoholic—and do anything," he said. "Certainly not golf. I'm a social drinker. I love people. Now, I'll be honest with you. I've overindulged some of the time. And stayed up too late. Probably cost me a few tournaments. I'm sure it has. But I'm not quite the rounder some people may think I am." From his seat, Demaret didn't believe he was in the 100-proof league of comedian Phil Harris, of whom he once said, "Phil Harris can drink more than Dean Martin with one lip tied behind his back."

When Demaret joined Snead to partner with him one year in the World Cup, Snead was worried that his nocturnal pace would affect their results. "That Jimmy, he wanted to go here, there, everywhere," Snead says. "He'd knock on your door at Augusta at 2 a.m. and say, 'Let's go have one.' But that World Cup, I told him I wanted him in bed by 10:30 every night. I didn't care if he was sleeping, as long as he was in his room. By God, he went to bed, played level par and we won by a bunch."

Burke, who spent more time around Demaret than anyone, says, "He never was stumbling around. He probably had a little too much every day, but it never did impair him." The truth was Demaret craved the company around him more than the drink in his hand. "He'd talk about going away somewhere where there was no phone or television," his daughter says. "He might go for two days, then he was ready to shoot himself—he had to come back to civilization."

There is the question of how much better a golf record Demaret might have achieved had he worked harder and socialized less, but there is no consensus. Snead says, "I think he would have won more had he tended to business, but that's just the way he was."

"I think he would have done things the same way," says his daughter.

"His career meant nothing to him," says Burke. "He enjoyed the people in it—the other things were a little bit boring to him." Demaret was an easy touch for anyone who needed a few dollars. "The dollar didn't really mean a lot to Jimmy," says Burke. "He was extremely generous. He was quick to the draw at a beer joint, would pick up everybody's bar tab. The only time Jimmy balked is when he and I had to buy a piece of equipment for the club or something. When you started talking about $10,000 for the tractor, he'd stutter a little bit."

Because he was so generous, when he died those who didn't know him well wondered about his financial health, but they need not have been concerned. He was a "secret saver," according to one friend, who steered clear of risky ventures. One of Burke's children, Mike, became Demaret's financial advisor in the late 1970s. He was fresh out of the University of Houston at a brokerage in Austin, where he was supposed to be selling tax-free municipal bonds but for the moment was making coffee and washing the cars of his superiors. One day Demaret called. "I told him I was making coffee," says Burke, "and he said, 'As soon as you figure out what you're selling, I'll take $100,000 worth.'"

In the aftermath of Demaret's substantial order, Burke's coffee-making and car-washing days came to a quick end. Demaret continued to do business with him, always insistent that his young friend do first-rate research first. One Christmas, Burke gave Demaret a small pair of scissors so he could clip his coupons. "Ahh, I like to just bite 'em off," Demaret said. By the time Demaret died, purses were going up and laughs were going away. Looking back on his career shortly before his death, Demaret wrote, "There was a lot more camaraderie then. We had more fun. The new players are shooting for so much money their eyes are pinched in like BBs. The numbers are eating them up."

Demaret paid attention to a different kind of number. At Champions they still play fivesomes regularly. It is an ode of sorts to Demaret, who liked the bigger group. The extra man afforded more games and more bets but, most important for the sunniest of golfers, more laughs.

March 31, 2000

No doubt Jimmy Demaret would be pleased at all the color that has popped into golf fashion the past few years—players like Ian Poulter, Rickie Fowler, and others dressing brightly in a new century. These young fashion plates have a long way to go, though, to catch up with the substance that accompanied Demaret's style—and all the fun Jimmy had along his journey.

CHAPTER TWENTY-TWO

A Fleck of History

It starts with the name. Jack Fleck. It is both sharp like his features and blunt like his personality. Jack Fleck. It comes off the tongue like a hard jab. If you're going to deprive a golf legend, as Fleck did to Ben Hogan in the 1955 U.S. Open—even if you do it fair and square with superior golf—something with a little more lilt or a few more syllables couldn't hurt.

Jack Fleck. He beat Hogan, but he couldn't control a couple of consonants.

Jack Fleck. It conjures up *fluke,* which his victory wasn't, and *underdog,* which he decidedly was. Through a combination of circumstance, perception, and in many ways his own volition, Fleck is the most enigmatic champion in a century of U.S. Opens. The title has been both claim and curse to him as to no other champion. Other long shots such as Sam Parks Jr. and Orville Moody have won the national title, but none combined an out-of-the-blue effort that also happened to topple a legend, as Fleck did.

"It didn't do Jack any good to beat Hogan because the whole world wanted Hogan to win his fifth Open," says Tommy Bolt, the 1958 U.S. Open champion. "And it made him a villain."

For the people who never forgave him or appreciated the magnitude of his upset or understood him when he wore the crown clumsily, here's where Jack Fleck is forty years after beating Hogan. He is at the wheel of a golf cart giving a tour of heaven—Lil' Bit A Heaven, that is, the golf course he built on a former cow pasture near Magazine, Arkansas, fifty miles southeast of Fort Smith. The layout, which plays around a practice range at which Fleck occasionally teaches, features double greens, multiple tees, and shared fairways. Golf Design of the Future, Fleck calls it.

Better still, call it ironic: the man who authored the most Olympian of upsets in golf history—a playoff victory over Hogan, at the Olympic Club, yet—hangs his hat at a truncated little course in the Arkansas woods. Fleck hoped his idea would take off. He thought land-starved Japan would love it. He believed there would be plenty of takers. So far, though, Fleck's vision of the future of golf course architecture begins and ends with this single, modest course in the shadow of the Ozark National Forest.

"We've got an area where we could put a lodge there," Fleck says, "or we could put some villas along the side. But that's all dream world."

Reality finds Fleck a few minutes later at the far end of the course pointing out a number of stumps and other trees whose trunks are wrapped with chicken wire. In a nearby creek just off Fleck's property, an enormous pile of logs and sticks clogs the flow of water. Beavers.

"It's unbelievable what those things can do," Fleck says. "Just unbelievable." But Fleck has taken out the beavers the way he took out Hogan. They won't be having any more tree times at Lil' Bit A Heaven.

A winner. A loser. Sometimes they give you the trophy and punch you at the same time, only you don't feel the pain until later.

Jack Fleck was born on November 8, 1921, in Bettendorf, Iowa. It was perfect timing, insofar as he was just learning what was what when the Great Depression hit. Years earlier Fleck's father, Louis, operated some touring cars in New York City. Yellow Cab bought him out. Then he worked as a photographer and became a truck farmer when he moved to Iowa. During the Depression, Louis Fleck, like everyone else in those days, did what he had to do to help his family survive.

"My dad had all kinds of jobs," Jack Fleck says. "And we had to go out and top onions, carry papers, shovel snow—anything we could to help out. It was rough, but you learn something in those times."

Fleck wasn't a poor student, but he was shy. When the time came for him to read aloud or voice his opinions, he fairly trembled. "I dreaded getting up in front of people and giving a book report," he says. "Scared to death. I would build guillotines, or whatever illustrated the stories we were studying so I could get credit and not have to get up in front of people."

Louis Fleck thought his son should find a factory job after he graduated from high school, but Jack had other ideas. When the Western Open came to Davenport Country Club in 1936, Fleck was a forecaddie. Before long he was caddieing there and using borrowed clubs from the members on Mondays. He got in the championship flight of the caddie tournament. Fleck liked this golf.

Fleck turned pro in June 1939, the day after his high school graduation. As a young assistant pro working for $5 a week, he had to steel his nerves just to leave the bag room and go into the shop to sell something. "I was afraid to come in," Fleck says. "I was so bashful. But I had to talk to myself—if I was going to be a golf pro, I would have to do it."

In 1940, with Iowa in the grip of winter, Fleck made some bus money shoveling snow off a bridge over the Mississippi River. He headed south, to San Antonio, to see what this winter tour was all about.

"I got down there and it was 89 degrees," Fleck says. "I said to myself, 'Why does anybody live in that cold country?'"

Although spectating there gave Fleck a taste of the tour that he liked, World War II delayed his plans. He was in the navy for almost four years, serving on a rocket ship that supplied supporting firepower for troops landing on Utah Beach on D-Day. Later he was in Hawaii about to go with his ship across the Pacific when news of the Japanese surrender was announced.

Back home it seemed to Fleck that the drinking and the card playing were going on too long. He didn't want to waste his freedom or his hard-earned navy pay. Early in 1946 he took a bus to San Diego. This time he entered a tour event. "I played the best I knew," Fleck said. "I shot a 93."

Throughout the late 1940s, even after he got a job as the pro at the two municipal courses—Duck Creek and Credit Island—in Davenport, Iowa, Fleck made occasional forays to Texas, Arizona, and California to try his luck on the circuit.

Although the rewards weren't great, neither was the cost. "I could take $200 and be gone for two or three months," Fleck says, marveling at the feat. He is still a man who cringes if a night on the road costs him more than $45. "We'd go to California and rent rooms in fine houses for $6 a week. And we could go to a cafeteria or a chuck wagon and load up a tray full of food for 69 cents."

All the while, Fleck's entwinement with Hogan was beginning. It started when Fleck perused the agate scores of golf tournaments in the Iowa papers, then copied the scores in a small notebook. "I'd record those eight or ten places, whatever the paper ran. Pretty soon, the name Ben Hogan comes up. Pretty soon after that, he wins three consecutive tournaments in the Carolinas."

When Fleck joined the winter tour in those days, he made an effort to watch Hogan, whose serious mien, dark hair, and thin build were similar to Fleck's—except the Iowan was much taller at six feet one inch and had a long, loose-jointed stride. "He never knew I was watching him," Fleck says. "He never knew me from a bale of hay."

Among the characteristics Fleck observed was Hogan's tendency to memorize club selection and how holes were best attacked. Knowing he was the kind of guy who remembered things best when he wrote them down, and because he didn't enjoy the best depth perception, Fleck decided to pace off the distances he hit each of his clubs. He then combined this knowledge with detailed yardages of courses by pacing off from landmarks to the front-third and rear-third of greens.

Although Jack Nicklaus is widely credited as the first big-name golfer to play by yardage—he learned the trick from an amateur named Gene Andrews—Fleck said he was playing by yardages as early as 1947. "I paced yardages when Nicklaus was still in diapers," Fleck says. "And after I won the Open, everybody started doing it."

But despite Fleck's meticulousness, he fought a bad temper and wasn't a wonderful putter because he opened the blade on the backswing and imparted sidespin on his putts. While his winter trips to points south and west were a heck of a lot more fun than shoveling snow in Iowa, they were neither lucrative nor particularly encouraging.

The closest Fleck got to a headline was on February 2, 1949. As he drove along a Texas highway from El Paso toward Van Horn, an ambulance escorted by a pair of motorcycles roared past his car. "The next morning," he recalled years later, "I'm having breakfast and I see a paper: 'Hogan Near Death in Bus Accident.'"

While Hogan bravely returned to golf after his devastating injuries, Fleck stayed in Iowa and ran the two courses—he wasn't a "driving range" pro, as some stories later described him—and ventured on tour part time. When Hogan won the 1950 U.S. Open at Merion, Fleck missed the cut. When Hogan prevailed at Oakmont in 1953 for his fourth Open title, Fleck tied for fifty-second. The 1955 U.S. Open would be Fleck's third appearance in the national championship.

Many expected the time was right for Hogan to claim his historic fifth Open title, and he even hinted that a victory might cap his great career. "I doubt if I ever will play in an important tournament again if I should be lucky enough to win here," Hogan said early in the week at the Olympic Club. "Oh, I may play somewhere for fun, but that would be it."

Fleck, with some help from a South Carolina pro named Melvin Hemphill, was quietly improving his play during the early 1950s. Hemphill worked with Fleck on his confidence and his tempo. Fleck also got longer off the tee. Like Hogan, he moved his shots slightly left to right. "But I hit a slider," Fleck says. "I could hit it a country mile when the ground was hard. I never crossed over until well past the ball."

Encouraged by his wife, Lynn, who helped him at Duck Creek and Credit Island, Fleck finally went out to play the tour full time in 1955. He was thirty-three, and his dream could not be deferred any longer. In those days you didn't have to go to qualifying school to join the tour; you just needed a good car. The pros had a phrase for those long drives between tour stops: "It'll take two days to get the wheel out of your hands."

"Try it for two years," Lynn Fleck told her husband. "I'll run the shops while you're gone. If you don't succeed, at least you'll have it out of your system."

In the first event of the year, Fleck tied for fifteenth at Los Angeles and won $386.25. He seemed destined to be a middle-of-the-pack kind of golfer. He finished twenty-sixth, twelfth, sixteenth, tenth, seventeenth, forty-fourth, twenty-fifth, twenty-second, twenty-fourth, seventeenth, and eighteenth, and, in his last appearance before the Open at Olympic's Lakeside Course, he tied for eighteenth in Fort Wayne, Indiana. It was worth $230, which boosted his 1955 earnings to $3,149.38. He did, however, have some new clubs in his bag—clubs made by Hogan's new equipment company.

Fleck had seen the Ben Hogan Precision model in mid-March in St. Petersburg. He opened a new set that had been shipped to

Tommy Bolt, but Bolt had switched to another manufacturer and was not using the Hogan brand anymore. Fleck liked the look and told skeptical friends he was going to write Hogan and ask for a set for himself. Presently Fleck heard from a Hogan Company general manager asking for Fleck's club specifications. When Fleck got an invitation into The Colonial in Hogan's backyard as a promising young player, he got the chance to visit the plant to pick up his clubs. By the weekend he had the set of Hogan irons. He got the woods two weeks later in Kansas City. Hogan himself brought Fleck's new pitching wedge and sand wedge out to San Francisco. In fact the only non-Hogan clubs in Fleck's bag at Olympic were a Tommy Armour driver and a Bulls-Eye putter.

Fleck and Hogan prepared very differently for the championship. Hogan spent much of his time on the Ocean Course, Olympic's other eighteen, practicing with Claude Harmon the kinds of shots he knew he would need at Lakeside. Fleck, upon his arrival the Sunday prior to the Open after a two-and-a-half-day drive from Iowa in his blue Buick sedan, played as much as he could—up to forty-four holes a day, the number resulting from two full rounds and then another partial round ending at the par-three eighth hole near the clubhouse.

Partly in response to Hogan's assault on par in 1948 at Riviera in Los Angeles, the only other time that the United States Golf Association had held the U.S. Open out west, architect Robert Trent Jones was hired to toughen the course. The layout was lengthened to 6,700 yards, and two holes, the seventh and fourteenth, were noticeably altered. Most important, the Italian rye rough was allowed to grow as tall as a two-year-old in places. The prevailing damp conditions made recovery even tougher; it was like striking a shot out of a deep bed of day-old linguini. The fairways were narrow, even by U.S. Open standards, and the greens small.

In practice Fleck paid close attention to getting all his yardages, but he wasn't playing well. With the exception of an Olympic member and tournament marshal, George Tompkins, who Fleck noticed watching him as he soaked his pant legs in the wet grass, he prepared in anonymity. Mike Krak, a fellow pro who sometimes shared the road with Fleck, recalled a Wednesday round.

"Walker Inman and I played [Fleck] and Al Mengert and beat 'em to death before the tournament," Krak says. "We were really shocked to see how well he played. But he was that type of individual. The way he hit the ball you could never tell how he was going to score because he was a real grinder."

With a three-under-par 67 on Thursday, Bolt led Inman by three strokes. Hogan was at 72. Fleck shot 76, but the trying conditions left him in twenty-second place. Sam Snead opened with a 79, which was a trifle below the first-round scoring average of 79.8. Fleck rebounded with a 69 on Friday for a 145 total after thirty-six holes. He was in a tie for second with Hogan, Inman, and Julius Boros, just one shot behind Bolt and amateur Harvie Ward.

Fleck is at a loss to explain exactly what happened, but on the fifth green on Friday, something changed with his putting. "I had some kind of a wonderful feeling in my hands over the ball," he says. "I didn't change my grip or stance—it was just a feeling in my hands. I don't think I three-putted a green from then on."

Even though he was now in the whirlwind of Open contention, Fleck had no trouble getting a good night's sleep at his motel room in Daly City. He would grab an early meal and return to his room to listen to some inspirational music on his record player. "He was one of the more straight-shooters when I traveled with him," Krak says. "He didn't smoke, didn't drink, didn't carouse, didn't chase women. So he wasn't the most popular guy with the writers."

Fleck appeared to shoot himself out of contention with a 75 in the third round Saturday morning. Hogan, with a 72, stood at 217, one better than Boros and Snead. Bolt and Bob Rosburg were at 219, with Fleck, Ward, and Jack Burke at 220. As the fourth round unfolded later that gray day, it appeared that Fleck, who teed off with Gene Littler at 3 p.m., an hour after Hogan, would arrive at

More Than a Score

the natural amphitheater of the eighteenth hole as merely an anti-climactic afterthought to Hogan's fifth championship.

A national television audience watching NBC's broadcast sure thought that Hogan, finished at seven-over-par 287 after a closing 70, had victory in hand. Gene Sarazen, missing from the U.S. Open field for the first time since 1920, was commentating for NBC. Sarazen congratulated Hogan on the air, and the broadcast ended well before Fleck finished his round.

Hogan himself had even given Joe Dey, executive director of the USGA, his golf ball beside the eighteenth green, telling Dey it was for Golf House, the USGA's museum. A bit later Dey proudly showed off the memento in the press room. In the locker room, Hogan had a shower and was having a scotch among supporters and reporters. He reiterated his pre- tournament pledge to retire from serious golf if he won. He began to hand out souvenirs. He gave away his white cap, some of his shag balls, and two full books of food and drink tickets.

As Fleck played his final nine holes, he was in position to make the actions of Sarazen, Dey, and Hogan seem very premature. After an outgoing 33, Fleck trailed by only two. A goodly number of spectators filtered out through the eucalyptus, pine, and cypress trees that filled the Lakeside Course and found spots behind the gallery ropes with Fleck. (It was just the second year such crowd control had been used in the Open.) There were few leader boards out on the course, but as he completed the thirteenth hole, Fleck's acquaintance, George Tompkins, the roving marshal, told him he needed a birdie to tie.

But Fleck hit a poor second shot on the difficult fourteenth hole and made a bogey. About the same time, Hogan said, "Hey, what's this guy Fleck doing?" Hogan was told his foe needed two birdies on the last four holes to tie. There was no question that Fleck knew where he stood.

"I was up in the clubhouse," says Bob Rosburg, who would finish in a fifth-place tie. "I had been a member there when I was a kid, so when I finished kind of early I went up and had a couple of beers with some friends. I almost left when Hogan finished, but I said, 'Nah, it looks like Fleck's still got a chance.' I was way up high, but I could see everything."

On the 144-yard fifteenth hole, Fleck played a six-iron shot just eight feet from the hole. He drained the putt. One back. Pars on the next two holes set the stage: Fleck needed that rarest of accomplishments: a birdie on the last hole to tie. He used his Ben Hogan three-wood to place his tee shot on the 337-yard hole just off the left edge of the fairway. Then, from a great lie in the light rough, Fleck hit a soft shot with his Ben Hogan seven-iron just over a pot bunker and only seven feet from the hole. With no deviation from his usual routine, he made the putt to shoot 67 and tie Hogan at 287, and the six thousand assembled fans cheered wildly.

"It was just deafening," remembers Stan Wood, a reporter for the *Los Angeles Mirror* who was in the clubhouse with Hogan. "The building practically shook. Hogan told his caddie to put his clubs back in the locker. That had to be the saddest day of his life, I guess."

Plenty of telegrams were sent to San Francisco that night from Iowans. Sarazen got them for prematurely crowning Hogan, while Fleck received messages and good luck. Hogan had primed himself for seventy-two holes and now had to summon the strength for another round.

The next morning, Fleck and Hogan spoke briefly as they put on their golf shoes. Fleck told Hogan about passing him in the ambulance in 1949 and how, like the rest of the country, he had pulled for Hogan's recovery. "You'll know what I mean out there," Fleck said to his idol, "so good luck and play well."

Early in the playoff, at the third hole, Hogan gave a hint that it might not be his day when he missed a four-foot birdie putt. He holed a long putt on the eighth, but Fleck countered from close range. Fleck shot another 33 on the front nine to Hogan's 35.

Despite a bogey on the demanding seventeenth hole, Fleck held a one-shot lead on the eighteenth tee.

Hitting first, Hogan's right foot slipped on the newly top-dressed back tee and his shot was pulled way to the left, into some of the tallest of the Italian rye. He needed three whacks just to move his ball back in the fairway and eventually holed a thirty-foot putt for a double bogey. Fleck reached the green safely and two-putted. Hogan, face pursed and arms folded, stood at the back of the green just out of Fleck's line of sight. Later Hogan playfully waved at Fleck's putter as if to cool it off.

Fleck 69, Hogan 72.

"People say Hogan was tired and all that," Rosburg says. "Well, what the hell? That's all bull. Jack played great and he deserved to win. It was unbelievable. Not only was it such a great last round, but to hang in there in the playoff head-to-head with Hogan was unbelievable."

Fleck's victory drew initial cheers, including a meeting with President Dwight Eisenhower, who was in San Francisco at a meeting of the United Nations, but his personality didn't encourage warm responses. He was essentially the same shy boy from Iowa who didn't like to stand up in class.

"I was thrust into something new, something foreign," Fleck says. "I got named Golf Professional of the Year by the *Los Angeles Times* and I had to get up there with Bob Richards, the pole vaulter, and speak. I died a thousand deaths that night."

Fleck didn't like making small talk or taking late dinners either. A religious man of intense routine, he was unsettled by the changes. He was hard on himself after poor rounds and could be curt to fans and reporters alike. He complained a lot.

"Fleck wasn't the easiest guy to be around," says Wood. "He was a very quiet guy, and he didn't get too much publicity—none of which was exceptionally pleasing to him anyway. He didn't go out of his way to make friends."

"I don't think he was rude," Rosburg says. "He was just a loner. You hardly ever saw him. I don't think anybody disliked Jack Fleck, it was just very hard to get close to him."

When Fleck's game suffered, so did he. "When Jack teed it up, it was work," observes Mike Krak. "So many guys seemed to really love the game and played it more for fun than Jack seemed to get out of it. I'm not saying he didn't enjoy it, but he was just so hard on himself. He was his own worst enemy."

Fleck won two more tour events, both in playoffs—he beat Bill Collins in Phoenix in 1960 and Rosburg at Bakersfield in 1961. He also figured in the 1960 U.S. Open at Cherry Hills, which was won by Palmer and remembered for the close calls by Hogan and a young Nicklaus. But Fleck himself birdied five of the first six holes during the final round, and if not for missing three short putts on the closing holes, it might well have been Fleck's second Open victory instead of Palmer's first.

Although others contend his putting wasn't as bad as Fleck says it was, he believes it kept him from following up his 1955 victory with more success. As evidence, he cites a stretch of four events in the Midwest in the late 1950s during which he says he hit every green in regulation for sixteen straight rounds—288 holes—but didn't come close to winning.

This much is certain: by 1963 Fleck all but left tournament golf. He had to qualify for the 1966 U.S. Open, which returned to Olympic. Hogan was given a special exemption, the first ever awarded by the USGA. Fleck gave a desultory performance, but on Thursday he had another encounter with Hogan in the locker room. "We were this close," Fleck says, gesturing a foot apart. "And he wanted to say something, but he couldn't. He just said, 'Good luck.' I have no way of knowing, but I think he wanted to know what I had meant when, eleven years ago I said, 'You'll know what I mean.'"

Over the next two decades Fleck held numerous club pro jobs in California, Illinois, and Wisconsin. None seemed to be a perfect fit for long. "I'd do real well, but then it would always be, 'You're making too much money,' from the board of directors."

Even his effort to design a little course for President Nixon at the western White House in San Clemente, California, in the early 1970s was dogged by bad luck.

"The people out there wanted to do something for him," Fleck says. "They donated all the stuff and the labor and I designed five holes that started at his swimming pool and crisscrossed. It would have been just for him and a foursome. But it never got done. Watergate blew it up."

Fleck's wife died in 1975. In the aftermath of her death, Fleck started playing and practicing again. He won the PGA Seniors Championship in 1979 and played a full schedule on the Senior PGA Tour for a decade, until his career money total no longer kept him exempt.

"Jerry Barber called it the Rollover Tour," says Fleck, who now gets in only the odd event, mostly late in the season when the wealthy seniors are ready for a rest. "Guys who made millions on the regular tour roll in there and continue making millions and squeeze everybody out. And they're letting all the club pros and all the foreigners and all the amateurs turning pro go in there, and the guys who really played years ago and didn't make any money don't have a chance."

Fleck and his second wife, Mariann, tired of the smog and the threat of crime in California, moved to rural Arkansas in 1981. When he was forced off the senior tour after the 1991 season, he started construction on his Lil' Bit A Heaven course, naming it after an exhibition of worldly treasures and curios that the Palmer College of Chiropractic maintained in his native Davenport.

It has come at a hell of a cost. Two years ago heavy rains washed out the greens and Fleck's construction costs soared. A soil study revealed that just beneath the surface of his land lay solid hardpan. Fleck needed money, and he reached into his closet.

"Oh, you've heard about that," Fleck says when the sale of his 1955 U.S. Open championship medal comes up. "I had financial problems. You used the word *sad*. I don't. I guess I'm a very, very different individual. I don't look back. I live for today and look forward to tomorrow. I wish I could do a lot of things—play the tour, do something, build something, build golf courses. I never had a trophy room. I guess that junk over there gives you some memories of it. I don't know."

Fleck is sitting at one of the three banquet tables in the Lil' Bit A Heaven clubhouse. At the far end, past the jumbo mustard containers for the microwave sandwiches, a small collection of trophies and crystal rests on a bookshelf. The nearby walls feature two oversize checks he won on the senior tour and some photographs. One of the pictures, water-damaged on the right side, shows Fleck playing the seven-iron shot on the seventy-second hole at Olympic. His winning medal that isn't there sold for $35,200 at a Massachusetts auction of golf memorabilia two years ago. It sold for so much, according to collectors, not because it belonged to Jack Fleck but because of its tie to Hogan.

"If I could sell the clubs, I'd sell them," Fleck is saying now. "They're always for sale."

The clubs, golf's version of the slingshot, rest wrapped in old newspaper in a brown cardboard box in Fleck's basement. The Armour driver and Hogan fairway woods are black. The chrome is worn away in spots on the Hogan irons, whose forged heads look minuscule compared to today's models. The Bulls-Eye putter that served him so well is also well worn. All the grips are wrapped in burgundy leather, the handles of the woods covered only far enough down the shaft to permit a grip; Fleck liked to feel the weight of the heads. When he handles the history-making clubs now, he seems no more attached to them than some he has for sale in his small shop, except for the realization of the sum a collector might one day pay for them.

"They'll never be put in the mail," Fleck says. "If anybody wants to come here and look at them, fine. But you're not going to get these clubs real cheap."

More Than a Score

On a typical day at Lil' Bit A Heaven, Fleck, who is fit at seventy-three—right at his playing weight of 160 pounds—will collect a few $8.25 green fees, sell some used golf balls, mow the grass, and perhaps give a lesson or two for $60 an hour. (John Daly's mother was a recent student.) He is on a one-man crusade to encourage the local golfers to abandon the scramble format. "As a golf pro, you're supposed to help amateurs improve their games," he says. "How can you improve if you play a scramble? But that's all they do around here. I'm the lone wolf, trying to introduce them to other games."

Some of the customers know that Fleck did something big in golf many years ago, while others see him only as a stern proprietor with a lot of rules. "People live today—what's happening on television and all the things that are happening in the world," says the man whose terse name is rooted so strongly to a weekend four decades ago.

At the end of the day, Fleck will plug in his fleet of eight power carts to charge overnight, lock the fence to the parking lot, and join Mariann for one glass of wine and an early, healthy dinner. He wants to live a long time, as much, it seems, to outlast his critics as anything else.

When he goes into his bathroom and looks into the mirror, Hogan will stare back. An advertisement for Hogan equipment is taped to the glass. Hogan is pictured swinging, and the copy begins, "I always outworked everybody."

What does Jack Fleck mean?

June 9, 1995

In 2012, when the U.S. Open returned to the Olympic Club, two excellent books about Jack Fleck's 1955 U.S. Open victory were published: *The Upset: Jack Fleck's Incredible Victory over Ben Hogan at the U.S. Open* by Al Barkow and *The Longest Shot: Jack Fleck, Ben Hogan, and*

Pro Golf's Greatest Upset at the 1955 U.S. Open by Neil Sagebiel. Both accounts detail the underdog and how he outplayed an icon. Fleck, then ninety and looking good, was in San Francisco in June 2012 giving interviews, a bit of amazing golf history in the flesh. A couple of months earlier, at the Liberty Mutual Legends of Golf, a Champions Tour event in Savannah, Georgia, I had come upon Fleck playing a practice round. He had the swing of a man decades younger, piping a drive more than two hundred yards down a fairway. On his head was a flat white cap, the kind favored by Ben Hogan.

More Than a Score

CHAPTER TWENTY-THREE

The Gospel according to Joe Dey

It is not easy to make a name for yourself in golf if you do not win important tournaments, give lessons to those who do, design courses, or invent a ball or club that is supposed to take five strokes off someone's game. Golf administrators and rules people work in the shadows, usually noticed only when something goes wrong. A person doesn't embrace starting times, hole locations, and the nuances of loose impediments to become famous. He does it because he loves golf, doesn't mind getting up early and staying up late tending to the tedious, or, in the case of the late Joseph C. Dey Jr., because he is on a mission.

A man on a mission is not to be taken lightly, and Joe Dey never was. In his thirty-five years as executive director of the United States Golf Association and another five as the first commissioner of the modern PGA Tour, Dey didn't run golf so much as he preached it. And as he spread the gospel, he was a symbol, a steadying influence, a beacon, and a man who checked his watch a lot.

For decades, to many people, Dey was the face of golf. "He was a symbol of the game for a long, long time," says Deane Beman, who succeeded Dey as PGA Tour commissioner in 1974. "He was the conscience of the game. He was a protector of the game."

Dey loved his work and respected his sport. That was clear to the golfers who revered him for his evenhandedness even as they struggled on a golf course he had set up to perplex them, and it was clear to his employees who rued the day they did something to irritate him. Sometimes the sermon came in a whisper and sometimes in a shout, but regardless of the delivery, the message was the same.

"The integrity of golf is all of golf," Dey told *Golf Digest* in 1973. "If you don't have that, it's no game at all." Says Frank D. (Sandy) Tatum, a former USGA president, "He lived and played according to the rules, and he certainly had a way of transferring that to golfers."

An interesting question is how the game's recent climate, in which confusion over equipment regulations created a deep fissure—between the USGA and the Royal and Ancient, and between manufacturers and the USGA—would have been affected if Dey were on the job. "I don't think things would be like they are today," Beman says. "I don't believe he would have let it happen. There has been a lack of strong leadership, a lack of a strong sense of right and wrong."

"My guess is if Joe were around," says Tatum, "he'd be a very important factor in pulling the game back together." That's exactly what Dey did in 1969, during another tenuous time in the game, by diplomatically leading tournament pros after they split from the PGA of America.

But Dey's iron will was forged in his lengthy career at the USGA, where he had a broad-reaching impact. He was heavily involved in the 1951 unification of the Rules of Golf between the USGA and the R&A, a huge step in the cohesion of the game worldwide, and he worked hard to promote and simplify the rules. He helped start five USGA championships and four international team competitions. And he became synonymous with the U.S. Open, where he was an omnipotent figure, whether it was as a first-tee starter in the early years or accompanying the leaders as referee in subsequent championships. It was under Dey that par became the

Open standard, fairways were narrowed, and rough was allowed to grow. "He set the courses up with a mind to being difficult but fair," says four-time U.S. Women's Open champion Mickey Wright. "He truly thought par was a sacred goal, not to be easily achieved."

But it was at the men's Open, where Dey often worked with architect Robert Trent Jones to toughen the layouts, that his philosophy was most evident. "Joe was always afraid someone would shoot 60 in an Open and he'd have to jump off a building," Jim Murray once wrote. Although Dey's power was theoretically muted by the structure of the USGA, whose volunteer executive committee makes policy decisions, at the Open, Dey was in charge. "His was a commanding presence," says Tatum. "You were aware of Joe in any setting. The president of the USGA is the CEO, but Joe was very influential on the presidents."

"He was tough as hell, but he had to be," says Johnny Bulla, who played in eighteen U.S. Opens starting in 1936. "There were no shenanigans, no favoritism with Joe. He set the foundation for the USGA." And he changed the look of the Open. Following Trent Jones's suggestion, he instituted gallery ropes starting in 1954. In 1962 he put scoring standards with every group so fans could tell easily how players stood.

Born in Norfolk, Virginia, in 1907 and raised in New Orleans, he was the son of Joseph Charles and Martha Dey. His father was a center for the North Carolina State football team in the 1890s who worked in the grain business. Always fond of words, Dey was a spelling bee champion and a part-time sportswriter by the time he was a teenager. He attended the University of Pennsylvania but dropped out to pursue journalism. He wrote for several papers, including the *Philadelphia Evening Bulletin,* for which he covered Bobby Jones's U.S. Amateur victory at Merion in 1930 to complete the Grand Slam.

He took the job as USGA executive secretary (later upgraded to executive director) in 1934, soon after deciding not to go into the ministry. The game became the pulpit for this Presbyterian-turned-Episcopalian. "He was very well read, much more than you'll find in sports managers now," says Frank Hannigan, who went to work for Dey in 1961 as public information manager and became the USGA's executive director in the 1980s. "But it all pivoted on his Christianity. He thought he was doing good deeds through golf."

Dey didn't possess a memorable golf game himself. He was a fifteen-handicapper who didn't generate a lot of clubhead speed although he stood a sturdy six feet. When he found out the R&A had named him captain in 1975 (only the second American, after Francis Ouimet, to be so honored), he hit a lot of balls to prepare for the driving-in ceremony. He played in a regular group at The Creek Club in Locust Valley, New York, and wasn't keen on big bets. "A golf ball was all he would bet at first," says friend Al Seaman. "But we worked on him and worked on him through the years, and by the time we stopped playing, he'd play two, two and four, with a couple of special bets. I had one called 'The Titanic,' a press at the end. He liked that."

While Dey governed golf at its highest level, he was also active at his club. In the early 1960s Dey was enamored with the look fescue grass gave to courses. On his recommendation, The Creek Club planted fescue, with bad results. "He screwed up the course," laughs member Innis O'Rourke. "He thought it would be a great idea, but it turned brown overnight. It looked like Shredded Wheat." It was an ironic twist for a man known for toughening U.S. Open courses by growing tall rough, a man *Sports Illustrated* a few years later called "the man who makes the grass grow."

By 1968 Dey had been with the USGA for almost thirty-four years. He was sixty-one. Thanks in large measure to his talent and labor, his job had grown, and so had the association. While many people were shocked he would leave the USGA, the opportunity to stabilize the tenuous state of the pro game was a strong lure. "He was really, really needed," says Jim Colbert, who was active in the pros' move to independence from the PGA of America. "His reputation, his character, his integrity—he was just so straightforward and trustworthy. The only question was whether he would do it."

But love the USGA as he had, Dey had been doing the same thing for a long time. "He had worked at the same place forever," says Hannigan. "The chance to do something new was exciting. Nothing else was really going to happen at the USGA. He would have just played it out. Plus the pros were getting a lot of bad press, being accused for the first time of being greedy. Joe had a chance to do his healing thing."

"I wasn't even thinking of retirement," Dey told author Ross Goodner. "I was quite active, my job remained thoroughly interesting, and I was happy. But I was disturbed by what the split between the touring pros and the PGA was doing to golf. I thought long and hard before making a decision, but it seemed to me this was an opportunity to help stabilize a very important part of the game. So I took the job."

Dey had seen amateur golf wane in popularity, usurped by pros who were playing for more money and on television more often. "Joe recognized before a lot of people the professional end of golf had a growing importance," says Beman. "He had lived through the years when amateur golf was king, but as the U.S. Open grew in relation to other USGA events, he recognized where the sport was heading. I think he thought his stamp of approval could help and that he could influence the tour in the right ways."

It also mattered, of course, that Dey knew the stars of the pro game well through their participation in USGA events. Jack Nicklaus, for example, met Dey at the 1953 U.S. Junior in Tulsa, Oklahoma. First off one morning, he cut it very close arriving on the first tee. "I walked up about thirty seconds before my time," Nicklaus recalls, "and Joe Dey gave me a good lacing down. 'Young man, if you had been a little later, you'd be going down the second hole one down,' and so on. That was my introduction to Joe Dey. I was thirteen, and that made me remember him pretty well."

Nicklaus got to know Dey better through further amateur play. It was Dey, with his eye for a good story in the days when U.S. Open pairings weren't made by score, who placed Nicklaus with Ben Hogan for the dramatic final two rounds of the 1960 U.S. Open at Cherry Hills. "The executive committee would have had the final say, but that pairing had Joe all over it," Hannigan says. "He had a great sense of drama. He was a showman." The occasion turned out to be Hogan's last good chance for a fifth Open and Nicklaus's first threat at winning. By the seventy-second hole, with Hogan having shot himself out of it by finding the water on No. 17, Nicklaus thought he had done the same when he was short and right of the final green.

"As I waited to play my chip, Joe Dey was picking up cigarette butts and paper cups in my line," Nicklaus says. "I wondered why he was doing it, but if I chipped in, I could have still won the tournament. After the round, in the clubhouse, 'Mr. USGA,' 'Mr. Stuffy' came in and gave me the biggest hug you've ever seen. After my dad and Jack Grout, he was like my third father. He really cared about a lot of people. He just always wanted to do the right thing."

When Dey accepted the job as commissioner of the Tournament Players Division of the PGA in 1969, circumstance dictated he be a conciliatory figure. "The tour was in a transition stage," Beman says. "Not much could be done. The policy board was set up with factions. Peace in the game was the most important thing. Nobody knows what Joe would have done in a different environment. He never had the opportunity."

But Dey made the most of the circumstances. Beyond blunting the criticism of the players and bestowing them credibility, he nudged the tour in several directions, improving the quality of courses and bolstering television and sponsorship deals. The Players Championship, which has grown into a premier event, was his idea. He also brought back a match-play event and attempted to set up designated tournaments that would guarantee the presence of the best players. As much as Dey treated all players alike when it came to administering rules—"He wasn't a guy who came up and said, 'Whose ball is it?'" notes Nicklaus—he understood the entertainment quotient of pro sports. And when it came to golf, he had a vision that was ahead of its time.

"I think a world tour is a certainty," Dey said in the early 1970s, "particularly so if the players continue their posture of independence as they seem determined to do. With the growing purses, the players can pick their spots, play where and when they want."

A new role didn't mean a new personality. Although Dey had to yield to his players when they balked at playing a smaller, 1.66-inch ball that was going to be a compromise between the USGA and the R&A, effectively killing the proposal, he remained a strong leader. "He had a strong sense of right and wrong, good and bad, good and evil," says Beman, "and I believe those are positives."

Colbert saw the stern Dey when he called him to ask about a release to play for a handsome guarantee in a Japanese event opposite the Las Vegas PGA Tour stop. "He said he had to protect his sponsors," Colbert says, "and the answer was no. I was hot. We hung up, and fifteen minutes later the phone rings. I thought he was calling back because he had relented. No go. Instead he read me the rule and told me what would happen if I went to Japan—which was a fine and a big suspension. I ended up playing in Vegas."

Dey was a complex man, with as many layers as the game he guarded. To the golf press, whom he was always able to court effectively, he was a literate spokesman who knew the rules inside and out. To the players and others in golf who valued his principled stewardship, he was an unwavering captain. To his friends, he was the guy singing Broadway show tunes. To his employees—particularly during his long reign at the USGA—he could be one tough boss.

When Dey wanted to see what time it was, which was often, he had a distinctive way of lifting his left arm to view his watch. You didn't want to disappoint him when he looked at his watch. He was always on time and expected everyone else to be too, which created a little friction in the Dey household. "My mother [Rosalie] was unbelievably unpunctual," says Dey's only child, Edward. "She was oblivious to the time. She could be an hour late and nobody was surprised but my father."

At the USGA office in New York, Dey told the receptionist to note what time each employee arrived for work. "You had to be at your post, was the way Joe put it," says Hannigan. "It was very Dickensian."

From his desk—where neat piles of stuff surrounded the typewriter at which he composed his voluminous correspondence with a hunt-and-peck fury—Dey approved expense reports with the care of a military general plotting a major operation. He was known to place ruler to map to confirm that someone wasn't fudging on a mileage calculation. He wouldn't hand out the annual holiday bonus check (along with a tie from Dey's preferred clothier, Brooks Brothers) until Christmas Eve.

Dey could be particularly tough on support staff and vendors. "He would drive printers out of business," says Hannigan. "He told me to do a big record book one time. When it was finished, I get a bill. I send it to Joe and it comes back: 'Pay him half.'" This was the same man who surprised strangers with hospital visits and devotedly taught Sunday school for years.

"I think there was the public Joe Dey, and there was the Boss Joe Dey," says current USGA executive director David Fay. "Apparently he could be just holy hell on the staff. Not just being a stern taskmaster, but beyond that."

"Joe had a lot of sides to him," observes Dey's longtime friend Bill Campbell, the 1964 U.S. Amateur champion and former USGA president. Campbell met Dey for the first time at the 1938 U.S. Amateur, when he was fifteen. "He never asked more of other people than he asked of himself. He would never agree to being less than perfect at anything, though he knew everybody falls short."

No one wanted to be on the receiving end of Dey's temper. Given the right motivation, his lips would twitch and even turn blue in

More Than a Score

anger. "He could totally lose it," says Nancy Boatwright, widow of P. J. Boatwright Jr., who worked under Dey and succeeded him when he left the USGA in 1969. When The Creek Club planted small trees as 150-yard markers before it was common to do so, Dey returned from a trip and was irate when he saw them. "He hit the ceiling, and the trees came out," says Bill Curran, a club member and former golf partner of Dey's. "Arguing with him on a golf matter was like arguing with the good Lord about the Scriptures."

Late on the final day of the 1972 U.S. Open at Pebble Beach, a couple of Vietnam War protestors chained themselves together in the drive zone on the eighteenth hole. "Joe was nearby and saw it happen," says Tatum. "He started to head for them with his shooting stick in his hand, and he created the impression that he was going to hit them all in the head. Another official had to physically restrain Joe. The playing field of the U.S. Open was being desecrated—it was just more than he could take."

For those who shared Dey's cause, who appreciated his unwavering dedication to a sport, who called him a friend, his strengths outweighed his failings. By example, without pep talks, he had a rare gift of motivating people, bringing out their best. "The possibility of disappointing him would appear like a dark cloud coming at you over the horizon," Campbell says. "A lot of people had their lives vastly enhanced by contact with Joe."

That list includes legends and obscure golfers alike. "I respected him, admired him, and felt real affection for him," says Mickey Wright. "He was one of a kind. All of us who knew him still miss him." Martin Roesink, who played the PGA Tour in the 1970s, has kept a letter of recommendation Dey wrote for him when he was job hunting. Roesink had been paired with Rogelio Gonzalez when the Colombian golfer was accused of altering his scorecard at the 1972 New Orleans Open; Gonzalez was subsequently banned from the tour during Dey's tenure. In the letter, Dey noted that Roesink handled a difficult situation well. "He was a class guy," Roesink says.

At the 1969 USGA annual meeting, when hundreds said good-bye to Dey as he left for the tour job, USGA official Phil Strubing paid tribute by noting that he had a special knack for making people feel they were involved in the most important venture in the world. Hannigan knew the feeling well. "It was absolutely true," he says. "I thought I was working on a mission when I was working for the USGA. It came from Joe. I would shake my head when he would do things that were unfair to some people, or be hypocritical, but he had a dignity. He worked terribly hard, wasn't on the make financially, and was all about making the sport as good as it could be."

The job took its toll on Dey's family life. Between the ninety-minute commute to his job and all the travel to tournaments, Edward Dey, now sixty-four and living in Paris, didn't see much of his father growing up. "If he wasn't a workaholic, he was close," he says. "We didn't see him in the summers, and he worked a lot of Saturdays. But my father liked his work. If he had been asked to write his perfect job description, I think he'd come up with about 80 percent of what he got to do."

When cancer claimed Dey on March 4, 1991, at age eighty-three, golf lost something it couldn't replace. There have been some great U.S. Opens since, but the game hasn't been the same. "It just hasn't seemed as important since Joe's not around, since they're not wearing coats and ties," says golf writer and author Dan Jenkins.

The Open, to be held next week not far from Dey's old Long Island home, has become a huge production: televised with the breadth of a 1960s space launch and including a Macy's-size souvenir shop, corporate tents full of food and booze, a set-for-life winner's check, and scores of computers and people running them.

It is tempting, but probably not accurate, to think Dey wouldn't recognize the event he used to run, the occasion where he got a bit famous himself. The golf will be hard, the rules will prevail, and the winner will get good bounces and bad ones. If you look hard enough, between all the tents and all the people and all the tidy grass, you'll be able to see the integrity Joe Dey nurtured those many years.

June 7, 2002

In 1981, not long after graduating from the University of North Carolina, I interviewed for an entry-level job at the United States Golf Association in Far Hills, New Jersey. (I recall my roundtrip airfare from Raleigh-Durham to Newark on Piedmont Airlines was $59.) I didn't get that position, or into golf administration, but always wondered how life would have turned out if I had. Few individuals, inside or outside the ropes, have ever had a more commanding presence in golf than Joseph C. Dey Jr. Many of the game's administrators and rules officials, though, on all levels, put in very long hours doing what can be a thankless job.

CHAPTER TWENTY-FOUR

The Mouth That Roared

They don't make Bob Drums anymore, not that they ever made many. To meet him was to remember him. "One of a kind, without question," says longtime friend Doc Giffin, who knew Drum for more than forty years. "That phrase is used a lot, but he truly was one of a kind. Nothing held him back—sometimes things should have."

Drum typed for a living much of his seventy-eight years ("He lost about fifty of those little portables [typewriters] on airplanes," says his older son, Bob Jr. "He bought one of those a month."), but he lived to tell stories and crack jokes. "When I think of Drum, I think of laughter," says Dan Jenkins, who met Drum in the early 1950s when he was the golf writer for the *Fort Worth Press* and Drum was with the *Pittsburgh Press*. "We found everything funny."

Drum's voice—deep, inflected with his Long Island roots, and unaffected by going to college in Alabama—was as large as his hulking six-foot-four frame, and it carried as if there were a bullhorn at his lips instead of a vodka and tonic. "If he was there, you *knew* he was there," says Arnold Palmer.

By 1960, when Palmer was making golf march to his enthusiastically muscular beat, he'd known Drum a long time. "He was around before the beginning," says Palmer, a teen golfer in

1946 when he met Drum. The next year Drum reported on the seventeen-year-old Palmer's victory in a regional event. "Arnold Palmer," Drum wrote, "stood out in the West Penn Junior tourney like a neon sign in a blackout." Drum soon opined that Palmer "ought to be quite a boy when he grows up."

"Bob was the first to notice," says Giffin, Palmer's assistant but once Drum's colleague at the *Press*. "He was predicting big things for Arnold when a couple of the other golf writers in town didn't have that clairvoyance."

As Palmer began attracting more attention for his play, Drum was along for the ride—not always as a passive observer. "Do you know how many Arnold Palmer stories I wrote? Five thousand, quoting him in every one and half the time I couldn't find him," Drum told *Golf Digest* in 1987. "Palmer still thinks he said all those things."

Drum was building a legend of his own in Pittsburgh, clocking more time in taverns than at the newspaper. "He would come into the office about 10 a.m., check his mail, make a couple of phone calls, and he was gone," Giffin says. One time Drum's stepfather, Howard Morris, happened to be in the city on business and came into the *Press* hoping to find Bob.

"He asked the executive sports editor, Al Tederstrom, if Bob Drum was there," recalls ninety-four-year-old Roy McHugh, a veteran Pittsburgh reporter. "The sports editor was editing a piece of copy. He didn't even look up and said, 'Nope.' 'Do you know when he'll be in.' 'Nope.' 'Do you know where I can find him?' 'Nope.' Drum's stepfather said, 'I'm passing through and don't get to see him very often.' For the first time, Tederstrom looked up and said, 'Neither do we.'"

Drum hung out at the Travel Bar in the Pittsburgher Hotel downtown by day and Dante's in the suburbs at night, when he wasn't listening to jazz at a nearby joint, sometimes with Pittsburgh Steelers quarterback Bobby Layne and a coterie of other Steel City notables. Sometimes Drum would write stories on cocktail napkins and send them to the paper in a taxi—collect.

"Bob was much funnier in a bar or at the dinner table than he was in print," says Jenkins. Drum's counterpart among golf pros when it came to living the good life on someone else's dime was putting savant George Low, a sometimes traveling companion. Asked what it was like to share a hotel room with Low, Drum quipped, "Taking a shower with your wallet in one hand is too much trouble."

"Dad didn't like writing. Writing was hard," says Kevin Drum, the youngest of Bob and M.J.'s five children. "There's a solitary writing life, and then there's being around people. One's easier than the other. He could hold court, no matter how big the place was."

Appropriately enough, in 1960 Drum achieved a lasting impact on golf because of things he said rather than wrote.

After winning the 1960 Masters with a fantastic finish, Palmer spoke about wanting to win the U.S. Open and PGA Championship. He didn't mention it at Augusta, but because the British Open was going to be played at St. Andrews, he had that tournament on his schedule from the start of the year. Two days after Palmer won the Masters, Mercer Bailey of the Associated Press wrote that Palmer "has charted a course which could carry him to the biggest grand slam in golf since Bobby Jones' feat in 1930."

Without a figurative kick in the pants from Drum, Palmer might not have won his second straight major. "They were very close," M.J. says of Bob's relationship with Palmer, "and Bob ragged him to death." Eating hamburgers in the locker room with Drum, Jenkins, and a couple of players between the third and fourth rounds of the U.S. Open at Cherry Hills, Palmer, who trailed Mike Souchak by seven shots, wondered if a closing 65 would do him any good. Drum dismissed the prospect as only he could.

"It really pissed me off, to tell you the truth," Palmer says. "When I asked him what he thought 65 would do for me, he got kind of sassy, like an old friend would, particularly when another friend of his, Souchak, was leading me by seven shots. The more he talked, the madder I got."

Motivated to prove Drum wrong, Palmer drove the 346-yard, par-four first hole that had flummoxed him for three rounds and two-putted for an easy birdie. He birdied six of the first seven holes and shot 65 to emerge the winner.

"Drum came up with a real snappy lead, something like 'Arnold Palmer wrestled with Cherry Hills for three rounds and then strangled it,'" remembers Giffin, forced to tinker with the beginning of Drum's story after an editor decided it needed a few more facts if it was going to run on the paper's front page. Moreover on the biggest story Drum would ever write about Palmer, his byline was inadvertently left off.

DENVER, *June 18—Arnold Palmer, who had wrestled with the Cherry Hills golf course for three rounds, caught it in a stranglehold on the final 18 today and pulled off one of the most unbelievable victories in National Open history.*

Drum soon made an important point.

The sensational victory moved him over the second hurdle in his bid for present-day golf's Grand Slam.

The idea of some sort of "Grand Slam" to supplant Jones's singular sweep of the U.S. and British Opens and Amateurs in 1930 had percolated sporadically since 1949. By then the Masters was gaining popularity and prestige among players and the public, and after Sam Snead won at Augusta and took the PGA (then played in May), interest was building. Heading into the 1949 U.S. Open at Medinah—where Snead would lose a heartbreaker to Cary Middlecoff—Will Grimsley of the Associated Press wrote that a win would give Snead "a professional sweep comparable . . . with amateur Bobby Jones' grand slam of 1930."

By 1960 it was possible for a golfer to compete in all four pro majors, which hadn't been the case in 1953, when Ben Hogan won his "Triple Crown" (Masters, U.S. Open, British Open), because the PGA overlapped with the British. Palmer remembered Drum on their transatlantic flight to Europe after the U.S. Open (Drum recalled it as being on the Denver–New York leg) affirming his belief that he was striving for a new achievement, a "modern" Grand Slam.

Drum talked up Palmer's plan in Ireland, where Palmer was teaming with Snead in the Canada Cup en route to St. Andrews, and at the Open, where Palmer lost narrowly to Kel Nagle. Although Palmer couldn't attain the slam, it would forever be modern golf's holy grail.

Eager for new challenges, Drum left the *Press* in 1963. For two decades he did freelance stories and held several golf marketing and PR posts, including in Pinehurst, North Carolina, where he settled. "[Fellow writer] Charles Price once said that he would have gotten me a job, but he didn't know what kind of work I was out of," Drum told the *Toledo Blade* in 1987.

Drum remained a familiar presence through the years, a regular at the Golf Writers Association of America annual tournament in Myrtle Beach, where he would emcee the dinner with the aplomb of an acerbic comedian. "He was really funny and totally irreverent," says retired Charlotte sports columnist Ron Green Sr.

Once, upset with another writer at the GWAA event, Drum smashed a windshield with a golf club. "He quit drinking for long periods," says Kevin. "He grew up in the martini and highball era. That's just the way it was. I don't think he'd change a thing about his life."

Drum certainly wouldn't rewrite what happened to him when he was sixty-six. He had long been a part of the CBS Television golf entourage as a writer, thanks to the generosity of producer Frank Chirkinian. In the summer of 1984, encouraged by a young producer named David Winner, Drum took his curmudgeonly act to CBS's golf coverage with three-minute features called "The Drummer's Beat."

"Lemme tell you something," he said to the *Miami Herald* in 1985, "I've been doing what I'm doing for 20 years in bars across America. Now, I'm getting *paaaaaid* for it."

"It never really mattered what the piece was about," Winner says. "What people remembered was the Drummer." Drum was nominated for a Sports Emmy in 1987, losing to ABC's Dick Schaap. "I think it made his life, and I also saw how disappointed he was when it all kind of came to an end [in 1988]," Winner says. CBS didn't pinpoint why it ended Drum's segments, but among his friends there was speculation he had rubbed the right CBS executive the wrong way.

Drum's health declined in the 1990s, but he managed to make final journeys to the 1995 British Open and the 1996 Masters. He passed away on May 8, 1996, of heart failure. "He died so gently," M.J. told Pittsburgh writer Marino Parascenzo. "So easy, so gentle, and that made me grateful. God knows, he sure didn't live easy and gentle."

One morning during the 1997 Masters, Drum's two sons hustled down to Augusta National's thirteenth hole. "It was a caper," says Bob Jr. "We slipped out there and spread some of his ashes in the azaleas by the green. We said some prayers and we cried a little. Then we thought it would be great to have a beer. Dad would want us to have a beer. So we went to a concession stand and had a beer."

March 29, 2010

When reporting this story about Bob Drum, I spent a lively evening with his widow, M.J., and their children listening to recollections. Bob was larger than life to his family as well as to everybody else. Occasionally when I go back to Southern Pines, North Carolina, my hometown, I'll tee it up with Bob Jr. and Kevin Drum, usually at a cool, old Donald Ross course, Southern Pines Golf Club. Bob Jr. looks and sounds—a lot—like his father. It is always a fun time.

CHAPTER TWENTY-FIVE

The High Life and Hard Times of John Schlee

He starts out as only a name in agate type, a runner-up, gone and almost forgotten. Then you start poking around, talking to people. You speak to the daughter who met him for the first time when she was ten. You learn that he was in the army, that he liked to drive fast cars, that after he quit the tour with a bad back he loved to teach. You discover how he got his college golf team kicked off country clubs, how he went to sleep with his hands taped together in a perfect impact position, how he swung the club so hard graphite shafts would snap in his hands. You find a letter he wrote to a magazine one March day in 1967 on stationery from the Thunderbird Motor Hotel in Jacksonville, Florida.

> Dear Gentlemen,
>
> I would like to thank Golf Digest for electing me the 1966 rookie of the year. With your help thousands of people across the country know that I am trying hard as I can to be a great golf [*sic*].
>
> One step down. One thousand to go.
>
> Sincerly [*sic*] yours,
> John Schlee

Behind the name in the golf scores and the bios in old tour guides, you find contradictions everywhere. He was tutored by

Ben Hogan but hooked on astrology. The biggest week of his golf life he credited to the stars, not supination, because "Mars is in conjunction with my natal moon." John Schlee was strong, funny, and hardworking, but he also could be rude, selfish, and eccentric. He stiff-armed his way through life but in the end got tackled harder than anyone deserves.

When he died of complications from Alzheimer's disease three years ago on his sixty-first birthday, frail and poor and alone in a California hospital while his former peers were playing for thousands of dollars in a senior tour event in Nashville, it was as if a tissue had hit the floor. Few people remembered that only Johnny Miller's final-round 63 had kept Schlee from winning the 1973 U.S. Open at Oakmont Country Club near Pittsburgh, that he won a PGA Tour event, the 1973 Hawaiian Open, or that he might have craved golf as much as anyone who ever played the game for a living.

"I knew him for a long time," says Ben F. Hill, a teammate of Schlee's at Memphis State. "He was probably the most self-centered, goal-directed person I've known in any walk of life. He was a total loner. I was as close to him as anybody, and you couldn't get that close. Nothing else mattered but being the best golfer in the world."

You're curious about Schlee because you know that 280, Schlee's seventy-two-hole total thirty years ago, would have been good enough to win sixty-nine U.S. Opens and to make a playoff in six others. "He had a big heart and was a good guy," says tour contemporary J. C. Snead. "Several guys, if things had gone their way at [a big tournament], they'd probably had a whole different career. But things happen. Some people are just not lucky."

Miller is up in a television tower for NBC, calling shots as well as he used to hit them. It'll come up next week, Miller's miraculous 63, still the lowest final round in U.S. Open history, a mark that has held up through titanium and Tiger Woods and sport psychologists convincing golfers to think big. Schlee will be a footnote, an interloper with his shirttail out who was keeping local favorite Arnold Palmer company that fateful Sunday. People will wonder how Schlee, a curly-haired, buffed-without–weight training six foot three, nuzzled so close to history in the first place, when in fact he'd been planning on it for a very long time.

About a dozen years earlier, Schlee and John Pepin, teammates at Memphis State, had been out on a quiet evening at an empty golf course trying to cram in as many holes as they could before dark. They were on the eleventh tee at the old Colonial Country Club in Memphis, nothing around except the birds and the wind, when all of a sudden Schlee asked Pepin if he felt what he did.

"Can't you hear?" Schlee asked him. "The crowd is lined up for the National Open. Can't you see the ropes? Can't you see 'em?"

He was known as Jack Schlee growing up in Seaside, Oregon, a sleepy tourist town that woke up during spring break and long holiday weekends. Schlee's mother, Mary, and stepfather, Carl, who everybody called "Lucky," ran a motel a few blocks from the Pacific Ocean that usually was too cold to swim in. His mother tended to most of the motel duties because Carl was stationed at the naval base in nearby Astoria. Jack is remembered as a lively kid, capable of mischief.

"I don't know how many people he alienated in his life in one way or another," says Dr. Jim Cartwright, a dentist who grew up with Schlee and whose family owned the golf course where Schlee played. "He seemed to step on his tongue every time he stuck it out. He was pretty aggressive, and he got in trouble with his aggressiveness."

According to the Seaside Police Department, Schlee committed a couple of offenses as a teenager, including disorderly conduct and noise disturbance. Cartwright says Schlee also stole some golf balls and was offered a choice. "He was between a rock and a hard place," says Cartwright. "He happened to have taken some golf balls from my father's place. The police found out. He was dating the daughter of the chief of police. The chief really disliked John. They reached an agreement, and he entered the army."

Schlee, who joined the army in 1957 and served for two years, acknowledged his troubles years later. "I was a pretty bad actor as a kid," he said in 1981, "and I think if I hadn't started playing golf, I would have been in a lot of trouble later on."

He went from the service to Memphis State, making a mark with his blunt and driven personality. "We had five country clubs at our disposal, and at one time or another I got us kicked off all of them," he said. "I was there to play golf, not socialize." When Schlee scrounged up some extra cash, he'd spend the money on alpaca sweaters so he could dress like a tour pro.

Schlee got club pro jobs after college, and in 1965 was a medalist in the PGA Tour's inaugural qualifying school. He had a consistent rookie year, making the cut in the thirteen events he entered and finishing forty-eighth on the money list. But he didn't fare as well the next several years, failing to crack the top sixty and gain his exempt status again until 1971. By then he had been getting help from Hogan for two years.

When he played well enough to get in the papers, Schlee often talked about two things: his love of astrology (he was a Gemini) and his affinity for Hogan. Hogan's book, *Five Lessons: The Modern Fundamentals of Golf,* had been Schlee's golf bible dating to the late 1950s. Hogan was hitting balls at Preston Trail Golf Club in Dallas in 1969 when he approached Schlee and asked him if he wanted to play. A friendship began, and Schlee's game started to improve. Hogan's word was gospel, right down to his advice that Schlee trim his sideburns and tone down his wardrobe.

"John was probably the type of player who fiddled a little too much with things," says 1971 Masters champion Charles Coody. "He tried to mimic beyond a reasonable amount somebody else rather than being himself. [But] if you couldn't admire Hogan, who could you admire?"

Everything started to click for Schlee in 1973. When a young Tom Watson faltered down the stretch at the Hawaiian Open, Schlee was there to shoot a final-round 68 and win by two shots. "He called me the night he won," says Hill. "Must have been 3 o'clock in the morning my time. He said, 'Benjie, I'm standing here looking at this big check [$40,000]. I used to live on $15 a month at [college]. All my dreams have come true.'"

Schlee played consistently through the spring. The week before the U.S. Open, he tied for fifth at the IVB-Philadelphia Golf Classic. At Oakmont he opened with a two-over 73, six shots behind Gary Player. After thirty-six holes, he was at 143, still six back. But a third-round 67 moved the thirty-four-year-old Schlee into a tie for the lead at three-under 210 with Palmer, Julius Boros, and Jerry Heard.

For the final round Schlee was in the penultimate pairing with Palmer. While Miller was getting off to a torrid start six groups ahead, Schlee had an awful beginning. He sprayed his tee shot on the 469-yard first hole to the right. Believing it could be out of bounds, he hit a provisional. Upon walking to his tee shot, he found it in bounds but in an unplayable lie by a hedge. Schlee returned to the tee to hit his third shot, and he made a double-bogey six.

From that point Schlee steadied himself. He quickly regained the two shots he had lost by holing a twenty-footer for an eagle on the 549-yard fourth hole. Despite the frenzy of being paired with Palmer, Schlee hung tough, the last man to have a chance to catch Miller. "That's the twelfth time I've been paired with Palmer and the last five times I've been under par, but I still think it's a two-shot penalty," Schlee said afterward. "It's so hard to concentrate with people yelling, 'Arnie, Arnie.' But I'm not blaming Palmer. It's not his fault."

With a birdie from ten feet on the sixteenth hole, Schlee pulled within one stroke of Miller. Left with a sixty-footer at the seventeenth, he burned the edge. After a good drive on No. 18, his four-iron from 188 yards hit the front of the green and bounced into the back fringe, fifty feet from the hole. With Miller watching greenside, Schlee chipped to within inches. He tapped in for a 70. "It's tough to take," he said, "when you come up one short."

In the USGA highlight film, Schlee can be seen walking off the eighteenth green as Palmer shakes Miller's hand. He casts a quick glance and keeps moving. Now and always, the fame would

More Than a Score

belong to someone else. "There is the biggest small word in the English language: *if*," says Coody. "If he had won, who knows?"

But Schlee put aside the disappointment, preferring to look at the next challenge rather than the last stumble. "When I think of John," says Bobby Cole, Schlee's best friend on tour, "it brings a smile to my face. He definitely saw the glass half-full." Cole and Schlee would scurry from one city to the next. "I had a little Porsche," says Cole. "It was pretty quick. He had a big, v-8 Mercedes with a CB radio and a radar detector. We'd race off to the next tournament and see who could get there first."

One time a sponsor gave Schlee a new Chrysler, says J. C. Snead, and Schlee raced it across a desert highway, "going about 140 or whatever it would do," melting the engine in the process. "He was famous for how fast he drove from one tournament to the next," recalls Bob Murphy. "I reckon if he was telling the truth, he got more speeding tickets than anybody in the history of the tour." Most players didn't know Schlee very well. "He wasn't an enigma," says Hale Irwin, "but he had his lifestyle, and he kept to himself."

Schlee's first marriage produced a daughter, Kendall, in 1965, but Schlee didn't have room for a career and a family. "My problems started in the fall of '66," he told a reporter. "I got a divorce from my first wife. She didn't realize how dedicated I was to golf, how much time I would have to spend." To another journalist he said, "It's something I had to do. It's a lonely life."

Kendall, now thirty-seven, says she met her father for the first time at the 1976 Phoenix Open. "I remember it was on the thirteenth hole," she says. "He walked up to me and shook my hand and said 'Hello.' I said, 'Mom, who is that?' She said, 'That's your dad.'" After the round, father and daughter went to a house and talked. They would stay in touch for the next dozen years. "He taught me a lot of things," says Kendall, who works at a power plant in Arizona. "He always had a plan and always had a goal. He always went after it. It amazed me—he bounced back from whatever was happening."

As vividly as his Popeye arms, friends remember his resiliency. "He never bitched about life," says Gene Dixon, another college teammate. "He'd take whatever he was dealt and play on." According to Hill, Schlee "would fail and jump right back. He'd go out and shoot 78 and come back and say, 'I'm going to be a great player.' He never had any doubts."

But the confidence came with a sharp edge. "He could get very short with people," says Pepin, referring to the time when Schlee mouthed off to a member at Memphis Country Club, which caused the team to lose its playing privileges. "The guy had a lot of talent, but he alienated so many people. He was a hard guy to help." Says Dixon, "He was a pretty cocky, high-strung person. If you knew him, he'd go to war for you. I always enjoyed him. I think he was just lonesome."

Golf was an all-consuming passion for Schlee. While his teammates frittered away time during the winter playing Ping-Pong, Schlee would hit balls off hard, dormant turf. He walked out once in the middle of a class, his books cradled in his arms, his hands in a new grip position. If he was fighting a hook, Schlee would set up outside his dormitory, six feet left of the wall, and strike shots down the length of it.

Several of his teammates couldn't recall Schlee ever traveling back to his hometown during college or ever talking about his family. "We never heard much from him after the service," says high school classmate Jack Burk, "because he never really came back to Seaside."

Once, while driving from Memphis to Jackson for the Tennessee State Amateur, Hill and Schlee had car trouble; they stopped at a gas station for repairs and went on their way. A couple of days later, returning along the same route, the car acted up again. "It's about 9:30 at night, by the same service station," Hill says. "Without a word, no emotion, [Schlee] gets out of the car, finds a rock, and throws it through a window [at the gas station]. He got back in the car and without any emotion said, 'Benjie, you can't let people take advantage of you.'"

More Than a Score

The mid-1970s were a time of mixed success for Schlee. He kept a close eye on the zodiac calendar ("There were guys I couldn't stand, then I charted their horoscopes, and I learned why they were the way they were," he said) and on his back, on which he had surgery in 1974. (He maintained he was born with an "extra vertebra" that, along with a pronounced reverse-c finish, contributed to his problem.) He tied for fourth in the 1976 PGA Championship and tied for eighth in the 1977 Masters, but his time on tour was coming to an end. He led the 1978 Masters with a first-round 68, but his back seized up overnight and he faded into a tie for forty-second. His last appearance was the 1978 Kemper, then he turned his energy to teaching golf, the lessons from Hogan having reverberated in him for years.

In 1980 he took his golf knowledge to Industry Hills Resort east of Los Angeles, recruiting several young professionals to teach in his schools. One of them was Greg Graham, now a teaching pro at Hacienda Golf Club in La Habra Heights, California. Graham worked for Schlee for four years, during which he saw Schlee's intensity and generosity. "He'd make a lot of money in his golf schools, but he'd spend it," says Graham. "He was great with us instructors. He'd pay us real well."

Schlee invented gizmos to help students learn: a strap to keep the arms close to the body, a device to get the right wrist in the impact position he dreamed about. He was frustrated by his inability to pass the PGA of America's written exam for certification, which was difficult for him, Graham says, because he was dyslexic.

While Schlee had his teaching curiosities—he wanted the address position to mimic impact, and he favored a very weak left-hand grip—Graham thought he had foresight. "John's philosophy was that the big muscles of the hips and the legs did the swinging and the arms were basically passive and followed them," Graham says. "He advocated a very physical type of golf swing, which more of the young tour players are doing today. I think he was ahead of the curve."

The golf schools were rigorous three-day affairs, short on cocktail parties and long on instruction. "I have never met a person who was insatiable about learning the golf swing and every characteristic of it, from your toes to the top of your head," says Pete Wilman, another Schlee protégé. "He knew what every body part was supposed to do." Schlee strengthened his upper legs by putting his back against a wall and crouching. Wilman was stunned the first time he saw him give a twenty-minute lecture in that position. "He'd do one-legged knee bends, whip off twenty like it was nothing," Wilman says.

Wilman remembers his boss as a private man of routine who would eat the same lunch—hamburger patty and large serving of hash browns—at the same time, 11 a.m., at the same table, in the corner of the clubhouse restaurant, every day. Schlee's enthusiasm would psych up his students, but his dogmatic style could turn them off.

"[This] is when people would think he was weird. He'd have a five-iron in his hand, and his focus would be on getting the ball in the hole," Wilman says. "His ultimate goal, his dream, was to play eighteen holes and not have to putt. That's why he rubbed people the wrong way. He'd wear people out. If we started out with fifteen people, by Sunday there might be ten left. He was like a college professor. The good ones—they grind you, but you learn."

Schlee collected his instruction theories in a 1986 book, *Maximum Golf,* which is in large measure a hand-off of what Hogan taught him. "It is impossible to put into words the care and concern and patience that Ben showed me," Schlee writes. "Much of what Ben shared with me was totally different from anything I had ever heard before, or since. And it worked. All of what Ben shared with me, I now give to you."

Maximum Golf is not only a glimpse at the Hogan who kindly taught Schlee and helped him become talented enough to nearly win the U.S. Open, but a window into Schlee. "Golf is like marriage: It tests our devotion and our ability to remember the good when things are less than pleasing. Just like a good marriage, a good golf game is a precious, fragile and complex thing. When handled in an indifferent way, it can become just like a marriage with problems."

In the late 1980s Graham started noticing that Schlee's demonstrations in golf schools weren't as crisp as they used to be. When he turned fifty in 1989, Schlee joined the senior tour. "I didn't win enough when I played the regular tour," he said then. "I'm mature enough to think I can let myself win. When I was on the regular tour, I tried to make myself win." But Schlee had little success, his best finish a tie for forty-second.

Schlee's third marriage ended in the early 1990s. He moved back in with his parents, and the Alzheimer's settled in. When they couldn't care for him any longer, he was institutionalized. "The last three years, they'd ship him all over the place, different types of government places," Graham says. "By '98 or '99 he'd gotten to be about 260 or 270 pounds. He'd smile when he saw me, but didn't really say much. Then it got really bad near the end. They shackled him to the bed. And he went the other way and only weighed about ninety pounds when he passed away."

Many people in golf found out about his death when Jim Achenbach wrote a column in *Golfweek* several weeks after he died, noting that in Schlee's last couple of years "he was stuffed away from society like a threadbare sock in somebody's bottom drawer."

Kendall Schlee had been out of touch with her father for more than ten years. "We just lost contact when I was about twenty-two," she says. "He was busy, I was busy." She found out the day after Christmas 2000, almost seven months after his death, that her father was gone. "A friend saw it in a magazine and called me at work. It hit me really hard." When she reached her grandfather, who is eighty-seven and has been battling kidney failure, she was told the Alzheimer's might have begun taking its toll when her father was in his late forties.

If Schlee had regrets about coming so close to winning the U.S. Open, he didn't voice them often. The most he would do was lament his pre-shot routine on his approach shot to the seventy-second green, needing a birdie to tie, when he forgot to take a deep breath before beginning his swing. "As he's telling me this story," says Wilman, "his eyeballs were bulging. He said, 'I never hit the ball thin. I think I was nervous and rushed the breath.'"

His best prize might not have been the trophy for winning the Hawaiian Open but a telegram he received from Hogan shortly after doing so. "ATTABOY. BEN."

Schlee was cremated, without a funeral or memorial service. "He was so young, and he was so alone," Kendall says. Last June, two years after Schlee's death, Graham decided to do something for his old friend. He obtained Schlee's ashes, and along with a small blue spruce Carl bought to honor his stepson, he took them to San Jacinto Mountain near Palm Springs.

"It's way up," Graham says, "about a two-hour hike. John had gone there a couple of times with me when he was healthy. Even though he smoked a bit and had a little trouble getting up, he loved it when he got there. He was like a little kid."

Graham planted the little tree, paused to say a few words to his friend, and spread his ashes. And with that, John Schlee had some space again.

June 6, 2003

John Schlee's poignant tale is proof that the most compelling stories, in golf or other pursuits, don't have to involve the biggest winners. Any golfer, on any level, is drawn to the game to some degree. Schlee's intense personality, as those who knew him told me, took that fascination to an obsession. But how many other golfers got a telegram of congratulations from Ben Hogan?

More Than a Score

CHAPTER TWENTY-SIX

Taking a Stand

Even during Oregon's rainy season, when people reflexively reach for a slicker before their first cup of coffee, it was a bad day— wet and raw and, in many places, muddy. This explained why Bob the cable guy, tool belt jostling, walked through this particular new townhouse in his stocking feet. As the homeowner, a twenty-six-year-old man with an easy manner and a limp, guided him inside, Bob noticed a set of irons lined up along one of the beaming white walls.

"Golfer, huh?"

Casey Martin, pleasantly surprised that someone knew him only as a customer eager to hand over $52.87 to get thirty-nine channels, kept moving past the shiny Yamaha baby grand piano in the living room. Had Martin taken his visitor to his second-floor study, he would have gotten more clues. A letter from former U.S. senator Bob Dole, a picture of Martin with Cindy Crawford, and laminated pages from *Golf Digest* featuring Martin's swing fill one wall. A large blanket with the insignia of Stanford University, Martin's alma mater, covers another, and a gold-plated Ping putter, commemorating Martin's victory in the 1998 Nike Lakeland Classic, rests beside it. On the far side of the room, above a small desk, is a small white cross.

But Martin walked instead down a dogleg of stairs to his basement den, where a new Toshiba set, big but not huge, joined only by a nearby pair of fifteen-pound dumbbells, was waiting to come to life. At this moment Martin didn't seem like everything he had been during 1998. He didn't seem like someone born with a rare circulatory disorder, Klippel-Trenaunay-Weber syndrome, which had ravaged his right leg and caused him not only to limp but to hurt, often excruciatingly so. He didn't look like the revolutionary who on February 11 won in federal court the right to use a motorized golf cart after suing the PGA Tour under the Americans with Disabilities Act. He didn't look like someone who had become a beacon for the disabled, someone whose cause divided his sport and prompted golfers to debate the innards of the game they play.

He looked like a guy who, after months of expectations, interviews, new riches, and old worries, wanted to channel-surf. "I've been waiting two weeks for this," Martin said. "You're going to hook me up right, aren't you?"

He also looked, still, like the younger brother of Cameron Martin, who unlike most everyone else, saw it coming. "I never dreamed there would be a lawsuit," Cameron says, "but I knew how Casey had struggled with pain his whole life yet still was as good at golf as he was. I thought the combination would make him well-known. I thought his story would get out."

Only a thousand people worldwide are afflicted with Klippel-Trenaunay-Weber syndrome. None of them has ever had a year like Casey Martin's. From his astonishing victory at the Nike Lakeland Classic in January to his victory over the PGA Tour a month later, from his U.S. Open appearance to his struggles on the Nike Tour and an unsuccessful attempt to secure a PGA Tour card for the 1999 season—nobody penetrated golf's conscience so deeply.

During the trial the strategies of the opposing sides made them seem like two boxers—gloves snug and mouthpieces in—ready to fight but entering rings in different cities. Bill Wiswall,

More Than a Score

Martin's old friend and lead attorney, is a wily, sixty-three-year-old personal injury pro who trades his corduroys and sweaters for something fancier only when he has to. The PGA Tour's attorneys dress in exquisite suits and carry the latest laptops. "I walked in with my yellow tablets," Wiswall says, recalling the first day in court. "My son, Mike, came up to me just before we got started and said, 'Dad, you're prehistoric.'"

Wiswall, fellow counsel Martha Walters (an ADA specialist), and the plaintiff himself believed the case absolutely was about Martin. His pain. His weakness. His awareness of the constant jeopardy of his frail limb, which at any moment could shatter to pieces as a result of the simplest action, much the way a two-iron can snap a golf tee on a long par three.

"During college a doctor looked at my shin and could not believe I hadn't broken it from swinging," Martin says on a recent day, the discomfort in his limb greater than at any time during the year. "When you hear that, you don't forget it. It makes me sick to my stomach thinking about it. I shouldn't be jumping over creeks."

Martin had pulled off the Bob Beamon act over a small ditch in Austin, Texas, in his first Nike tournament after the trial was over. Until he played in the U.S. Open, that week represented the crescendo of attention, a time when some journalists tried to bribe the club's cart boys with $20 bills to find out where Martin was staying, and photographers followed the disabled golfer right to the Port-o-Let door.

There would be plenty of dramatic pictures, but none nearly as compelling as the x-rays of Martin's right shin taken over the years. As the bones deteriorated and the blood pooled, the pictures evolved like developing storm clouds. "They go white, white, white, off-white, gray, more gray," Martin says. "Now they're almost black."

The night before Martin got his own television connected, he sat in a hotel room discussing his year with one eye on a Monday night football game between the San Francisco 49ers and New York Giants. Suddenly he blanched. Bryant Young, the 49ers defensive star, had gone down with a gruesome compound fracture of his lower right leg.

"He really did get hurt," Martin said as the television screen filled with Young's agony. "We don't want to see this stuff. Turn the channel. Or turn it off."

When it came to legal strategy, the PGA Tour turned away from Martin's medical records, declining to look at a here's-what's-beneath-my-stocking-and-slacks videotape of Martin's condition, or show it to Arnold Palmer or Jack Nicklaus, both of whom testified before the trial in support of the tour's no-carts position.

After urging the tour (to no avail) to show the elder statesmen of the game the footage of Martin's leg, Wiswall gave Palmer a copy of it after the King offered his deposition in January in Palm Springs. "I was always curious to know if he ever looked at it," Wiswall says. What is known is that the revered superstars received their share of negative mail for their position on the issue, particularly after they appeared later in the year, along with Gary Player, in an advertisement for a brand of motorized golf carts. "It didn't shock me that they were against me," Martin says. "But it disappointed me, obviously, that they felt so strongly they had to testify against me."

The tour tried to take the emotion and pain out of play, like some fairway bunker that could be carried with a big drive. Its corporate response of ignoring Martin and focusing on its right to make the rules, and its argument that allowing anyone to use a cart would skew the competition, polarized the issue and helped stir the very emotions the tour was trying to skirt. To some, the tour's strategy—not considering the individual in one of the most individual pursuits in sport—was ironic. Nine months after case 97-6309-TC went his way, Martin is still perplexed.

"Their legal tactic was to make no exceptions," Martin says. "But I at least wanted those guys to understand what I go through. I would have loved for them to have seen [the leg] and said, 'Okay, we're still going through with it.' But they wouldn't even look at

More Than a Score

it. Nicklaus or Palmer, had they had the opportunity to look at it, who knows? Maybe the PGA Tour wouldn't have had any support and they would have done things differently."

It is hard not to look back and wonder how Martin's life would have played out in 1998 had the PGA Tour found a way to accommodate him with a cart before the matter went to court. Martin certainly has thought about it. "My life would have probably been different," he says. "People might watch me, but not because of this controversy. [The notoriety] would eventually blow. Instead, it's been the story. If I continue to do well, it'll continue to be the story."

There would have been no trial, of course, and Martin probably wouldn't have gotten the healthy endorsement contracts with Nike, Hartford Insurance, Spalding, and Ping, nor would he have been named honorary captain for a football game by his beloved University of Oregon Ducks, competed in the Skills Challenge with established players (he finished second), or been asked for autographs while shopping for lamps at the Target in Eugene. He wouldn't have a new piano in a new house and would likely be getting his cable connected in a rental apartment somewhere. And the PGA Tour wouldn't have had to hear Bob Dole wondering aloud if PGA stands for "Please Go Away." But there was a trial.

"It bummed me out how the PGA Tour handled it, but they put me on the map," Martin says. "People have this perception that I'm making millions and millions of dollars, and I'm not. But compared to what I've achieved in golf, I'm getting paid far in excess of what I'm worth as a golfer. There have been some blessings. What can you say?"

Mostly Martin moves on, one labored step at a time. "I don't wake up in the morning and think, 'I'm courageous,'" he says. "It's just what I deal with." He moves on buoyed by two things that are hard to see: a resolute faith and two $300 custom-fit Jobst support stockings. The tightly fitting wraps, which have covered his right leg every minute of every day for years (except when he showers), have enabled him to lead an active life by doing part of what his missing venous system cannot manage: force blood back up his leg.

"But there is still a reality check," says his father, King. "The reality is not going to change. It is literally what they call a dying leg. It's an issue of how much time he has. It could be three days or three years. I suppose it could be five or ten years. I've been shocked he's been able to do what he's done."

Before the x-rays started to look so bad, Martin wouldn't consider what his life would be without his leg, but that has changed. "Now," he says, "if I see someone playing golf with a prosthesis, I'll go up and talk to them. I'm kind of feeling them out. I'm like, 'Someday, maybe that will be me.'" He believes he could still play competitively with an artificial lower leg but knows that his condition might ultimately demand a greater loss. "If I could have [amputation] done above the knee, it would take care of the bulk of my problem, but my golf career would be done. It's a debate. I'm not near the point where it has to be done, but if I were to break my leg, I think that's what would happen. You see how thin my leg is. Imagine how it would be after six months in a cast. It wouldn't be worth it." When he returned home in late November, Martin was troubled by some alarming pain in his right knee, which has also deteriorated over the years. "The cartilage is so tweaked in there," he says. "This thing is so fragile. A couple of days ago, I couldn't even lift my leg. It's been brutal."

Shifting from side to side on a couch, constantly rearranging his restless leg, Martin was asked whether golf is better off for what happened to him this year. "I don't like to think it's better off with me," he says. "It would have been plenty good without me, and it'll be good when I'm not out there. The purists probably don't like it. But that doesn't bother me. It depends on who you speak to."

"He brought a lot of media attention to the Nike Tour," says PGA Tour commissioner Tim Finchem. "He created a lot more fan interest. There may be some negatives, but I don't know what they are. He's great to have playing—the courage he's demonstrated, the ability to strike the golf ball, his qualities as a fine young man. But that doesn't have anything to do with the fundamental issue."

The PGA Tour's appeal of the verdict could be heard sometime next year by the U.S. Court of Appeals for the Ninth Circuit—the opponents have already filed written briefs—although both sides also acknowledge it may drag into the millennium. "We really don't know," says PGA Tour spokesman John Morris. "There is no indication that it will be heard [in 1999]." Regardless of the appeal's outcome, there is a strong sense the case will wind up in the U.S. Supreme Court. "No question," says Wiswall. "I think the aggrieved party in this appeal will keep pursuing it."

Martin's brief, written by his new counsel, Simpson Thacher & Bartlett of New York, cites scores of cases and runs 13,745 words. Cameron Martin, sitting in his office at Salomon Smith Barney in downtown Eugene, where he works as a stockbroker for his father, speaks more succinctly. "Golf is an extraordinary sport," he says. "It's not a bad thing that golf can accommodate a disabled person when other sports can't. Why not let golf do that?"

Speak to Craig Loest of Fort Worth, Texas, whose nine-year-old son, Kern, also is affected by K-T in his right leg, and you hear this: Since going to watch Martin play in Nike Tour events in Austin and Shreveport, Louisiana, since meeting him and getting an autographed cap, since finding someone like him who can hit golf shots as if nothing was wrong, Kern Loest has been a different little boy. He is more willing to wear his compression stocking, even though it's tight and makes his leg hot and sticky, because Casey Martin told him to. More than he ever did before, Kern deals with his disability rather than letting it control him. Kern plays golf whenever he can at a little par-twenty-nine course near his home. His best score is a 41.

"The impact of Casey Martin, not just on my son's life, but on our whole family, has been unbelievable," says Craig Loest. "The inspiration Kern got from Casey helped him overcome his inhibitions. He has confidence in his leg now. He's got a desire to try things he never would."

On Halloween night Kern Loest put on a cap that used to be white, signed by a golfer who used to be just like him, a fourth-grader whose dreams find a way through the pain. He put on a golf shirt and shouldered his tiny golf bag that holds his four small clubs. He *was* Casey Martin. He went trick-or-treating, and there wasn't a fundamental issue in sight.

It is the same way Martin feels when he sits down at his piano. It is a feeling he can't get from a costume, a court case, or a golf cart. There are days, simply, when "Great Balls of Fire" or "Jesus, Jesus, Rest Your Head" work better than Advil. Someday, he is almost certain, the pain will no longer exist.

December 18, 1998

PGA *Tour Inc. v. Martin* was argued in the U.S. Supreme Court in January 2001, with Martin asserting that the tour could not legally deny him the option of using a golf cart. On May 29, 2001, the Supreme Court ruled 7–2 in favor of Martin, who continued to play professionally until 2006, when he became men's golf coach at the University of Oregon in his hometown of Eugene. His right leg still brittle and his game rusty, he managed to qualify for the 2012 U.S. Open at the Olympic Club. The forty-year-old shot 149 for thirty-six holes, missing the cut by one stroke. The cart didn't seem nearly as big a deal as it had been at the 1998 Open.

More Than a Score

CHAPTER TWENTY-SEVEN

The Detour of a Phenom

Plenty of professional golfers misplace their talent from time to time, but after hitting three hundred balls, trying two dozen putting strokes, sitting through six sessions with a sport psychologist, or having one conversation with a spouse who reminds them how much the mortgage is, they usually find it. Sometimes they don't.

There is no reason to feel sorry for a healthy forty-one-year-old man who has a wife and three children, a comfortable home, and a steady, well-paying job on network television describing how other people play golf. It's a nice life, a lucky life. Bobby Clampett owns a resolute faith, a six-seat Piper Malibu that can fly at twenty-five thousand feet, a head full of curly hair, and memories of the once-upon-a-time when he was going to be the world's next great golfer.

It is completely appropriate, though, to ponder what happened, especially with a new generation of grooved swings and great expectations—much like Clampett's—hitting the tour. Listening to Clampett work as an announcer for CBS, it is difficult for a viewer to tell what kind of golfer he once was. From his perch on a tower at one of the closing holes, he rarely brags and seldom dissects a player who has blundered. Occasionally he'll reach for a cliché or impose an aviation term on the audience. As do many announcers, he has a supply of pet phrases. "Unforced error" is one of his favorites.

Two decades since Clampett struck golf shots with dictatorial authority—the sound alone made old-timers recall Ben Hogan—he thinks about the swing every day. Clampett lives in Cary, North Carolina, not far from Research Triangle Park, where many high-tech ideas are hatched. His own are still fermenting. "I enjoy the challenge of continually figuring it out," he says. "When I practice these days, I usually have a video camera with me. Some people say, 'What are you bothering to do that for?'"

The answer is fairly simple. "I was asking him not long ago if he wanted to be remembered as Bobby the announcer or Bobby the golfer," says Lee Martin, Clampett's first golf instructor, "and he didn't hesitate."

Bobby the golfer was a young man without peer, someone who had all the shots, the touch, and the drive to become the best. "He was a notch above everybody else," says contemporary Bob Tway, the 1986 PGA champion. "I remember talking to him once, and he was saying that he never thought he really hit the ball that well. I had to call him on that. I never saw anybody hit the ball better."

Clampett beat Tway in an epic extra-holes match in the semi-finals of the 1978 Western Amateur at Point O' Woods Golf and Country Club in Benton Harbor, Michigan. In the final, Clampett squared off against Mark Wiebe, who led through seven holes. No. 8, a tight par four of about 270 yards, was within reach with a bold tee shot. Clampett took out his driver. "I remember it clearly," says Wiebe. "I took a big gulp when his ball left the tee. That hole was as narrow as a lane at a bowling alley. He just hit a rope."

A skinny eighteen-year-old from Carmel, California, who was enjoying one of the best summers an amateur ever had, Clampett hit a shot that never left the flag. It flirted with going in. Clampett made an eagle, won the hole, and went on to take the match. "I was focused in," Clampett says, smiling at the memory. "Tiger

[Woods] talks about this. I always had it. You absolutely picture the swing and the feel and visualize the shot."

When Clampett was ten, he hit balls until his hands were raw in order to learn a particular shot. In a couple of years he'd worn down the grooves in a set of irons. "First time I'd ever seen that," says Martin, who taught him for three years. When Clampett was thirteen, he met Ben Doyle, an instructor who swore by *The Golfing Machine* by Homer Kelley, a revolutionary book that explained the swing in terms of physics and geometry, broke it down into twenty-four components, and detailed a cause and effect for everything. Its subtitle is *The Computer Age Approach to Golfing Perfection*.

It was gospel to Doyle, and it became the road map for Clampett, who came by his analytical bent naturally. His father, Robert, who died when he was eleven, was an aviation engineer. The book, first published in 1969, is filled with technical terms, and it is not for everyone. In the preface Kelley urges readers to be open-minded to the scientific terminology. "After all," he writes, "complexity is far more acceptable and workable than mystery is."

Accepting and mastering the complexity, Clampett became a young legend around the Monterey Peninsula. He won two California Amateurs. At Brigham Young University he was a three-time All-American and twice winner of the Fred Haskins Award, college golf's Heisman Trophy. Karl Tucker, who coached BYU's golf team from 1961 to 1992, hadn't encountered another golfer quite like him.

The team would hit balls in a football practice field adjacent to Smith Fieldhouse on campus. From his office Tucker had a good view. In two hours Clampett would hit just twenty-five balls, each shot preceded by phantom swings, position checks, analysis fit for a science lab. Although no one was going to mistake Clampett for Sam Snead as he settled, machine-like, into a shot—his right elbow quivering until it was set just so, his back tilting, his head shifting—he wasn't without flair.

"He was phenomenal," says Mike Holder, the longtime coach at Oklahoma State University. "He was a shotmaker who had a great short game. He had everything." If Tucker told his No. 1 player that the team needed a really low score, Clampett would deliver. "If we needed a 65, Bobby would shoot 65," Tucker says. "He was magic."

After three seasons at BYU, in the summer of 1980, Clampett turned pro. The precocious kid who could hit shots two hundred yards left-handed off his knees was going to bring the competition to theirs. Clampett seemed inoculated from the vagaries of a fickle game, but if you looked closely, there were storm clouds. "I'm probably more of a student of the game than I am a player," he said early in his pro career.

No one knew so at the time, but the 1982 British Open at Royal Troon, on Scotland's west coast, would be the beginning of the end of Clampett's path to greatness. The man with the enviable lag in his downswing, the delayed hit that golfers craved, would get in a hurry—to seize the championship that week, to modify his swing soon thereafter. "I think Bobby was always an impatient guy because he grew up without a father," says Tucker. "He wanted to get things real quick. And he was a mix of confidence and a belief that he had a lot to learn. In college, he'd come into my office after having done something goofy, and say, 'I know you're going to chew my ass out, but before I leave tell me you love me and that everything is going to be okay.'"

At Troon, from a 67-66 start and a five-stroke lead through thirty-six holes, Clampett enlarged his lead to seven strokes after five holes of the third round. Then, at the par-five, 577-yard sixth hole, he drove into a fairway bunker. Trying to advance the ball far enough down the fairway to reach the green in three shots, he played boldly and caught the lip, the ball settling not far away in a nearby bunker. From there he repeated the mistake, staggered to the green, and carded a triple-bogey eight on a birdie hole. Clampett's lead and spirit had been sliced considerably.

"That was a critical mistake," says Nick Price, who was paired with Clampett for the final two rounds and had his own problems over the closing few holes Sunday, handing the championship to Tom Watson. "Up until he didn't get out of that bunker, he had played perfectly. All of a sudden, his confidence was questioned. That eight seemed to take all the confidence out of him."

After his torrid start, Clampett closed with 78-77 and tied for tenth place. His breakthrough trip to Britain, which had bulged with long interviews with an intrigued press corps and photo ops with his girlfriend and future wife, Ann Mebane, turned to disappointment. "I feel very sorry for Bobby," Watson said after collecting the Claret Jug for the fourth time. "He may be crying right now, but I've cried before, and he'll learn to be tough."

Instead of chalking up his troubles to nerves or inexperience or pressure—"Sometimes you can go from shooting 65 to 75 and the problem isn't your swing," says Tway—Clampett blamed his technique.

"I was hitting too many shots a day that were costing me," he says now. "My swing relied too much on timing, and I had some compensating moves going on. Essentially, I was too steep coming into the ball." At first Clampett stuck with Doyle, who was worried about Clampett's attitude, not his mechanics. "Bobby's problem at Troon was that he lost respect for the golf course," Doyle says. "He got a little greedy. Bobby thought he knew it all. One time he played a round with Jack Nicklaus, and he told me he didn't watch a shot Jack hit. Well, that's a lack of respect. You watch Jack Nicklaus, and you learn something."

At the end of 1984, Clampett's fourth full year on the PGA Tour, he expanded his search to improve. Enthralled with the way his good friend Mark O'Meara had modified his swing working with instructor Hank Haney, Clampett turned to Haney. Soon he would work with Jimmy Ballard and supplement that help with what fellow players, who were always intrigued by *The Golfing Machine*, had to offer. In contrast to the lone wolf personality that has been the hallmark of many of the best golfers, Clampett was a gregarious, friendly man eager to listen. When his game deteriorated, the cocksure attitude that had marked his brilliant play was replaced by uncertainty.

"He got the ultimate case of rabbit ears," says respected instructor Chuck Cook. "Everybody started giving him advice. He got to where he wasn't sure what to believe and began using a combination of things in his swing that didn't fit together." Bogged down by too many swing thoughts, Clampett floundered, his swing an awkward parody of the clinically precise action it had been. "He had more moves than an erector set," was Ballard's ignominious appraisal.

An unquenchable quest to get better, which always had been as much a part of Clampett as his Harpo Marx hair and his breadstick build, helped make him a prodigy. But that same desire ultimately worked against him and made him little more than a puzzled plodder.

"I thought that with the swing I had, I couldn't be the best player in the world," Clampett says. "There were two ways I could go: I could stick with what I had and be satisfied with second best, or I could try to make some monumental changes to get to the next level. That is just part of my nature." Clampett was fourteenth and seventeenth on the money list in 1981 and 1982 but was dissatisfied. "That wasn't my comfort zone. Was I really good? Really good compared to what? Tiger Woods? I don't think so. To when I was a junior? Yeah. To half the other players on tour? Maybe. But I knew what my potential was, and I wasn't reaching it."

Unlike Ralph Guldahl before him and Ian Baker-Finch after him, the two men who authored golf's most infamous disappearing acts, Clampett didn't have a major title before he started tinkering. If Price could go back twenty years, he would tell Clampett to infuse into his swing a bit more rhythm, one more similar to his demeanor. "Bobby had a real slow backswing, which is okay," says Price, "but most great players swing the way they walk and

More Than a Score

talk. Bobby walked one way and swung another." Holder, who is a devotee of *The Golfing Machine*, believes Clampett gave too much credit to the book and Doyle. "A player has to constantly build his belief system," Holder says. "A player has to take responsibility for what goes on inside the ropes, and he needs to take all the credit when he plays well."

If, twenty years ago, someone had predicted the summary of Clampett's PGA Tour career would be what it is—387 events, thirty-three top-tens, six second-place finishes, only one victory—he would have been accused of not knowing his golf. But that's the record, the lone win coming at the 1982 Southern Open just a few months after his collapse at Troon. Wearing the same gray plus-twos, argyle socks, and white shoes he'd worn on that disappointing Sunday in Scotland, Clampett closed with a 64 to defeat Hale Irwin by two strokes. "I had people saying the reason I had lost the British Open was because of the stupid knickers," he says. "I was always against superstitions, and I wanted to make a point. I don't know what happened to that outfit. I think it went to Goodwill."

When Clampett was unsuccessfully trying to recycle his game, he kept his angst in check. "Bobby has always been a positive person," says Wiebe. "He wouldn't walk around with his head down thinking his life had ended. But to go from being as great as he was to struggling like he did had to be tough." When Clampett got the chance to work full time for CBS in 1995, he had no reservations. "With great players," Clampett says, "there is almost something wrong with them. They've got tunnel vision. There isn't much roundedness in their life."

It is a brilliant December morning in North Carolina, the air clear and warming. If Clampett decides to hit some balls later, he'll need only a lightweight sweater. He is caring for his wife, Ann, who is recovering from recent surgery, and minding their children, Katelyn, fourteen; Daniel, twelve; and Michael, ten. The kids want to measure themselves, and Clampett points them to a closet where there are already some marks on the wall. These days Michael is going at the piano the way Bobby went at golf when he was a boy—practicing without being prodded, eager to learn something new, thirsting to get better.

Ann and Daniel have just taken up golf. "My wife's got a backswing to die for," Clampett says. "On plane, rotated, the clubface is absolutely perfect. It's so natural for her. I just sit there and marvel. My older son is the same way. Of course, they haven't gone to the extent of working on their games and learning the downswing yet, either one of them, but when they do, it's going to be fun to watch."

He has an eye on the new wave of can't-miss kids flowing onto the tour—players such as Charles Howell III, David Gossett, and Ty Tryon—who are as eager to make their mark as he was a generation ago. "Some people were shocked that Ty was able to qualify for the tour at seventeen, but I'm not really surprised," he says. "With better understanding of the swing and more training, we're setting the stage for kids to have more success. Golf has transitioned into a mechanical art form, or, as *The Golfing Machine* says, it's about translating the mechanics into feel."

When Clampett's peers who are still on tour—men who saw him soar and struggle—glimpse him in the TV tower, they have mixed feelings. "I really felt sorry for him because he had all the ingredients," says Price, who recovered from his Troon disappointment to win three major championships. "It's terrible when everything you believe in and everything that has worked stops working. But it happens all the time in golf—very few golfers go through life without trouble in their swings or their short games. It depends on how you deal with those things."

But what of the new breed of barely legal golfers loaded with length, potential, and expectations? When they see Clampett, should they be seeing something more than a man in a headset talking behind a sheet of Plexiglas? "Could they learn something from what happened to me?" Clampett says. "That's a good question." He pauses for a couple of seconds, as long as the trademark pause he used to make before beginning his backswing. "Probably not. Because every person is so different, he has to make his own decisions, has to figure out what his goals are, who he is, the way he's made up. You put ten players in the same situation I was in twenty years ago, a couple would do what I did. But most of them are going to do like Bruce Lietzke—just keep going, not try making any changes, stick with what they've got. Neither way is right and neither way is wrong."

Clampett's balanced view of golf comes from his religion and his experiences on and off the golf course. He believes it takes more strength to stand up to a slump than to lift a trophy, and compared to the punch he discovered real life could deliver, golf wasn't very important. In September 1986, when his golf game was already a maze of mixed messages, he endured the death of the couple's first child, Sara Elizabeth, a few days after she was born. "That event changed me in a lot of ways," he says. "I ran to God for answers. I started studying the Bible. What was revealed gave me a much healthier perspective on life. I looked at things in a totally different way."

He still loves golf, and hopes one day, when the kids are out of the house and he is eligible for the Senior PGA Tour, it will love him again. "If Bobby could get an exemption on the regular tour right now," says Doyle, "he could be very successful. He'd have to work at it, but it's all in there." Clampett trades emails about the swing with Martin and has renewed his friendship with Doyle, but he goes to the range alone. "The last four or five years," Clampett says, "I've actually made more progress working on my own."

After improbably qualifying to compete in the 2000 U.S. Open at Pebble Beach Golf Links, where as a twenty-two-year-old he had finished third behind Tom Watson and Jack Nicklaus in the 1982 Open, Clampett—competing for the second time in twenty-one months—went out in the first round and didn't miss a green or a fairway while going four under par through ten holes. It was textbook golf, that sweet blend he was always looking for, the way ice cream becomes a shake. He got on the leader board, dabbed tears from his eyes, finished with a 68, and reminded everyone of an earlier time.

"Life is made of dreams," Bobby the golfer told reporters that afternoon, "and a lot of dreams have happened on the golf course."

Clampett doesn't talk much these days about what might have been, but he doesn't have to. If he thinks he made an unforced error along the way, he's not saying.

January 11, 2002

Bobby Clampett left full-time golf broadcasting and returned to regular competition in 2010 when he turned fifty, joining the Champions Tour. In his first three seasons as a senior, he tied for fourth place in two events, the 2010 SAS Championship and 2012 Insperity Championship. He was thirty-ninth on the 2012 Champions Tour money list. Clampett and Andy Brumer wrote an instruction book in 2007 called *The Impact Zone: Mastering Golf's Moment of Truth*. Anyone who reads it will benefit from his serious, lifetime study of the golf swing.

CHAPTER TWENTY-EIGHT

The Journey of Jim Simons

Deliberate and cautious as a golfer, Jim Simons was known for his precision, as someone who enjoyed peppering the hundred-yard flag on a practice range more than hitting tee shots toward its distant end. "Jim could really get the job done," says Ben Crenshaw. "He could pick a course apart." But Simons's exacting style, which very nearly earned him the 1971 U.S. Open title at Merion when he was a twenty-one-year-old amateur and resulted in three victories on the PGA Tour, belied the fact that he was a man of extremes.

"[He believed] if two aspirin were good for you, let's take four," says Jesse Haddock, Simons's golf coach at Wake Forest and his former father-in-law. "He was that way."

In college Simons traveled with a satchel full of vitamins and supplements. "He took vitamins back before we knew what vitamins were," says Lanny Wadkins, a Wake Forest teammate. "He was always big on what could do you some good." He was one of the earliest pros to try metal woods, and his win at the 1982 Bing Crosby National Pro-Am helped popularize the clubs. Later on Simons put his faith in exotic contraptions that he hoped would improve his fitness, balance, or vision, such as getting in a "spinning chair" that twirled at hundreds of revolutions per minute and then immediately trying to focus on an eye chart. "To me it was just nuts," says his close friend Gerry James, a golf and fitness instructor. "I tried it and got dizzy and almost puked. But he was always a seeker on how to get better."

At his house in southeast Jacksonville, Simons also had a "gyro gym," an apparatus that spins a person up and down and all around, something an astronaut might use when training for space flights. He even owned a hyperbaric oxygen chamber that one would more likely find at a medical or sports-training facility.

But Simons's favorite thing, according to friends and relatives, was his custom outdoor hot tub, which he equipped with jets powerful enough to bruise and filled with water as hot as he could stand, 105 degrees. A longtime night owl who often didn't go to sleep until three or four o'clock in the morning, he loved to soak in the wee hours looking for relief from the discomfort of fibromyalgia—a chronic condition characterized by fatigue, muscle pain, and tender points—and a body banged up by a lifetime as a professional golfer.

"He had that hot tub put in special," says Simons's eighty-one-year-old father, Ralph. "I guess it helped the pain. He wasn't one to tell you his problems. He went to all kinds of doctors and tried everything over the years, and all of them were going to get him well—but none of them did."

In the early morning hours of Thursday, December 8, 2005, Simons, fifty-five, twice divorced and the father of three sons, followed a familiar routine. First, he emailed friends. At 1:30 a.m. he sent a message to James, whom he had known for nearly three years after meeting him on the practice range of the TPC at Sawgrass. James characterized it as "a real positive email"; it included a photograph of Jesus from the movie *The Passion of the Christ* that was indicative of Simons's recently renewed faith. "Jim recommitted his life to Christ about nine months ago," says another friend, Ernie Vadersen. "He came to Christ one night about eight o'clock in the parking lot at the TPC."

Simons was a regular at Sawgrass. He went there four or five days a week to hit balls or play, often working with James and Vadersen, a golf club designer who developed the Snake Eyes wedges in the 1990s, to get better. Even though any realistic chance to sharpen his game enough to perform on the Champions Tour probably had passed—he didn't break par in six appearances from 2002 to 2004—the light-hitting Simons had picked up more than twenty yards with his driver in the past year, according to Vadersen. He still enjoyed practicing, and if someone asked for help with his swing, Simons was eager to assist and would patiently make his point several different ways if needed.

Friendly, talkative, and a big tipper to the TPC employees, Simons sometimes would help the range staff pick up balls. They might well have hoped to see him that Thursday, but a light rain fell throughout the day, so his absence would have been unremarkable. His phone went unanswered. He did not show up as expected early that evening for a small group meeting of men from the Southpoint Community Church, which had become a focal point in his life.

Concerned about his friend's absence, Vadersen went to Simons's house that night to check on him and discovered his body in the hot tub. Shortly after emailing James, Simons apparently had gone alone to soak in his hot tub like so many nights before, and he died there at approximately 2 a.m. The Jacksonville medical examiner's office ruled it an accidental death caused by "multiple drug toxicity."

A complete report is pending, but James says Simons, who had gone to rehabilitation for alcohol and prescription drug abuse a decade ago, "was hooked on painkillers really bad," including OxyContin and Ultram. "When he went into his hot tub, I think the combination of him taking all the drugs with the hot water, probably seized his heart."

"He had some prescription medicines," says Ralph Simons. "There were no illegal drugs involved at all. It was a bad combination, I guess, the medicines and the hot tub. That's a no-no. He had a tendency to do everything to extremes."

Ralph Simons learned early of his son's tenacity. Jim had been an overachiever from the day when he was three years old and his father took him to Butler (Pennsylvania) Country Club. Ralph gave Jim his adult-length three-iron and told him to choke down, try to keep pace, and pick up when he got to the green. The elder Simons didn't know how long Jim would keep swinging, but a couple of hours later, the little boy with the strawberry blond hair and broad, toothy smile was making his way up the last hole.

"He was a hole behind us, but he played the whole eighteen," Ralph remembers. "I couldn't believe he could hit the ball that far, that many times."

Ralph Simons and his wife, Orpah, had a 130-acre farm about thirty-five miles north of Pittsburgh but didn't farm for a living. A Carnegie Tech graduate, Ralph was a successful businessman, having invented with a colleague the first electric commercial deodorizer. Jim had a steer of his own to look after and an egg route with his sisters, but from that first day at the country club he developed a hunger for golf that his dad was eager to cultivate.

"I didn't have much problem with his behavior," says Ralph, "but I'd punish him by not letting him play golf. That was the most effective punishment." Ralph was health-conscious, and Jim once confided to a friend that he played poorly at a junior event in Hershey, Pennsylvania, because he was tortured by the air's scent. "He had never had candy, and if you're in Hershey you can smell the sweetness," the friend recalls. "He said it was the worst tournament he played because he could smell that chocolate and wanted it so badly."

Jim got good at golf, fast. He routed the competition in tough conditions to win the 1966 Pennsylvania state high school championship as a sophomore. In 1967, when the event conflicted with U.S. Open qualifying after a rainout, Simons chose the latter. "There were seven spots," recalls Ralph. "He tied with seven people for the seventh spot and won [the playoff] on the fifth extra hole." When the crew-cut seventeen-year-old teed off at Baltusrol Golf Club (he shot 86-79), he was one of the youngest players to compete in the event.

And his talent was just starting to blossom. He qualified again for the 1968 U.S. Open at Oak Hill, where he made the cut and got a fourth-round pairing with Arnold Palmer. Simons went off to the University of Houston that fall but became disenchanted with the golf-factory feel. He transferred after one year to play for Haddock at Wake Forest, where the team was equally strong and the atmosphere more diverse. Simons began dating Sherry Turner, a Meredith College student and his coach's stepdaughter, whom he would marry in 1973, the year after he turned pro. He roomed for three years in Davis dormitory with Bob Hook, a Demon Deacons basketball player from Louisville, and loved being a member of Kappa Alpha fraternity, whose smooth chapter-room carpet was marked by a hole Simons had gouged out with his wedge so he could practice his putting.

"We had fun," remembers Hook, now a Kentucky car dealer. "We'd try to hit the library bell from in front of the house. Jim was the only one who could do it. It was about a four-iron for him. I'm not sure where the rest of our balls went—we hit cars and windows. Fortunately we didn't kill anybody."

Many of Simons's more serious swings were taken in the company of Wadkins, who was as fast as Jim was slow. "I think playing with him all those years is probably what helped me tolerate all the slow play on tour," Wadkins says. "I used to throw stuff at him when he was over putts. I'd fall in his line." (None of Wadkins's tactics had much effect. Simons was one of the slowest players on tour since Cary Middlecoff. When the tour cracked down on dawdlers in the late 1970s, Simons began walking briskly outside the ropes with the gallery between shots before his partners hit so he could still have enough time when he got to his ball.) But their disparate pace of play didn't keep them from becoming fast friends. "I lived off him," says Wadkins, recalling their daily matches. "I had no money; Jim's dad had some money. We'd play a dollar or two-dollar Nassau a day. If I won six bucks off Jim, that was a burger at McDonald's and dinner on the way home from Henny Penny chicken."

While Wadkins consistently got his meal money from Simons, the outcome was different when the two hotshots, who traveled the summer circuit together in Simons's Volkswagen Beetle, met in the first round of the 1970 Trans-Mississippi Amateur. "He was my pigeon for a while, but the one time the match meant something he beat me one up," Wadkins remembers. "He was the ultimate grinder, no question."

All-out was all Simons knew. As he once explained to *Golf Digest*, "You take what God gives you—hey, an eagle seeing a mouse from 200 yards, only God gives that—and try to improve on it. It's criminal not to."

But Simons could speak of keen vision only as a wishful hypothetical, because since elementary school he was saddled with terrible eyesight—10 diopters nearsighted in both eyes, about three times worse than most nearsighted individuals. His glasses were as thick as a beer mug and didn't offer a crisp view. His contacts—he tried dozens of models—gave him better vision but bounced out of position when he blinked and could be nightmarish in the wind or during pollen season.

"He fought his contacts all the time," recalls Logan Jackson, another Wake Forest teammate. "His contacts hurt him so bad, I can't believe he wore them. Nobody else would have worn them if they hurt that bad, but he felt he could see better with them than [with] glasses."

When Simons shot a third-round 65 while paired with Lee Trevino to take a two-stroke lead in the 1971 U.S. Open, he was in position to become the first amateur since Johnny Goodman in 1933 to win the title. With three holes left on Sunday, now paired with Jack Nicklaus, Simons trailed by only one shot. After narrowly missing birdie chances at Nos. 16 and 17, his drive took a bad kick into the left rough on the eighteenth. Simons chose a three-wood, a shot Wadkins taught him to use to pop the ball from the thick grass, but he hit it poorly. A double bogey dropped him to a tie for fifth place, and Trevino outlasted Nicklaus in a play-off the next day.

After turning pro, it took Simons nearly five years to win his first title, at New Orleans in 1977. His second victory came the following year at The Memorial, where he prevailed in a final-round grouping with Nicklaus. "He really only talked about one thing [he did] on tour," says Vadersen, "his win at Muirfield. He said he snuck it by Jack a couple of times that last round and got the giggles all the way around."

Simons believed his lack of power caused stresses in his game that would cause his "nerves to wear out before the next guy." In fact shoulder, wrist, and back injuries—as well as a job in the bro-kerage business and a desire to spend more time with his family—had more to do with his leaving the tour after the 1988 season.

Trading the pressure of the tour for postdinner play illuminated by cart headlights with his boys, Bradley, Sean, and Ryan, at the golf course community where the family lived in Jupiter, Florida, Simons liked his new life. But trouble was brewing. Sherry was diagnosed with stage-four breast cancer in 1990 when she was thirty-eight. Surgery, chemotherapy, and radiation prolonged her life, but the stresses on their marriage were adding up. "We both lived for the boys and let the marriage go," Jim told *Golf Digest*'s Tom Callahan in 1998.

While Sherry was battling her disease, Jim was struggling with alcohol dependency. "Jim had another side of him that a lot of people didn't know," says a longtime acquaintance. "I don't think he could handle the alcohol." Says Hook, "She had cancer and it wasn't something she could control, and she never forgave Jim for not being able to control himself better. Neither one was there for the other, and you need help to get through those things."

About the time Sherry's cancer recurred, early in 1996, Jim was receiving treatment for alcohol and drug abuse. He filed for divorce on November 27, 1996, and Sherry's health worsened as the case worked its way through court. The divorce was finalized just two days before Sherry, forty-five, died on May 7, 1997, in Winston-Salem, North Carolina. The minor Simons children, Sean and Ryan, who were sixteen and fourteen at the time, chose to live with Jesse Haddock and his wife, Kay, in North Carolina, near where they had been living with their mother.

The fissured relationship with his children weighed heavily on Jim. "I think he went through some things that no one deserved to, really," says Hook. "It made it really tough on him the last few years of his life." Friends say Jim longed to be fully reconnected with his children. Sean Simons, now twenty-five, speaking on behalf of his brothers, declined to elaborate publicly, beyond saying all three, to varying degrees, had reconciled with their father. "We resolved our conflict years ago, and he was long forgiven," Sean says of his relationship with his father.

According to several people who knew him, Simons was in good spirits in the weeks leading up to his death, while continuing to deal with the effects of fibromyalgia, whose symptoms can include sleeplessness and headaches in addition to muscle aches. Friends and relatives are convinced, as the official investigation concluded, that Simons did not kill himself. "I just never felt it was a suicide," says Hook, who saw Simons three times in 2004 and frequently exchanged emails with him until his death. "He was frustrated and battled some depression, but in all the times when he was down, he never indicated that [desire] to me. I just never felt it was a suicide." Simons's second marriage, to Sally Davidson, ended in divorce on February 10, 2005, but sources say it was an amicable parting.

Says Ralph Simons, "I can guarantee this was no suicide. If he had gone that way, I'm sure he would have left notes for people. His wallet was laying in the house with a lot of money in it. Lot of different things."

But the fact that Simons didn't purposely end his life isn't much comfort. James regrets that his efforts to get Simons to stop taking prescription painkillers did not work. "I did my darndest to do everything I could do to clean him up," James says. "This past summer he swore to me he was only taking a very minuscule amount of painkillers, and I actually saw a dramatic change in his reaction time and well-being. Quite frankly, Jim hid his drug problem extremely well. He lied to everybody about it. After his death, we found out how severe it was."

If there is a lesson in Simons's death, James hopes it is an awareness of the potential danger of prescription medication. "People don't realize how addictive prescription drugs are," he says. "Anybody can get hooked on them. I don't care how strong mentally you think you are."

Amid the pills and the exercise equipment Simons left when he walked out to his hot tub for the last time were many festive bags filled with candy and trail mix. That was his holiday tradition, packaging and delivering the sweets to friends, neighbors, children at his church, even area golf pros who had extended a courtesy. "He'd make up bag after bag," says James, "and give them to everybody he knew."

January 27, 2006

I won a first-place award in the Golf Writers Association of America writing contest for this article, but given that it was prompted by the early and unfortunate death of a one-time golf golden boy, I wish I hadn't had to write it. That said, as my story revealed, Simons was a complicated individual, his life not nearly as neat as the game that offered so much promise when he was a young man. In the decades since Simons came so close to winning the 1971 U.S. Open at Merion Golf Club, no amateur has had a better finish in the national championship than Simons's tie for fifth place that year.

CHAPTER TWENTY-NINE

Still Driven after All These Years

A lifetime of practice has resulted in a détente between Deane Beman and his height. "When you are smaller you have to be better, you have to be tougher," he says, an admission that will surprise no one who ever faced him on a golf course or in a board room. "I think smaller people are fortunate because they have to drive themselves harder."

The peace, however, is not always and forever. During a recent round at Cape Arundel Golf Club in Kennebunkport, Maine, not far from his summer home, for which his pregame meal was a hot dog from the local convenience store, the five-foot-seven Beman drove the ball as straight as a testing machine. He nearly holed a three-wood for a double eagle, peppered wedges close to the flag, and shot his age, sixty-six, on the par-69 course. He could not resist making an observation to his six-foot-two guest.

"If I had been as big as you," Beman said, "they might not have heard of Jack Nicklaus."

Retirement can't stop a man from dreaming, but Beman always did have a way of making hypotheticals sound like the last word. "There were no arguments to be won when talking to Deane," says player and broadcaster Gary McCord. "[People] knew he was tenacious, but I don't think they knew *how* tenacious. He had teeth, serious teeth." Ten years since stepping down as PGA Tour commissioner, Beman has learned to put his feet up, but he prefers to-do lists over bingo and is often closer to a legal pad than a lounge chair. "I'm a substance-over-style kind of guy," Beman says. "I'm a results-over-talk kind of guy."

Beman's late father, Delmar, was a public relations man, but the youngest of his three sons never saw the joy in trying to sway others with slogans. He doesn't enjoy idle chitchat, but that is not to say he doesn't have lots of opinions. A decade removed from being one of sports' most powerful figures—a man who transferred his competitive fire as a golfer into an innovative, twenty-year, take-no-prisoners reign as commissioner—he is full of them, from how beginners should learn golf to what can be done to motivate schoolchildren. Nothing revs him up quite like a discussion of why he believes the United States Golf Association has let technology overrun the sport.

"There is not strong enough leadership to bring perspective," he says of the USGA, "and there is a great tendency for no one to be responsible. [The USGA's] role is to preserve and protect, not to preserve and protect [its] treasure. They either think what is happening now is right, or they don't think they have the authority, or they are afraid of losing money. I maintain the money the USGA has is not worth a nickel if they don't use it to protect the game. Better that they should get in a lawsuit and lose it all than to allow ourselves to go where we are going."

When Beman delivers a point he particularly fancies (and thinks you should too), his arresting blue eyes, set off now by a head of white hair, fix the listener like a neon sign on a lonely highway. They are the eyes that saw a way to beat bigger, stronger opponents despite an unorthodox swing and injury-prone body, that charted a course to bring the PGA Tour into the modern sports marketplace, that envisioned how a north Florida swamp could be developed into the home of one of the game's premier events, that stared down icons who thought he was too omnipotent and wanted his hide midway through his tenure.

They are the eyes of a man who never wanted to lose. "Deane was always confident in whatever he wanted to do," says Beman's old friend and rival Nicklaus, who along with Arnold Palmer challenged Beman's authority in 1983 before backing down. "Deane thought he could beat the world in whatever he was doing. He always did."

If Nicklaus could see him now, he'd say nothing has changed. It is another peaceful New England summer morning, but shortly after seven o'clock noises coming from Beman's exercise room, which doubles as a playroom for his ten grandchildren, puncture the stillness. When he was a crew-cut teenager growing up in suburban Maryland in the 1950s, Beman jogged carrying a small sledgehammer. Today he is on a treadmill, the motor whirring louder as he goes from brisk uphill walk to moderate run. Having built up a sweat, he stretches, the start of a golf-specific workout program prescribed by a new friend in Ponte Vedra Beach, Florida, long-drive champion and trainer Gerry James, who is getting short-game instruction from Beman while helping him gain distance. "I've probably given it 50 percent effort, and it has increased my clubhead speed to the point where I carry the ball ten to fifteen yards farther than I could last November," says Beman, who is hitting his driver 240 to 250 yards in the air now. "By next January or February, I think I can add another ten to fifteen yards."

Before long Beman is laying back on a two-foot-tall Swiss ball, rapidly turning his torso back and forth, simulating a golf swing and beating the hell out of the ball with a 4.4-pound weight on a rope each time back and through. When he has finished two twenty-rep sets of the "tornado rotation," Beman is breathing hard, sweating, pleased with his effort. "An exercise program," he says, "is about continually overcoming your failure to hang in there."

Beman and his second wife, Judy, bought their Maine place, on eight acres a couple of miles from the water, in 1997. It has a screened-in porch, Adirondack chairs, a garden, and enough room in back to set up a Lilliputian golf course for family tournaments. Two Cairn terriers, Yankee and Dixie, are nearly always underfoot. In the attached garage there is an artificial-turf mat and a practice hitting net. If Beman isn't in there grooving his swing—on a recent day he had to fess up to Judy that he'd sent a ball through a hole in the net, breaking a window—he often can be found in the separate, larger garage that has a comfortable guest apartment on the second floor.

It is home to Beman's favorite diversions. (Golf is more than that, way more than that, still.) There is a gleaming white 1953 Buick Skylark convertible, the same type car Beman squired his girlfriend in to her senior prom when he was a sophomore, thereby acquiring instant cool. There are his and hers motorcycles and a bizarre, limited-edition creation from the 1980s called a Pulse. It resembles the cockpit of a fighter jet on wheels and looks like something to be raced across the Bonneville Salt Flats, and when Beman takes it out it turns the heads of the blueberry- and lobster-seeking set. His pet project, nearly five years in the making, is a black 1935 Ford convertible. "I built [that] car from the absolute frame up," he says. "I've never done that before. It isn't quite finished, but almost. When the weather isn't good, I work on the car."

The Bemans named their home "Too Wonderful Farm" for a remark one of the grandchildren, twenty-year-old Sarah Clark, made when she was a tot. "One time when she was little," says Judy, revealing the origins of the name, "she said, 'You make everything too wonderful.'" Twice in the past few years the home has been filled with a different mood. Sarah's mother, Amy—the oldest of Beman's five children with his first wife, Miriam—was killed in an auto accident in North Carolina in the fall of 2001. "It was devastating on a lot of levels," says Judy. "You have to soldier on. You're not given more than you can handle." While the Bemans were coping with Amy's death, son-in-law Peter Kyros, who was married to Beman's daughter Valerie, became ill with cancer and passed away late last year. "I have had two terrible family tragedies," says Beman, who has another daughter, forty-three-year-old Priscilla, who has mental retardation and lives in a group home in Florida. "It is more helpful when you go through something like this when your time is your own."

The recent traumas have been the nadir of Beman's decade-long transition to a new life. Although he was fifty-six when he retired, Beman intended to compete full time on the senior tour that was created on his watch. He has had three top-tens in sixty-eight senior events since 1994—playing more than ten times only in 1995 and 1996—a bad left shoulder and arthritic back limiting him more than the sniping from some pros who resented his presence on sponsors' exemptions. Over dinner at a little restaurant in Cape Porpoise he says of the chilly reception, "Hurt isn't the right word. Let's just say it didn't lessen my desire."

Once Beman's former deputy, Tim Finchem, replaced him in 1994, Beman contends he moved on without reservation, intent on spending the time with his grandkids that eighteen-hour days and nonstop travel didn't allow with his five children. He also made sure not to shadow his successor. "I was second-guessed for twenty years," Beman says. "It's a tough job. He's going to be second-guessed—he doesn't need it from me. I was determined not to put him in that position, and I haven't."

Beman was too busy getting instrument-certified to fly ("I can fly when the weather is bad,"), reestablishing friendships ("You may call yourself friends, but you are really acquaintances until you spend enough time with people"), and coming up with a plan, as yet untested, in which elementary school students would have the incentive of earning merchandise if they do their assignments ("You need to directly motivate the kids; you can't depend on the parents. They see things on television, they want stuff. You complete a task, you get a credit. You learn to earn."). He also codesigned Cannon Ridge Golf Club in Fredericksburg, Virginia, with architect Bobby Weed.

Plus his understudy was ready. As Finchem says, "I had already been running the day- to-day operations of the business for five years. He gave me a lot of responsibility. You can't say too much

More Than a Score

about that in terms of preparing somebody. When he left, he did make a clean break." While Finchem might have had to smooth some feathers Beman had ruffled along the way, he took over a corporation that was in high gear. "Tim Finchem's doing a great job," Peter Jacobsen told *Sports Illustrated* in 1997, "but it's like Deane left him a Mercedes with the tank a quarter full, and all Tim has to do is keep putting gas in it."

Finchem likens Beman to the late Pete Rozelle and himself to Paul Tagliabue, the last two National Football League commissioners. "Rozelle took it up a notch," he says, "and Tagliabue was there to build upon it." He says Beman "brought the PGA Tour into the modern world of sports, and he did it with a lot of obstacles. He had to argue with players about whether we should do marketing deals. He had to argue with players about whether we should do Tournament Players Clubs. He had a lot of people who didn't see the vision."

Beman was not quite thirty-six when he replaced Joseph C. Dey Jr. in 1974 after six years on tour in which he won four times and finished second in the 1969 U.S. Open despite his lack of distance. Says Jim Colbert, a longtime ally, "I used to accuse him of hitting it even shorter when he played against Nicklaus so he could stick it in there with a five-wood before Nicklaus hit his eight-iron." More than his power deficit, Beman was sabotaged by recurring injuries, his hands in casts nearly as often as they were healthy.

Upon taking over the PGA Tour, he set out on a furious pace to improve and modernize it, a four-hundred-meter sprinter in a setting that had been used to a leisurely stroll. Perhaps it was because after waiting until he was twenty-nine to turn pro, after a successful amateur career (two U.S. Amateur victories, one British Amateur title, four Walker Cup appearances), he was shelved so often by injury. Maybe it was because he had seen one of his brothers, Del, die in his early thirties from a cerebral hemorrhage. Whatever the genesis, for a guy whose game lacked horsepower, he always loved speed. He summed up his get-it-done-now philosophy once by saying, "If you play eighteen holes and make only one birdie instead of two, it doesn't mean you saved one for tomorrow."

So much of professional golf as it is known today—wall-to-wall corporate sponsors footing the bill for television broadcasts, stadium golf, the PGA Tour as a brand, an all-exempt structure that allows more pros to escape a gypsy life, tours for fledgling (Nationwide) and aging (Champions) players—came to fruition while Beman headed the PGA Tour that the accomplishments tend to blur like the individual successes of a straight-A student. He considered reflecting on his career in a book but says it didn't happen because he wasn't willing to produce a "kiss-and-tell" tale detailing who got fined and for what. "They really wanted more [about what I did] with John Daly and Mac O'Grady," Beman says. "I wasn't going to do that. Having gone twenty years without discussing any of those things, I'm damn sure not going to discuss it now."

Beman may yet write an autobiography, especially if he ever decides to stop working hard on his game, but don't expect it to be filled with regrets. He is not sorry he took on Karsten Manufacturing over square grooves, which resulted in a time-sapping lawsuit that eventually was settled. He doesn't think he was wrong in not embracing foreign stars such as Seve Ballesteros, who wanted to compete on the PGA Tour without playing the minimum number of events. "He was out for himself," Beman says of Ballesteros. "He didn't care about the rules, the organization, or anything else. You have to have rules for everybody. If you don't administer the rules impartially, across the board, then you don't have rules."

Ask Beman about any specific mea culpas as commissioner, and he cites not a major initiative but a fight between Dave Hill and J. C. Snead on the driving range of a 1991 senior tour event in California. "I took an action with both players," Beman remembers. "[The fine] wasn't going to break anybody, but Dave Hill took it like a man, and J.C. was successful in his appeal. I felt they were equally wrong, that J.C. was actually the instigator. I wish I'd given Dave Hill his money back, even if I had to write a personal check."

More Than a Score

To those who would nitpick his record, Beman tells a story. "I [was talking] to a couple of buddies one time, probably 1989 or 1990, who were complaining about us [the tour] losing some money somewhere," he says. "I said, 'Yes, I've probably lost ten million dollars running this place, but I've made a billion and a half making good decisions.'"

These days Beman thinks much less about his legacy than about the current state of the game—his own and that being played at the highest level. "I'm highly motivated," he says. "I can still play. And I play better when I need to, not worse." For all he accomplished as commissioner, there is a slight yearning for what might have been inside the ropes. He says, "I certainly was not a better executive than I was a competitor. Had I been as injury-free as Jack [Nicklaus], my heart tells me I would have performed in golf as well as I did as commissioner." Had he not left competition in 1974? "I think I would have won two or three majors and one tournament a year over the next ten to fifteen years. There wasn't any reason to believe I wouldn't."

In the winter and spring at home in Ponte Vedra Beach, the forty-four-year-old James, who is six feet five inches and 240 pounds, is a frequent opponent. "He's a consummate competitor," says James, who recorded a 473-yard drive in 1997. "I'll shoot 70, and Deane will shoot 69. I'll shoot 68, and he'll shoot 67. I'm outhitting him by a hundred yards sometimes. When I play with a lot of guys, if I get a couple under early and I'm bombing it by them, they just give up. With Deane, it just inspires him."

Beman's bag is full of lightweight graphite shafts and lofted fairway woods, but his putter is a Ping Anser that Karsten Solheim gave him in 1973. Most of his golf is social, but none of it is pointless. "I consider the journey as much of a pleasure as the destination in golf," he says, "even if it is only getting ready to play your best for nothing." He has played for more than pride a couple of times this summer, failing to qualify for the U.S. Senior Open by two strokes, finishing tied for fortieth in the Greater Portland

(Maine) Open, and tied for thirty-third in last week's Greater Bangor (Maine) Open against many golfers half his age. He would play on the Champions Tour if he could get in some events. In the meantime he also watches a lot of golf. While acknowledging he views the game through the prism of his talents and limitations, he believes modern balls and clubs have diminished the sport by changing the skill set required to succeed. "That's what's so bad about the new golf ball," he contends. "It diminishes your mistakes, and the more powerful you are, the more important that is. Golf used to have a wonderful balance between power and precision. Now [power] is an overwhelming part of the game."

To him, the current generation of balls, with their improved aerodynamics, is akin to playing with the 1.62-inch-diameter ball formerly played outside the United States. "The modern ball plays better [easier] than the 1.62 ball used to, the one that required less skill," he says. "So from a skill level, we've gone backward. Real ball-striking ability that comes with playing unforgiving equipment is going backward. The players aren't as good as they could be if they played less forgiving equipment. And I think it takes away from golf."

Although Beman says the USGA is "responsible for where we are, and they won't own up to it," many USGA defenders, including its executive director David Fay, have argued that equipment regulations of tour pros is the domain of the tour, not the USGA. The tour's experience with the Karsten lawsuit, which filled Beman's last couple of years as commissioner, left it with little desire to wade into equipment controversies. Some equipment manufacturers, most notably Acushnet's Wally Uihlein, contend there is no evidence the game is in need of equipment regulation.

Beman, though, is not swayed. He would not limit distance but mandate balls that curve more, that are more vulnerable to the side spin imparted by a misstruck shot and less impervious to the wind. Grooves would be limited as to the amount of spin they can impart, making shots from the rough harder to control.

"It would still be possible for somebody who is bigger and stronger to play better," he says. "It just gets rid of the free pass."

By the fall Beman will still be five-foot-seven, but he plans to be stronger. He plans to be playing better. Some things, after all these years, haven't changed a bit.

July 30, 2004

The PGA Tour continued to click along as the first decade of the twenty-first century came to an end and a new decade in golf's burgeoning global era commenced. Deane Beman's successor, Tim Finchem, has ably guided the enterprise Beman launched on such a sound course forty years ago. In 2012 there were forty-five official PGA Tour events offering total prize money of approximately $279 million. Adam Schupak detailed Beman's long, instrumental reign as PGA Tour commissioner in the fine 2011 book *Deane Beman: Golf's Driving Force*.

CHAPTER THIRTY

The Man Who Loved Golf to Death

Whether it was when he was a boy growing up in the Florida panhandle, or as one of the best players in the world in the late 1960s and early 1970s, or as an aging pro trying to hang on to a senior tour exemption, Bert Yancey could never get enough golf. Above almost everything else, the people who loved him remember this. Often the recollection comes with a smile, but sometimes with a tear.

Yancey's twin brother recalls the sticky summer mornings on a public course in Tallahassee. They were only five or six years old, dropped off most days by their father, Malcolm, the city manager. "Bert took it seriously from the very beginning," Bill Yancey says. "We used to get in arguments on the course. I'd be down in the creek chasing frogs, and he'd say, 'Get up here, play golf.'"

It was a spirited love that accompanied him to the sport's peaks and into its depths, a journey that mirrored a more powerful duel going on within, a struggle that on a good day could only be wrestled to a draw.

"Around and around we'd play," says Mark McCumber, recalling as many as fifty-four holes a day in the 1980s when he was being tutored by Yancey. "He'd beat balls and play, beat balls and play. I've never known anybody who loved to play golf as much as he did."

Frank Beard was one of Yancey's good friends on the PGA Tour. "Sometimes he got too intense, got in his own way," Beard says. "He'd be fumbling around with all these different golf swings and forget to play golf. It didn't seem to bother him—it was like he was on some mission to find the perfect golf swing."

Yancey's mission—to play, to teach, to be a golfer—was fueled with both public bravery and private risk. Sidetracked many times by manic depression, it ended August 26, 1994, about the only place it made sense that it end for him, at a golf course, a bucket of balls at his feet.

The Franklin Quest Championship, a Senior PGA Tour event, was going on, a tournament Yancey didn't want to withdraw from despite the chest pains, despite a warning earlier that morning not to play, despite the fact he was fifty-six years old and many Yancey men had been taken down early by heart disease.

There is a plaque affixed to a boulder at Park Meadows Country Club in Park City, Utah, near the practice range where Tom Weis-kopf heard his best friend collapse to the ground and soon saw the paramedics rush forth. The words on the big rock read, "Bert Yancey was a tenacious champion with unusual courage, deter-mination, wit and wisdom. . . . His quest for excellence remained remarkably intense and focused as he executed his final shot from this area."

The seniors still play at Park Meadows each summer, and spec-tators who notice the memorial sometimes stop in the pro shop with a question: Did he die right there? "He never made it to the helicopter," says Scott Yancey, one of his four children. "Died in the ambulance. As far as we know, his last words were, 'I have to play.'"

The best time of the year to remember Bert Yancey is the spring, when golf is breaking out all over and the Masters beckons. He all but had one arm through the sleeve of a green jacket several times, including 1967, the first year he competed at Augusta, as a twenty-eight-year-old tour pro on the rise who finished third. He was third the next year too, and fourth in 1970. "He was almost a darn good enough player to have won," says Weiskopf, who knows the feeling, having been a Masters runner-up four times himself.

When top players rent a home while playing in the Masters these days, it is usually one that's tucked away on a quiet block, an ample dwelling owned by a doctor or lawyer who has vacated to Hilton Head or Sea Island. When Yancey and his wife, Linda, arrived the week before the tournament in 1967, they settled into a room of a modest house owned and occupied by Mr. and Mrs. J. B. Masters located at 315 Berckmans Road, a busy thoroughfare across from the Augusta National Golf Club property.

To Yancey, it was the happiest of coincidences that his landlord had such a surname. He had always been fascinated by the Masters. Although his parents held badges for many years, he vowed not to attend until he earned an invitation to play, and he did not. Enthralled with golf history, he was wild about the Masters: Yancey made it his business to know the plots of all the finishes, the slopes of the tricky greens, the pattern of the clubhouse silverware, the manufacturer of the green jackets.

"When some player remarks that 'the Masters is just another tourney,'" Yancey told *Golf World* in 1977, "I have to think he is just fooling himself or has never been there. It is unique. The U.S. Open is, too, but that's like comparing soup to nuts. Augusta has a different style and quality to it. If you aren't among the best in the game you simply aren't there."

Once, in the early 1960s, the Yancey twins killed time during a long drive by debating the merits of the country's best courses. Bill defended some other well-known layouts and questioned his brother on what was so all-fired hot about Augusta National. "There are no azaleas at Pebble Beach," Bert said, ending the discussion.

Some of Yancey's peers on tour also recognized the Masters for the plum that it was, but they soon discovered Yancey's feelings ran deeper than theirs. Jack Nicklaus played a sparse schedule to peak come Augusta, but almost every other pro stayed busy to

More Than a Score

pay the bills. But Yancey would tinker with his technique during tournaments or duck off the circuit altogether to get ready for his biggest tournament of the year. Fellow pros would describe Yancey's preoccupation as his "Masters fog," but they seldom teased him because it seemed so sincere, so true.

"It became apparent that all Bert wanted to do was win the Masters," says Beard. "The healthy side of the line is called a passion, and the unhealthy line is called obsession. Palmer and Nicklaus had a passion to win the Masters, but it wasn't obsession. Bert's was an obsession."

That first trip to Augusta, Yancey bought forty-two cans of Play-Doh, paint, plastic straws, and a sheet of plywood about the size of a pool table. Staying up late into the night, sustained by cold cuts from Mrs. Masters's kitchen, he studied his extensive notes about Augusta National's tricky putting surfaces and constructed replicas. "It was a matter of putting this information in my head and doing it physically with my hands to memorize the greens," he later said. Yancey knew nothing so much as that there were positions on those greens to be avoided at all costs. And by making the miniatures, by caressing the slopes that mimicked the real ones, he believed he would be better prepared to win the title more dear to him than any other.

"The models were very well done," says Weiskopf, remembering the time, probably after a bridge game, when Yancey said, "Take a look at this," and slid his moldings out from under the bed in the Masters's guest room. "Each one was about the size of a pie plate. They were painted but pliable enough that he could move the little flagsticks around. He would look at all these hypothetical situations."

Fantastic at bridge and great with numbers, Yancey would fill the hours of a long flight by doing calculus problems. "For a hobby he would take these medical quizzes," says Weiskopf, "and he'd know the answer 90 percent of the time." Building model airplanes was one of his favorite pastimes long before he shaped his first Augusta replica. But his analytical bent coexisted with an uncommon touch, one Dave Stockton recalls once allowed Yancey to play nine hundred holes on tour without three-putting.

"Doing the model planes was an exercise for his hands," says Scott Yancey, thirty-two, who followed his father into golf as a club professional. "He thought of himself as a great putter, almost to the point where he thought he was a surgeon. His hands to him were so important."

Yancey's older brother, Jim, who taught him how to play golf, lives on a peaceful street in Ocala, Florida, with his wife, JoAnne. As far as physical reminders of Bert, they don't have many. They have a few family pictures, a couple of magazine articles, a first-place trophy he won at a local invitational in 1957; the gold-plated golfer is missing his tiny club. But Jim, who has gotten to seventy-three having survived cancer, a heart attack, and a stroke, and his wife have plenty of memories.

The phone calls would come in the middle of the night, rambling calls from a man who couldn't sleep. If Bert was visiting, there was another way they could tell something was going on. "He always had to be dressed perfectly," says JoAnne, "so the first way to tell he was getting sick was that he would start dressing peculiarly. He'd wear a scarf, or put a feather in his cap."

The first time they might have sensed something was different about Bert came in the spring of 1960. The West Point golf team had traveled south to Miami, where Jim and JoAnne were living. "Bert kept me up late into the night talking," JoAnne says, sitting in her quiet living room at home. "That was a symptom, but we didn't know it at the time."

A few months later, back at school, where Bert had scored one of the highest entrance exams at the academy and was on the dean's list, his sleeplessness soon escalated into outbursts that led to a nine-month stay at a psychiatric hospital in Valley Forge, Pennsylvania, one of those months in a padded cell. Instead of completing the customary training of a fourth-year cadet en route to becoming an officer, Yancey received electroshock treatments and a medical discharge.

The doctors called it a nervous breakdown. It was terror for the whole Yancey family, but it went away. His military hopes dashed, Yancey focused on golf. After one failed attempt, he got on the tour and stuck. After a brief first marriage, he met Linda and they wed in 1963. Yancey was tall, blond, and handsome and possessed a flowing, upright swing. He was businesslike. "He didn't say funny things, he didn't dance on the greens," Dave Kindred wrote of Yancey in 1978. "All he did was pull a white visor low over his eyes and walk slowly around a golf course, walking so smoothly he seemed to float, a man in a dream world."

Even before the dream was not yet a nightmare again—before bizarre episodes that reoccurred in 1974 and 1975 were correctly diagnosed as manic depression—his brain chemistry was affecting him and his golf. Yancey led Lee Trevino by one stroke after fifty-four holes of the 1968 U.S. Open at Oak Hill Country Club in Rochester, New York. "Going out there the last day, he was saying, 'Who am I to win the U.S. Open?'" says Linda Yancey Makiver, who divorced Yancey in 1977. "I'm like, 'Well, who is Lee Trevino?' I think this was part of his illness. He was a perfectionist, yet if things were going well he had a way of destroying it."

Yancey looked out of his element that final round, "as pale as a prison guard" on the first tee, wrote Jim Murray. The grace misplaced and his swings uncertain, he shot a 76 to Trevino's 69. Ten years later Yancey attempted to explain what might have gone wrong that Sunday, and it had nothing to do with fairways and greens. "What happens," he said, "is that when you succeed, believe it or not, you become depressed. For me, anyway, you become depressed again because your body feels it has to succeed again and again. You win a tournament, you've got to win another, then three or four. You win a major, then you've got to win another major. I mean there's no end to it."

The lithium that would keep Yancey from thinking he could save the world or preaching from a workman's ladder at a major airport (two of the episodes that hospitalized him in his darkest hours) gave him a slight hand tremor. To a pro golfer, it might as well have been a broken arm. Returning to the tour in 1976, Yancey was a slim shadow of his old self, unable to make a cut. Paired with Jack Nicklaus and Lanny Wadkins at the Sea Pines Heritage Classic in March, he shot 90-80. His bravery notwithstanding, Yancey's struggles that abbreviated season became the shorthand recollection of him for some. When a punter double-clutched in a *Monday Night Football* game last fall, Dennis Miller made a joke at Yancey's expense.

"We felt for him because it was a cycle," says Charles, his oldest son. "He wanted to play so bad, but he knew he couldn't play well taking the amount of medication he was supposed to be taking. So he'd lower [his dosage] and play. And then he'd get a little high. Once he got a little high, he thought he didn't need to take it any more, and pretty soon he's back in the hospital. Then he'd have to receive higher doses to get him back to normal. Going on and off the medication, having to get the higher doses, can't be good. I think he killed himself over golf, really."

As a teacher, Yancey could be blindingly complex. As much as Jim Yancey loved his brother, when Bert visited and insisted on tutoring one of Jim's and JoAnne's six sons, it wasn't a banner day. "He couldn't resist messing with their swings," says JoAnne, "and Jim would tell the boys not to listen to Bert. He was on a totally different plane."

But Yancey was also an enthusiastic and smart man, stressing the importance of pre-shot routine before many other instructors did. McCumber, still trying to hone his routine and play better under pressure in 1982, turned to Yancey. At their first session, McCumber and Yancey talked for a quarter-hour, then McCumber hit balls for forty minutes while Yancey sat silently on a shooting stick behind him. McCumber was growing anxious when Yancey finally spoke.

"He said, 'Okay, that's eighty-three shots. On the fourth shot you took three waggles. On the eighteenth shot you took four waggles. On the forty-second shot you took one waggle. Other than that, you took two waggles. That's normal for you.'" Taking care to make two waggles, McCumber won ten PGA Tour events and became close friends with Yancey. "I grew to love him like a family member," McCumber says. "I could sit and listen to him talk all evening. He was a brilliant man, and he knew how to inspire me."

Even when Yancey was teaching golf full time, he couldn't resist playing in the couple of PGA Tour events (he won seven titles) he could get into because he was a past champion. Scott, born in 1968, wasn't able to see his dad compete in his prime; he was the Yancey child who "couldn't get enough of the scrapbooks." Once he got the golf bug, he couldn't wait until Bert finished his lessons so they could play a few holes before dark. One summer, when Scott was in junior high, he accompanied his father on a drive from their South Carolina home to Memphis.

"He wanted to stop in Augusta," Scott says, "and I thought we were going to see the course and everything. We get to the front gate. I jump out. I'm ready. We're chatting with the security guy, who seems to know Dad. And then Dad goes, 'If you want to go through these gates, you've got to earn your way through.' We stood there for a minute, gazed down Magnolia Lane, then we drove away."

When his condition was in check, Yancey had a pleasant voice as calm and smooth as a farm pond at midnight, hardly a trace of the South, though he had grown up there. It was always a comfort to Weiskopf, especially at the end of a day when his short fuse had gotten the best of him. "He was a tremendously loyal friend," says Weiskopf, "and he had a lot of compassion for me, and he understood me. He went out of his way to help me. Many a night, after he'd heard that I was upset about something, he would call and say, 'Tell me about it, T.'"

And just as Yancey saw through the sporadic petulance and temper of his buddy, Weiskopf embraced the frailty and accepted the disorder that manic depression caused in a man who otherwise was all military corners. "Bert represented the game, he represented character, he represented everything a tournament player should be," Weiskopf says.

Although Weiskopf knew Yancey was in grave trouble when he collapsed near him that Friday at the Franklin Quest Championship, he didn't know he had died until after completing his own round. Like many of the senior pros who had known Yancey for decades and been aware of what he'd been through, Weiskopf didn't want to continue playing but was talked into it by Jim Yancey.

What happened two days later—eight months before most of the world knew Ben Crenshaw had ever taken a lesson from Harvey Penick—was enough to make golfers believe in much more than a straight left arm. Weiskopf trailed Dave Stockton by three strokes but holed improbably long putts on the last three holes, including an eighty-footer on No. 16, to force a playoff. On the first extra hole, Weiskopf rolled in a twenty-foot birdie putt to claim his first senior victory, Yancey's voice with him the whole miraculous time, telling him the same old advice, to keep his head still when he putted.

Weiskopf was never one to surround himself with the trophies that came with his victories—"I always sent them back to the clubs because I figured they'd enjoy them more than me," he says—but this was different. The Franklin Quest trophy sits opposite Weiskopf's desk at his golf course–design office in Scottsdale, Arizona. "Bert's Trophy," he calls it, his voice hushing a little. "It's unique, really a work of art. It looks like it could be part of a golf swing, or an upside-down question mark without the dot. I look at it, and I remember him."

He wishes that Yancey's defiant brain chemistry hadn't ever become part of the public record, that no one ever thought his friend was crazy when he was merely sick. But it is not an all-

More Than a Score

encompassing regret. It doesn't extend to Yancey's tendency to finesse or abandon his medication so he could play golf. "The unfortunate thing is because of his passion and love for the game, Bert created a problem for himself," Weiskopf says. "That was his decision."

Yancey's daughter, Tracy Defina, believes her father is with her every time she goes into the Pennsylvania preschool where she teaches. He was good with kids, frequently wrapping something about the game he cherished with a larger truth. "People say he accomplished so much, that everybody can't be Jack Nicklaus, that you can't have regrets, but I do for him," Defina says. "But golf was the world to him—the history, the mechanics of it, the people. I see his early death as a blessing. Had he gotten to be an old man in bad health and not been able to have golf . . ."

At his California home, Beard reflects on the young Yancey: all the practice rounds and the oh-so-normal twilights by motel pools watching their kids, the friend who enjoyed a laugh but "always had a reservation and seriousness about him." The golfer "who'd go all winter into the spring not playing worth a crap, then get to Augusta and play well." And the older Yancey: the stickler for the rules who was having a manic episode and hitting practice shots during play at a senior tournament in Los Angeles, an ambulance soon taking him away to a place where there was no golf.

Bill Yancey, a sociology professor at Temple University, tells a sweet story about his boyhood bonds with his brother. If anyone picked a fight with one twin, they were soon scrapping with both of them. And a sad one about the distance that grew between them once they were older. "There were times we got together, but they weren't easy times," he says. "I was never sure when Bert would get mad. I remember I mispronounced *Baltusrol* one time and he got angry." There is regret for the long sit-downs they never had, "a couple of beers under us," talking about life.

In Augusta a businessman named Dan Cook, a manic depressive like Yancey, remembers his friend each summer by conducting the Bert Yancey Memorial, a golf tournament to raise funds for three local mental health agencies. "You don't outgrow manic depression," Cook says. "He was still trying to get it together when he died. He still had ups and downs. But he achieved so much by helping get the word out that we're not nuts, that it can be controlled."

Every second week of April, Berckmans Road bustles with people in cars and on foot heading to one of the Masters parking lots or one of the walk-in gates. They go right past the house where seven of the eight times Bert Yancey played at Augusta he rented a room and tried to absorb a landscape, until one day it crumbled in his hands, and where his landlady sewed him a tiny green jacket and hung it on the wall.

Into the fragrant, green oasis of Augusta National they'll stream. Laden with folding chairs and sunblock, intent on watching the best golfers in the world, a good portion of the patrons will meander through the tall pines to camp out at the sixteenth hole, a cozy devil of a par three with a green that pitches like an angry sea, where one of the best made a deuce four days running back in 1968. Scott Yancey will watch from a distance, on television, keeping a promise that must last as long as his father's dream.

March 30, 2001

A few years ago Augusta National Golf Club built a large, state-of-the-art practice range on land where thousands of cars used to be parked during the Masters. The club bought up houses and land for new parking along Berckmans Road. The home where Bert Yancey stayed during the tournament he loved so much, where he made his Play-Doh replica greens, is no more. His legacy lives on, bravely, in the form of golfers like Steven Bowditch and Christina Kim who play professional golf while battling depression as Yancey did.

More Than a Score

The Tiger Era

I met Tiger Woods on a magazine assignment more than twenty years ago, in the fall of 1991, when he was a skinny (six feet, 137 pounds) fifteen-year-old on the ascent. I played with his dog, Genie, and posed Tiger in front of a fraction of the golf trophies—the kind with miniature clubs that tend to fall out of the tiny gold-plated golfers' grips—he had won to date. We ate breakfast on a Saturday morning at a golf course restaurant. Tiger had an appetite; he had a three-egg omelet *and* an order of chipped beef with cream gravy on toast.

From that first encounter, I would see Tiger a lot over the next two decades or so, as he became to his era what Bobby Jones had been to his and Arnold Palmer to his: the face of golf, but in Tiger's case, the first multiethnic face of golf. I watched Woods at college tournaments, the U.S. Amateur, and his first event as a professional, the 1996 Greater Milwaukee Open. I saw his historic maiden Masters win the following spring, quite a few stops during his magical 2000 season, and his miracle at Torrey Pines in the 2008 U.S. Open, where neither a badly injured left leg nor Rocco Mediate could interrupt Tiger's willpower or mess with his mojo. Then, after a personal scandal erupting in late 2009 that changed so much for Woods, I have trailed him at major championships as he has sought—unsuccessfully, through the 2013 season—to recapture his former gloss in the events that have shaped his life since he was an underweight and heavily hyped teenager.

For all those observations, though, I don't know Tiger. Few, if any, golf writers do. We've watched and we've written and we've theorized and we've judged and we've ranked and we've predicted and we've doubted, but we don't *know* him.

What is known *of* Tiger, however, as he's defined an era and we've tried to define him in the process, is fascinating.

Years before it was a Twitter acronym (GOAT), something hashtagged to Roger Federer that had been said by, and about, Muhammad Ali, Tiger Woods wanted to be the Greatest of All Time in his sport. How much of it was Earl's dream, and how much of it was Tiger's? Whatever the role of the father—and mother, Kultida, from whom her son got much of his competitive doggedness—in planting the seeds of his ambition, I am certain he soon took it over, driven to achieve an unforgettable chapter of golf exceptionalism.

No one could have shown the focus Woods displayed, time after remarkable time in tense and intense moments on the course, living out someone else's idea of a career. Individuals with that unfortunate burden, whether in tennis or golf or other sports, end up by the athletic wayside sooner rather than later, frustrated and burned out because their dreams really weren't their own. As he nears forty Tiger might still be trying to "own" his golf swing, à la the sweet spot–hitting troika of Ben Hogan, Lee Trevino, and the eccentric Canadian shotmaker supreme, Moe Norman, but I'm convinced he has long possessed the deed to his aspirations.

When I visited Tiger those many years ago, there was a small newspaper clipping tacked to his bedroom wall listing some of Jack Nicklaus's golf milestones and how old Nicklaus had been when he achieved them. But the destination that would define Woods's journey was Nicklaus's record total of eighteen professional major championship victories (six Masters, four U.S. Opens, three British Opens, five PGA Championships).

Becoming golf's GOAT, to Tiger, would mean winning nineteen (or more) majors. Anything else would be setting out from New York for Los Angeles and making it only as far as El Paso or Phoenix.

There had been a succession of "Next Nicklauses" in the latter part of the twentieth century, from Tom Weiskopf to Ben Crenshaw to Hal Sutton, men who carried the onerous label to fine but ultimately lacking records compared to the Golden Bear. Woods, however, seemed comfortably fueled by the most concrete, and lofty, goal any golfer ever had.

Good under pressure?

A few months before I met Tiger in 1991, he had won the first of three consecutive U.S. Junior Amateur titles, an unprecedented feat. He rallied from three down after six holes in the final against Brad Zwetschke—there is a name for a trivia contest—en route to a sudden-death victory.

Woods's subsequent junior conquests in 1992 and 1993 were followed by another historic trifecta: consecutive victories in the U.S. Amateur in 1994, 1995, and 1996. In winning the first and last of those national titles, against Trip Kuehne and Steve Scott, respectively, Woods fell behind but rallied dramatically. Not even Nicklaus himself, the king of sinking putts that had to be made, had anything on Tiger's knack of coming through in the clutch. To boot, he had Nicklausian power and Palmer's ability to scramble smoothly out of trouble.

By the time Woods played in his first tournament as a pro after signing endorsement deals reportedly worth more than $40 million, expectations for his game—and *the* game—were soaring. He made only $2,544 in his first play-for-pay foray, finishing twelve strokes behind Loren Roberts's winning total at Brown Deer Park, but Tiger had his moments.

I still have a crinkled pocket notebook from that week, a souvenir of his debut. In my scribblings about Tiger's opening round at the GMO, I see in faded ink that on his very first tee shot, with so many eyes focused on him, he drove the ball 336 yards down the middle. On the par-five sixth hole, he hit a 235-yard five-iron twelve feet from the flagstick after a 330-yard drive. John Elliott, the good-natured journeyman, deadpanned to the greenside gallery, "Pretty good, isn't he?"

On Sunday, out of contention but still in the spotlight, Tiger made an ace at the fourteenth hole. Yes, he had all the shots.

His push to earn a PGA Tour card for the 1997 season by making enough money in an abbreviated schedule turned out to be a breeze. In eight events that fall, Woods won at Las Vegas and Disney World and had three other top-five finishes. Not only did he finish in the top 125 money winners, but he ended the 1996 season inside the top twenty-five. (He would not rank lower than fourth in earnings for the next thirteen years, a span in which he was leading money winner eight times.)

The bar, it began to seem, could be raised to the clouds and Woods would clear it.

Out in forty strokes on the first day of the 1997 Masters Tournament, Tiger didn't look invincible. But he roared back in thirty. Three days later, after a power-and-touch display eclipsing even Nicklaus's landmark rout at Augusta National in 1965, Woods won a record twelve-stroke victory, putting the biggest log yet on the fire that was Tigermania, stoking his growing legend.

The color of his skin and the ferocity of his fist pumps drew attention, but those ingredients were underpinned by Tiger's skill, grit, and cool. The awesomeness of his physical and mental arsenal, so evident when he was an amateur, just kept getting better once he was on the main stage.

Phenomenal putts. Fantastic flop shots. Ball-striking—such as the wow-that-can't-be-done six-iron from the sand and over the water on the final hole of the 2000 Canadian Open—that turned the heads of golfers accustomed to turning heads themselves.

Amid Tiger's monster 2000 season, when his nine PGA Tour victories included a sweep of the schedule's last three majors (blowouts at the U.S. and British Opens, at Pebble Beach and St. Andrews respectively, and a tense playoff win over upstart Bob May at the PGA Championship), Hall of Famers such as Tom Watson raved at this guy whose game had no limits.

Indeed, much like his multiethnic heritage, Tiger's game was a melting pot of attributes from earlier legends. He captured the fancy of the public the way Bobby Jones did in the Golden Age of Sports. His knack for winning tournaments in bunches recalled Byron Nelson. His focus and desire seemed every bit as keen as Ben Hogan's, even if he didn't hit as many fairways and greens. His dominance intimidated foes much like Nicklaus's had. He was a striver, like Gary Player, always trying to improve. Tiger scrambled marvelously, often better, even, than the go-for-broke Palmer or inventively opportunistic Watson.

It was authentic athletic genius, as deep and as broad as golf—perhaps any sport—has ever seen. That made his fall from grace—when he was revealed, through actions at sharp odds with his public image, to lack authenticity as a person—that much more of a shock.

Before Tiger's life erupted in a tabloid frenzy late in 2009 over revelations of serial affairs that eventually led to a divorce from his wife, Elin Nordegren, criticisms about him had been pretty narrowly focused: he cussed too much on the course and didn't sign enough autographs off it; he failed to help B-list tournaments with an occasional appearance, especially ones that had given him a chance in his early months on tour; he was given early-bird starting times in nearly every pro-am and therefore was done with his day when many spectators were just arriving at the course.

His peers—who as a rule found Tiger a pleasant fellow competitor and had benefited enormously from purse increases that his presence and popularity brought about through much higher television rights fees the PGA Tour negotiated in the wake of his 1997 Masters win—largely did not join in the Tiger-bashing after the scandal broke. (Nor, it should be said, did Woods encounter much negative reaction from galleries after he returned to action in the spring of 2010. There was the occasional yahoo, but most fans, at tournament venues anyway, were willing to forgive if not forget and are fascinated by his quest to come back to his previous heights.)

No athlete, however, had ever taken such a publicly embarrassing hit to his reputation. This wasn't as simple as coming back from an injury. Having observed Woods a fair amount at major championships from 2010 through 2013 since he returned to competition following rehabilitation and his "blue curtain" mea culpa speech, it seems evident the personal upheaval took a toll. When it comes to winning more majors, time may or may not heal what ails Tiger.

Post-scandal, through the 2013 PGA Championship, Woods got himself in very good position to win several majors but was lacking in the clutch on weekends, formerly his wheelhouse. There was no single missing element; it was a blend of shortcomings, from mental lapses to poor shots to missing putts that he used to make. He made his reputation by being comfortable at the pivotal junctures in a tournament when others were anxiously unsure. Despite winning regular events, he was still looking for that competitive serenity in the majors.

I am writing these words a few days after the 2013 PGA Championship at Oak Hill Country Club in Rochester, New York. It was the eighteenth major Woods had played since winning his fourteenth at the 2008 U.S. Open and one of his worst performances in that span. His tie for fortieth place was particularly confounding given that it came on the heels of winning the WGC-Bridgestone Invitational at Firestone Country Club. That was his fifth PGA Tour triumph of 2013, which boosted his career total to seventy-nine victories as he arrived at Oak Hill. That many w's, to use Tiger's jock shorthand, is jarring to write, to read, to try to comprehend. On a single professional tour, there have been only three more prolific winners: the LPGA's Kathy Whitworth (eighty-eight titles) and Mickey Wright (eighty-two) and the male legend now squarely within Woods's sights, Sam Snead, who finished his amazing career with a record eighty-two PGA Tour wins.

There was a stunning footnote to Woods's 2013 achievements. His victory at the Farmers Insurance Open was his seventh at that event. When he won the WGC-Cadillac Championship, it was also for the seventh time. By claiming the trophy for the eighth time at both the Arnold Palmer Invitational and the WGC-Bridgestone, Woods has thirty victories in those four tournaments. His bounty on *those favorite stomping grounds alone* exceeds the career PGA Tour résumés of all but seventeen golfers all-time. At just that quartet of events, Woods has won more than did Hall of Famers Lee Trevino, Tommy Armour, Gary Player, Johnny Miller, Raymond Floyd, Hale Irwin, Greg Norman, and Davis Love III in their whole PGA Tour careers. These comparisons, like so many numbers Woods has put up, go to the heart of his golf brilliance.

Given Woods's focus on Nicklaus's eighteen major championships, Snead's all-time victory record has been a secondary, and often underappreciated, target. But as Woods closed in on Snead, the iconic Virginian's milestone seemed more relevant. It could well be that Snead is the golfer Woods will catch, not Nicklaus.

My *Golf World* colleague David Barrett, by analyzing early in 2013 what skilled players after World War II have done before and after their thirty-seventh birthday (Woods turned thirty-seven on December 30, 2012) in regular events and majors, predicted that Tiger would retire having shattered Snead's record but having come up just shy of Jack's.

Barrett projected that Woods will finish with ninety-four victories and a total of seventeen major titles. The wildcard, he was clear to state, is to what extent the psychological residue of Woods's scandal and the possible physical limitations caused by his various injuries will affect him for the rest of his career. Then there are much younger stars, led by Rory McIlroy, who have talent to burn and don't have the layers of competitive scar tissue some of Tiger's peers accumulated when their peak performances fell far short of his.

There is the old saw that a golfer, regardless of his greatness, has a finite quota of clutch shots and pressure putts—that no one is immune to the inevitably hard slap of age. Seve Ballesteros won his last major at age thirty-one, Tom Watson at thirty-three, Arnold Palmer at thirty-four. Tiger was thirty-two when he outlasted Rocco Mediate in the 2008 U.S. Open.

Finally, could the favorable winds of golf karma simply have ceased blowing in Woods's direction after years of being with him? Had his third shot to the fifteenth hole during the second round of the 2013 Masters not caromed off the flagstick and into the water he would have likely been in command of the tournament and poised to end his major drought. Instead he took an incorrect drop, found himself at the center of a rules imbroglio, and tied for fourth—his ninth top-six major finish during his Grand Slam dry spell.

Given Woods's strong play outside the majors through the summer of 2013, Snead's victory record should be eclipsed soon. As to scaling Mount Nicklaus, it remains possible if not as probable as it once seemed. Woods will be thirty-eight by the 2014 Masters. Nicklaus won the British Open at thirty-eight, the U.S. Open and PGA Championship at forty, and the Masters at forty-six. Nicklaus won his professional majors over twenty-four years; 2014 will mark seventeen years since Woods won his first. Despite being shut out in the majors from 2009 through 2013, Woods is still mathematically on pace with Nicklaus, who did not win his fifteenth major until his sixty-seventh attempt as a pro. The 2014 British Open at Hoylake would be Tiger's sixty-seventh pro start in a major. Yet a six-year drought is a long one; as Jaime Diaz pointed out after the 2013 PGA Championship, only Raymond Floyd and Gene Sarazen have won majors separated by half a dozen years and then proceeded to win at least two additional majors. Rare air, indeed.

As sure as Woods wears a red shirt on tournament Sundays, there will be intrigue as long as there is a quest. If Tiger were to be able to reach eighteen major victories, at whatever age, and be all square with Jack, what a plot would then be presented. Will even the bar-raising and moment-seizing Tiger have the appetite for that dimension of pressure? As a dreaming boy, could he have imagined the burden of a man on such a verge? How many times would he try before acknowledging the good fight is over? Counter to the surety of his many successes, it is anyone's guess. No one, even this colossus of a golfer himself, knows.

ACKNOWLEDGMENTS

First and biggest thanks go to Condé Nast, which publishes the best magazines in the world, for permission to reprint the stories in this collection. Former *Golf Digest* brand editor Bob Carney and Julie LaPointe and Lindsay Herron were especially helpful. My editors in chief at *Golf World* (the late Dick Taylor, along with Terry Galvin, Geoff Russell, and Jaime Diaz, the magazine's current leader) have been generous in assignments given and guidance offered, which is all a writer can ask for. Jerry Tarde, longtime chairman and editor in chief at *Golf Digest*, has steered the mother ship smoothly for many years.

All my past and present colleagues at *Golf World* (including the current cast of David Barrett, Kerry Brady, Tim Carr, Jennifer Corsano, J. D. Cuban, Ryan Herrington, John Huggan, Christian Iooss, E. Michael Johnson, Brendan Mohler, Tim Murphy, Tim Rosaforte, Geoff Shackelford, Dave Shedloski, Ron Sirak, John Strege, Lisa Vannais-Shultz, and Ron Whitten) are special folks with whom it has been a pleasure to work on a great publication the late Bob Harlow had the vision to launch in 1947. Putting out a magazine is one of the most collaborative things in the world; sincere thanks to my coworkers for all the help over all these years. I spend a lot of time in the *Golf Digest* resource center, where Cliff Schrock is always eager to assist.

I've been lucky to have many good friends in the words business who have offered sound advice and genuine thoughtfulness over the years. Besides being a fantastic writer, Jim Moriarty has been a buddy, a sounding board, a booster, and a fellow lover of chicken vindaloo for thirty years, and knowing Jim has meant knowing his wonderful wife, Audrey. Mike Dann, whom I mention in the introduction to this book, was a true friend and key role model when I was a teenager wondering about the future, always encouraging my dreams.

It's an honor to know sportswriting icons Tom Callahan and Dan Jenkins, who have generously told me when the work has gone well. One of my journalism heroes, Frank Deford, even though he doesn't like golf, was once nice enough to critique a handful of my articles, which meant the world to me. I would not have been able to write well about golf history if I hadn't worked for and studied the impressive writings of Al Barkow, whose *Golf's Golden Grind* and *Gettin' to the Dance Floor: An Oral History of American Golf* are must-reads for serious golf fans.

Thanks to the golfers who have shared their stories with me, with a special nod to those wise folks who played before the sport was a multimillion-dollar business. The late Johnny Bulla, who saw and knew so much, comes to mind.

As a college student at Chapel Hill, when I could sneak away from the clatter of all the manual typewriters at the *Daily Tar Heel*, one of my favorite things to do was go to the quiet of the Wilson Library periodicals room and read the columns in the *Charlotte News* by Ron Green Sr., one of North Carolina's best all-time sportswriters, hoping some of his insight and humanity would rub off. More recently, thanks to the talented novelist and nonfiction writer Roland Merullo for his advice and encouragement.

My sisters, Dianne Broyles and Sadie Carter, have been very kind to their little brother. The same goes for Dianne's husband,

Bob, and Sadie's late husband, Bill. Dianne recently retired from teaching, but she is also an ace copy editor and provided a careful reading of the manuscript, for which I am most appreciative. My mother, Juanita, would tell you I have never written a bad story, which isn't true but speaks to her love.

My journey would not have been as meaningful or enjoyable without having known at one juncture or another these folks, some for many years: the late Marianne Ballard, Jim Boros, Bernie Carr, Dick Coop, Jen Dayton, Chuck Ellison, Mike Fields, Dom Furore, Rusty Jarrett, Chris Mackie, Barry Matey, Karyl McGill, Brad Murchison, Lee Pace, Larry Petrillo, Helen Ross, Lorne Rubenstein, Dave Senko, Phil Stambaugh, Mary Beth Stark, David Steen, and Steve Szurlej.

I am indebted to Carly Thurlow and Byrute Johnson in the production department at *Golf World* and *Golf Digest* for their considerable help in gathering my stories from the company archive.

This book wouldn't have happened without the efforts of my agent, John Monteleone of Mountain Lion, Inc., and Rob Taylor at the University of Nebraska Press, who saw potential in this anthology. Thanks also to Rob's assistant, Courtney Ochsner, for her assistance. Kyle Simonsen and Judith Hoover steered the project down the homestretch. Two-time Masters champion Ben Crenshaw, one of the game's good guys who shares my love of golf history, didn't pause when I asked him to contribute the foreword. Neither Ben nor I had gray hair when I saw him for the first time, at the 1973 World Open in Pinehurst.

Somewhere my father, Gene, who put the sports pages of the *Greensboro Daily News* under my nose when I was a little kid and loved to play golf in his last years, is happy about this.